Bill Brown was a finalist in the 'People's Author' national writing competition as featured on *The Alan Titchmarsh Show*. Bill retired in 1984 from the Fire Service, having responded to a total of 21,000 incidents and saved many lives. Today he lives in East Sussex with Jane, his partner of twenty-one years. He has two children and one grandchild.

Billy Brown,
I'll Tell Your Mother

BILL BROWN

First published in Great Britain in 2011
by Orion
an imprint of the Orion Publishing Group Ltd.

An Hachette UK company

5 7 9 10 8 6 4

A CIP catalogue record for this book
is available from the British Library.

ISBN 978-1-4091-2094-0

Typeset at The Spartan Press Ltd,
Lymington, Hants

Printed and bound in Great Britain by
Clays Ltd, St Ives plc

The Orion Publishing Group's policy is to use papers that
are natural, renewable and recyclable products and made
from wood grown in sustainable forests. The logging and
manufacturing processes are expected to conform to
the environmental regulations of the country of origin.

The Orion Publishing Group Ltd
Orion House
5 Upper Saint Martin's Lane
London, WC2H 9EA

www.orionbooks.co.uk

For
Stephen, Tanya
and
Sophie

Acknowledgements

First, to my partner of twenty-one years, Jane, without whose love, support, patience and typing skills this book would not have been possible. To Alan Titchmarsh and all at Spun Gold TV Productions, especially Sinead and Sonny, who made the whole television experience such an enjoyable one. To all those involved in The People's Author competition, in particular Amanda Harris, Luigi Bonomi and Gervaise Phinn for believing in my story. To Susanna Abbott, Juliet Ewers and all the staff at Orion Books and my amazingly talented editor, Celia Hayley, for all her wonderful help and advice and for managing to make order out of chaos. To June, Gloria, Shirley, Rose, Rachel, Saskia and Steve for their brilliant support. Finally, to the amazing people of Brixton I grew up with, who were the inspiration for writing this book.

PROLOGUE

Billy Brown, I'll Tell Your Mother

Captain Brown, of the 7th US Cavalry, reined in his panting steed. The fine mount was eager to charge, snorting with impatience.

'Easy, Thunder,' the captain whispered softly, patting the black stallion's neck. 'Easy.'

Peering ahead through the runner-bean rows, he could clearly see the two savages with their bright green headdresses blowing in the breeze, unaware of his presence. Slowly, he drew his trusty sabre, taking a moment to watch the afternoon sun glinting on the polished steel. Even alone, without his troop, he knew these two Indians were no match for a captain in the US cavalry. Digging his spurs in, he gave the magnificent charger his head. Thunder responded instantly, galloping down upon the terrified enemy. With two deft slashes of his sabre, the Indians were dead before they could draw their tomahawks. Restraining his mighty steed once more, the captain surveyed the carnage. Both Indians had terrible splits to their heads and had died instantly. He allowed himself a smile of satisfaction but reminded himself that this would be a long campaign.

Suddenly the silence was shattered by a terrifying cry, striking fear into his very soul.

'Billy Brown, I'll tell your mother!' Turning, he looked up towards the sky. There, on a second-floor balcony, a lady in uniform was shaking her fist at him.

'That's right – I can see you, Billy Brown.'

In an instant, the wonderful horse evaporated from his imagination. The glinting sabre returned to its original stout stick disguise and Captain Brown was immediately demoted to a seven-year-old boy. Me. Oh bugger, I thought. Of all the people to spot me, it would be Dolly Hammond, owner of the allotment. I surveyed my victims; not two fierce Red Indians from the plains of nineteenth-century America, but two of Dolly's prize cabbages each with its head split open, lying on their sides in a 1949 Brixton allotment. I tried to shrink lower amongst the gooseberry bushes, but soon realised that my white school shirt was not helping me stay undetected.

'Just you wait 'til your mum gets home – I'll be round to see her.'

I didn't bother arguing. Standing up, I walked out of the allotments. At the gate a large thistle had grown about three feet tall. Venting my frustration, I cut it down at the base.

Out of the corner of my eye I could still see Dolly watching me, the row of pencils glinting in their big steel clip on her jacket. I thought she looked like a prison warden, only needing her bus conductor's cap to complete the picture. Closing the gate I turned towards her. Standing to attention with my trusty sabre over my shoulder, I saluted her. Instead of returning my salute she shouted at me, 'Just you wait, Billy Brown.'

I turned away, smiling. I was in trouble again. Wasn't life great!

Hiding the stick under my usual hedge I headed to the front gate – walking past the four-storey blocks of flats, built as affordable housing for the working classes – to wait for my mum. Each block was separated by allotments. Originally lawns, they had been dug up as part of the 'Dig for Victory' campaign. There were ten blocks in all, housing four hundred families, and in the centre were two playgrounds and a community hall. As I reached the front gate, the clock on the super-intendent's office chimed five o'clock. Mum would be home in twenty minutes. I climbed the six-foot high iron gate and sat on the supporting stone wall, giving me a better view up Loughborough Park Road. The road ran all the way from Loughborough Park Junction to our flats, which were boxed in by the railway to one side and at the back. In its heyday it had been a very desirable road. Alas, time and Hitler's bombing had taken their toll, and its heyday had long since passed. Most of the large houses had been divided up into flats to help with the shortage of housing following the war.

People came and went, most said hello to me in a friendly manner, although Mrs Thompsit, an elderly lady who had lost her husband on HMS *Hood*, tipped her hat back to see me better and wagged her finger at me. 'Billy Brown,' she berated me, 'one day you'll fall off that wall and kill yourself. Then where will you be?' A daft question, I always thought, as everybody knew where I would be. Even at the tender age of seven I'd been referred to as a 'little devil', so it wasn't hard to work out where I was going to end up in the next life.

Up the road I spied Mum carrying two large bags of shopping. She was easy to spot amongst the group of residents returning home from their day's work. Mum was nearly six feet tall and well built, coming from good country stock. She made a point of always standing straight and tall, carrying herself with dignity, proud of her height. Even taller with her light straw hat on to protect her from the summer sun, she was always telling me what a fair English rose she was. As usual she was smartly dressed, her light cream dress complimented by white open-toed shoes and matching handbag.

'Mum.' I got down and ran to her, greeting her as casually as I could manage. 'Hello, Mum. Give us a bag.'

She gave me one of those quizzical looks mums are good at. It said, 'This isn't like you, what have you been up to? You'd better tell me now because I'll only find out later.' All that without the power of speech. Fancy. Maybe mums are telepathic. 'Here, you can take a handle.'

I grabbed the handle of the big canvas bag, slipping it over my shoulder.

'What's that green stuff all over your school shirt?' she asked.

I looked down at the evidence. Damn, cabbage stains, I thought to myself. Not for my mum the science and analysis of DNA or fingerprinting. Just one look from her and I knew it was confession time.

'Well, you see . . . I was playing in the allotment and I fell over on one of Dolly's cabbages. She said she's gonna speak to you about it later.'

'What do you mean, you fell?' The look had now hardened to full interrogation mode.

'Well, you see, I had this stick . . .'

'Stop right there, young man. What have I told you about sticks?' Now I was in big trouble. Once Mum went from 'Billy' to 'young man' it was serious.

We walked back home together, passing the superintendent's office, the clubhouse and playgrounds on our right. The third block was ours: Ashford House. By each entrance was a dust chute containing the rubbish trolley.

'Sit right there, you,' she commanded, 'and look after the shopping. I am off to see Dolly.'

I sat for what seemed like an eternity. Several people passed by on their way home. I knew all of them, especially those who were my pals' mums and dads. Most of the women were carrying their daily bags of shopping back from nearby Brixton market. A young man in uniform carrying a large duffel bag waved hello to me. It took me a while to recognise my own cousin Peter, home on leave from the navy, complete with his new beard.

'Can't stop, Billy, I'm off to surprise Mum!'

All over the flats ordinary people were making their way home, not just to their own flats but to the community of the Guinness Trust Buildings where they shared a common bond with their neighbours; some with tragedy and loss from the war, but most with the knowledge that they'd survived through self-sacrifice and hardship. Neighbour had helped neighbour. And although the war had been over for five years, that spirit had continued.

Barbara Blake passed, coming home from high school. She was very pretty, with jet-black hair and dark eyes. 'Hello Billy. You in trouble again?' She didn't wait for an answer, just breezed past into her ground-floor flat. The only reason she even acknowledged my existence was because she had a crush on my older brother, Bob.

Then Mum came back. 'Get the stick, now!'

I duly obeyed, trotting across to the hedge to get a stick. And that's what I got, *a* stick. Because under the hedge I had a selection. I wasn't going to give her my best one. Taking it from me, she made a gesture as if she were going to beat me with it. She wouldn't have, of course, but just for a moment . . . Then she snapped it in half and put it in the rubbish trolley.

'No more sticks,' she warned.

'Yes, Mum,' came the compliant reply, as I mentally went through my depleted stick collection. We carried our shopping up the nine flights of granite stairs to flat 242, Ashford House. Home.

'Now, young man' – bugger, I thought, I'm still in trouble – 'go and get your money box and take out two shillings.'

'Oh, but Mum,' I began. My protestations were soon cut short.

'Now!' came the order. Reluctantly I removed my

6

hard-earned cash. 'Right, now go and give that to Mrs Hammond.'

'Oh, but Mum.' I pleaded. 'Can't you pay her?'

'No, Billy,' she said firmly. 'You must learn to pay for your own sins.'

I skulked off with the two one-shilling coins in my hand, walking as slowly as I could across to Dolly's block. Arriving at her door I pushed the bell, announcing to the executioner that her next victim had arrived.

'Ah – the cabbage-smasher – and to what do I owe this pleasure, Billy Brown?' She knew very well to what she owed this pleasure; the pleasure of seeing me squirm.

I held out my hand with the two one-shilling coins.

'Thank you, Billy,' she said, taking my money. 'And now what do you have to say?'

This was humiliation beyond endurance. 'I'm very sorry, Dolly,' I whispered, looking down at my feet.

'Mrs Hammond to you, if you don't mind. Now once again and louder, so I can hear you this time.' Oh no, this was evil at its best, I thought. Why couldn't Hitler's Luftwaffe have hit her bus?

'I'm very sorry, Mrs Hammond,' I almost shouted.

'There, that wasn't too bad, was it? Now give these to your mum.'

She offered me a large bag and I peered inside. There, staring back at me, were the heads of the two dead Indians. Taking the cabbages, I walked back down the stairs and slowly began to smile, remembering that on my way to her I had spat several times on the one-shilling coins.

I

Saturday Boy

'SATURDAY BOY WANTED'. The sign was scrawled in thick chalk on an old roof slate propped against the open gate to the yard. I picked it up and walked in. I could hear someone banging away in one of the sheds, and was about to head in that direction when I heard another noise close by. It sounded like hundreds of steel ball bearings being emptied into a metal dustbin. I turned just in time to see the source of the noise, and quickly flattened myself against the corrugated iron gate. The biggest, fiercest, dirtiest dog I had ever seen was rushing in my direction, dragging a huge chain behind her. I knew now what the ball-bearing noise was. Frozen to the spot with fear, I closed my eyes and waited to be torn to pieces.

I could hear her barking and snarling in an absolute frenzy just inches away from me, but no attack came. Opening my eyes, to my relief I saw she had reached the limit of her chain. My knees started to give way when, out of the blue, a voice to my left boomed, 'Stand still, lad, she can't reach you.' Turning my head, I looked towards the voice. Once again my knees started to turn to jelly. Not only a rabid killer dog, now I had a giant bearing down on me.

Michael Gallagher was six feet six inches tall and weighed eighteen stone. He had come over from Ireland after the war for all the rebuilding work in London, but had found running a demolition and reclamation business far more profitable. Seizing the dog by her collar he commanded her to sit. The dog obeyed instantly, but still growled and snarled at me.

'Home,' said the giant. To my utter relief my would-be killer trotted back to the forty-gallon oil drum, which served as her kennel and home.

'Didn't you see the RING BELL sign on the gate?'

'No, sir, only this one.' I held out the roof slate still in my hand. He looked at it, then back at me before roaring with laughter.

'By God, lad, you must have been born lucky. Another foot and old Jessie would have had you for breakfast!'

'My mum says it's better to be born lucky than rich.'

The giant stopped laughing. 'Your mum's a very wise woman, lad. Now, what do you want?'

Once again I held up the slate. 'I want the Saturday Boy's job.'

'Oh, is that right? And how old are you exactly?'

'I'm nearly ten,' I replied, lying as convincingly as I could. I was, in fact, only seven and a half, but very tall for my age.

He gave me one of those knowing looks, just like my mum did. This one meant, 'I know you're lying, but I'm not going to pursue it further.'

'What's your name, lad?' he asked.

'Billy Brown, sir.'

'OK, Billy Brown. Put that damned slate down and follow me.'

Dropping the slate by the gate, I followed him into one of the open-fronted sheds. As he walked in front of me I couldn't help noticing his huge boots. They must have been size twelve or more, without laces, so that they made a sort of slopping noise as he walked, while his huge blue and white checked shirt flapped open like one of Mum's tablecloths on the line.

'Right, Billy Brown, let's see if you can tie a knot properly.' Picking up a bundle of kindling in his huge hand, he placed it in a piece of six-inch steel tube welded to the bench. The tube reached exactly halfway up the bundle. He formed a slip knot and pulled it tight, securing the sticks. Taking out the tied bundle, he placed it in an old baker's tray with some others.

'OK, Billy. You try!' So, scooping up some sticks he put them in the tube. Taking the string, I made an attempt at the knot like he'd done. As I lifted them out, they fell everywhere.

'No, no, Billy. You missed the last bit,' and he demonstrated the knot again.

On the third attempt I got it. 'There you are, sir,' I announced proudly, holding up my secured bundle for his approval.

'Look, Billy, you should understand one thing. Your nice king hasn't seen fit to knight me yet, so you don't have to call me "sir". Mike will do. I'll see you Saturday morning, eight thirty sharp until four thirty. The pay is two and six. Do we have a deal?' He spat into his huge hand and offered it to me. I looked back at his smiling face. He gave a short nod indicating I should do the same. I spat on my palm and shook his hand or, rather, he shook mine. To any passers-by it must have looked like David and Goliath before the fight. Now shake hands and may the best man win.

Safely back at the gate, he stopped. 'Don't forget, Billy,' he reminded me, 'ring the bloody bell next time.'

The two of us parted company, both laughing as we went.

'Mum, I've got a job.'

'Wait a minute, Billy. Let me get my coat off. I've only just got in.'

'But, Mum . . .' I protested.

'Look, you go and put the kettle on while I get my slippers on. Then you can tell me all about it.'

She went off to her bedroom at the end of the hallway while I went to the kitchen. Being on the fourth floor I had a good view of the rear blocks and allotments, plus the railway yards of Loughborough Junction and Herne Hill. Having filled the kettle, I put it on the stove and lit the gas with a sudden pop which I knew was coming but still made me jump. Blowing out the match, I smelt the smoke from the spent matchstick. It wasn't a particularly good or bad smell, but it was to become one I'd remember all my life and remind me of home and warmth, and cups of tea with my mum.

Once the tray was filled I carried it into the lounge/diner, placing it on the table. Dad had made a room divider with a plant trough, separating the dining table and chairs from the sofa, two armchairs and open fireplace. The mantelpiece was stacked with Dad's certificates from smoking Kensitas cigarettes. These he would exchange for gifts from a small catalogue. Smoke 500 ciggies – get a pair of pruning shears! Added to this was a shelf unit he'd made to house the record player, and his collection of over four hundred 78 records with our Decca radio on top.

Although the room was small, everything had its place and there was still a good amount of carpet space for me to lay out my Hornby o gauge train set. The walls had been papered with panels of two different designs of wallpaper, as that was all Dad could get due to the shortages. On the opposite side to the hallway a glass door led out onto our balcony which was open, being on the top floor. Two large rabbit hutches sat against the wall, at present unoccupied, the previous residents having been eaten several months previously.

Mum returned and helped lay out the teapot with its knitted tea cosy, the milk jug, sugar bowl, tea strainer and saucer, two china cups and saucers and two teaspoons. In our house, the afternoon cup of tea may not have been as elaborate as a Japanese tea ceremony but it was just as important. It signified to Mum, and thousands like her, that their working day was over: they were home. Mum worked full-time as a shop assistant for Woolworths on the Walworth Road near the Elephant and Castle. She left before eight o'clock each morning and wasn't home until five thirty, having been on her feet for most of the day. Dad wouldn't be home until at least seven, sometimes later, having left home at six forty-five to travel twenty-seven stops on the Underground to his job as a foreman maintenance engineer at Hoover at Perivale in north London. He'd worked there before leaving north London to take the two-bedroom flat in Brixton as it was too good an opportunity to miss. His job paid well and gave a pension so he'd stayed, even with the horrendous travelling.

The biscuits were in a Huntley and Palmers tin depicting a yellow horse-drawn coach outside a seventeenth-century inn. Pulling off the lid, I offered them to Mum. Once she had selected her Rich Tea biscuits I began my quest, sorting through the selection until I found a custard cream and two chocolate wafers, which I arranged around the edge of my saucer in order of devourability. Settling in her favourite armchair with her feet up she drank her tea in silence, finishing it off with a long sigh and an 'Ah, that's better . . . put one back.'

'Oh, but Mum . . .' I whined.

'Put one back or have none.'

I reluctantly returned the custard cream, making a mental note of its position in the tin.

'Now then, Billy, what's all this about a job?'

'I've got a Saturday job at Mr Gallagher's yard. By Somerleyton Passage.'

'Doing what, exactly?' she enquired.

'Well, I'm going to do firewood and stuff. Look, I'll show you.' And before she could object I was off to the kitchen for a tin of beans and some string. In one of the

14

kitchen cupboards was a drawer full of 'come in hand-ies', as Mum called them. Opening the drawers revealed many small neat hanks of string which had been wrapped around Mum's fingers and tied in the middle, elastic bands, half a box of carpet tacks, some brass picture hooks and other items. Virtually every household in post-war Britain had a similar collection. I often thought that if all the 'come in handy' drawers were emptied in Trafalgar Square, Nelson would be standing on the world's biggest pile of assorted string.

I deftly showed Mum the amazing knot around the tin of beans.

'See, Mum. Easy, ain't it?'

'Easy, *isn't it?*' she corrected. 'Well, we must ask your dad, but wait until after he has had his dinner, Billy. Give him a chance to get through the door!' Even at my tender age, I understood the reasoning for this.

'That sounds like a good idea,' I said, gesturing with the last of my now melted chocolate wafers. 'After dinner.'

Later that evening, Dad settled in his armchair with his long legs up on the pouffe. He was over six feet tall, of muscular build and had huge hands. My auntie Eaddie had once described them as being as big as kitchen tables. Dad was handsome, and always popular with the ladies at any of the events organised within the Guinness Trust flats. He always sold the most raffle tickets for good causes. Apart from music, Dad's other passion was his allotment, where he would spend his weekends in the fresh air tending his prize roses and dahlias, and nearly always winning the competitions with the other one hundred allotment owners in the flats. Now, seeing him relaxed with his tie and collar off, his shirtsleeves rolled up and his second cup of tea and cigarette, I thought it would be the perfect time to bring up the subject of my job offer.

'Dad, you know how you're always saying that money doesn't grow on trees and has to be hard earned?'

'You're not getting any more pocket money,' he cut in, before I could continue.

'No, Dad, I don't want any more, I want a job.'

Suddenly I had his full attention. 'A job, eh? But what kind of job?'

'I'll show you,' and once again I performed the amazing new trick on the tin of beans.

'How will that get you a job?'

'I've already got one. With Mr Gallagher, every Saturday for two and six, bundling up firewood. Can I do it, Dad? Please, can I?' Pleading with my eyes, I looked from him to Mum and back again.

'What do you think, Eileen?'

'Oh, please, Mum, I'll be ever so good if you let me.' Mum gave me one of her fixed stone stares.

'You'll be ever so good if I *don't* let you, young man.'

Oh, bugger, I thought. I'm 'young man' again. This is never a good thing!

'Oh please, Mum, *please*?'

'Big Mike's a good man,' Dad interceded. 'I'm sure Billy will be looked after, and it may teach him the value of money, that's if that bloody dog doesn't eat him first, of course.'

'Jack,' Mum scolded. 'Mind your language.'

Dad looked at me. 'OK. You can do it. So long as your mum's jobs come first.'

'Ah. Thanks, Dad, thanks Mum. Don't worry. I'll make sure all your jobs are done.' This was said as if I would be completing the tasks of Hercules each day, but in fact it meant anything Mum needed help with, plus making sure we had a bucket of coal brought up from our pram shed in the single-storey block across the service road opposite the entrance to our stairs. By a bit of negotiation we had managed to get two sheds. One stored coal for the open fire in the lounge and the small stove in the kitchen, which supplied the heat and hot water, while the other housed Dad's bits and pieces and garden tools. All the flats in the Guinness Trust buildings had coal fires, although one or two had had new electric fires installed. All us kids thought these privileged tenants seemed very rich indeed!

Saturday morning came and I was up early. Mum had made me a plate of Scots porridge oats and a cup of tea. Outside, it was a bright September morning. She got me dressed in my old clothes and had found some really long football socks that I could pull up over my knees, as I still didn't have long trousers. Before leaving, she wrapped a knitted scarf around my neck and made me put my woolly gloves on, ignoring my protests.

'It's cold out today, Billy; if you don't look after

yourself, who else will? Here, take this.' I looked in the brown-paper bag she'd given me. Inside, awaiting their fate, were a cheese sandwich, an apple and two chocolate wafer biscuits. 'For your lunch. Don't eat it all at once, and mind your manners with Mr Gallagher.'

I peered into the bag again, then back at Mum. She read my thoughts.

'Yes, Billy Brown, a secret supply. If you knew we had more chocolate wafers there wouldn't be any for you now.' She bent down and kissed me on the cheek. 'Now, off to work with you, oh, and bring your money home safely. No spending it on sweets on the way back.'

'Yes, Mum,' I replied, descending the sixty-eight stairs from our flat. I wondered how she knew I'd already worked out how far two shillings and sixpence would go in Mr Snook's sweet shop on the other side of Somerleyton Passage, under the railway.

The instant the yard bell sounded, the ball bearings started emptying into the tin can. This time Jessie came from under a nearby lorry stood on jacks. I stood well clear of the gate as she skidded to a halt, showing me what a ferocious set of teeth she had. Once again, on command, she returned home.

'Morning, Billy. That's a good start. You're five minutes early.'

'Yes, sir. I mean Mr Mike.'

'Right, then. Follow me,' and off he went with his huge sloppy boots, galloup, galloup, galloup. In the open shed I was introduced to Pop, an old man wearing a faded red boiler suit with a huge leather belt and steel toe-capped boots. Covering his bald head, he had an ex-US army knitted hat on with ear pieces, designed for wearing under steel helmets.

'Pop, this is Billy Brown. He's our new Saturday Boy.'

'Don't look much, does he?'

'Never mind all that. You just look after him and show him what to do. I'm going back to that sodding differential on the Bedford.' And with that he was gone, leaving me with Pop.

'Right, young man. You can put your stuff in here,' he indicated an old tin locker painted in drab army green. 'You may as well leave the gloves or you won't be able to tie the bundles.'

'Yes, sir,' I replied, putting my lunch, gloves and scarf inside as instructed.

'And don't call me sir. You can call me Pops, and you do exactly as I tell you. See?'

'Er, OK, Pops.'

'Good. Let's get going then. I chop, you tie. Got that?'

'OK, Pops.'

'Good. Wait there. I'll be back in a minute.' He soon returned with a large wooden box for me to stand on which he placed close to the bench. 'That's better. Always be over your work if you can, lad. Can you tie a slip knot?'

I swiftly demonstrated with a perfect knot. If he was surprised he didn't show it.

For the next hour he chopped pre-cut timber into

kindling sticks while I filled the tube and tied them. The wood was old and rough and I got one or two splinters, but I didn't stop. This was my first proper job, and there would be plenty of other boys ready to jump at the chance to take my place, so I didn't complain.

After a while Mike came over to see how I was doing. Although Pop's kindling was piling up, he seemed pleased that I'd filled two baker's trays with tied bundles. Suddenly he noticed my hands. They were red on the backs and dirty, and there was a splinter or two on the palms.

'Where's his bloody gloves, Pop?'

'He only brought woolly ones,' the old man replied. 'They're no good.'

'You stupid old bugger!' Mike seemed very cross.

'Sorry, Mike,' I said, apologetically. 'I didn't have any other gloves to bring.'

Calming down, he placed a huge hand on my shoulder. 'Not you, Billy. Don't worry. I've got some here from when the women did the bundles. They should fit you.' Rummaging in an old tin box, he brought out the smallest pair of gloves he could find.

'Here, try these on.' I pulled on the gloves but they were still too big.

Mike pulled them back off me. Taking Pop's axe, he laid the gloves on the upturned log and, with two deft strikes, cut the fingers and thumb off each glove, turning them into mittens. 'Here. Try them now.'

The mittens fitted quite well now that my fingers

didn't have to reach the tips. 'They'll protect your hands and keep them a bit warm.'

'Thanks very much, Mr Mike. They're great.'

'Pops, give me a hand with this bench.' I stood aside as the two men lifted the bench and turned it 180 degrees so my metal tube was now on the other side. It was then that I noticed the pot-bellied stove stood on a large sheet of rusty steel.

'Why isn't the stove lit, Pops?' Mike enquired.

'It's not cold enough yet.'

'Jesus, give me strength,' Mike replied, getting cross again. 'Billy, any time you come here and it's cold, light the stove.'

'I'm alright,' I protested, but my bright red hands and legs had already given me away. With a look that could kill any mortal man, he spoke calmly to Pop.

'Now listen to me. This lad isn't here to take your job. He's here to *help* you. He's just a boy, but a boy I already like, so show him how to do the stove and stop sodding about!'

If Pops wasn't scared, I was. Even at my age I'd already realised that Mike Gallagher was not a man to be argued with. He went back to work on the Bedford lorry.

Pops took off a glove and offered his hand.

'Sorry Billy. I can be a miserable old bugger sometimes.' I removed my mitten, then suddenly remembering the procedure, spat into my dirty palm and offered him my hand. Pop spat into his and grinned, his teeth looking like misplaced yellow tombstones in a churchyard. 'We'll get along fine,' he said.

'Oh, I'm sure we shall, Pops, 'cos any friend of Big Mike's is a friend of mine.'

For a minute he gave me one of those quizzical looks. Then he grinned again. 'Billy Brown, you're not as daft as you look!'

Lighting the stove was easy. First Pop cleaned out the old ashes and raked out underneath for good airflow. Then, taking a few thin sticks from the kindling pile, he cut shavings down each side of the stick without actually detaching them. Once he had three or four done he placed them inside the stove, lighting them with a match. The thin shavings caught immediately, with no need for paper to ignite the sticks. More sticks were applied until the stove was roaring away. Pop closed the damper and the stove settled down.

'Right, Billy. It's your job to keep it going or light it. We use all the old crap timber. Anything I can't chop goes in that oil drum for the stove. OK?'

I peered into the open drum. It was half full of odd bits of wood, some with nails, bolts or screws, and some just with big knots. Pop took a large piece and showed me how to open the top of the stove with a tool and drop in some wood. I took a piece and did the same. 'That's it. Back to work. It'll soon be time for breakfast.'

We went back to chopping and bundling while I thought about the breakfast remark.

'Billy, I have a job for you,' said Big Mike as he walked back over to his van. Reaching inside, he brought out a parcel wrapped in newspaper. 'Do you know the Primrose Café?'

'Yes, Mr Mike. The one next to the water tank in Railton Road?'

'Right, good lad,' he said, giving me the parcel. 'Take this to Rose in the café; tell her three sandwiches with mustard and sauce and not to be mean. OK?'

'Yes, Mr Mike. Three sandwiches with mustard and sauce, and not to be mean?' The mean part I repeated more as a question.

'That's it. Now, off you go and don't forget the sandwiches.'

'But, Mr Mike, I haven't any money to pay for them.' I wasn't sure about the smile he gave, nor about his answer. 'No money needed, Billy.'

The Primrose Café wasn't even five minutes away through Somerleyton Passage, under the railway, over Mayal Road to Railton Road and turn right. The café stood on a corner painted primrose yellow, and had half-height lace curtains so you could look in but not see the seated customers. Inside, I was greeted by a nice, jolly lady with bright red cheeks wearing a flowery apron just like the one Mum always wore.

'Please, Miss. I was told to ask for Rose.'

'I'm not a miss, I'm a Mrs, but you can call me Rose. Who are you?'

'I'm Billy Brown and I work for Mr Gallagher.' She looked at me with a kindly smile. 'You – work for Big Mike? He's employing young.'

'I'm the Saturday Boy,' I announced with great pride.

'Well, good for you, Billy Brown – the Saturday Boy. Is that my parcel?' She gestured towards the newspaper parcel I was carrying. I handed it over and repeated the message. When I got to the bit about 'and don't be mean', Rose fell about laughing.

'You tell him he's a cheeky bugger. No, on second thoughts, you best not! Well, sit down Billy, and I'll do his sandwiches. Do you want a cup of tea while you wait?'

'I'm sorry, Rose. I haven't any money.'

She laughed again. 'That's just like him to send you out without a penny. Do you take sugar?'

I watched as she held the huge chrome teapot under the hot-water geyser for a few seconds, then, giving the pot a good shake, poured me out a cup of tea, adding two sugars as requested.

From where I sat I could see her in the kitchen. Unwrapping the parcel, I stared as she produced a dead rabbit and a long string of pork sausages. I hadn't seen sausages for at least three weeks. Rationing was still in force following the war and meat was in very short supply. Deftly she cut six sausages from the string and put them in the pan where they sizzled away, filling the café with a wonderful, mouth-watering aroma.

'Now, what sauce do you want, brown or tomato?' I looked up, bewildered. Rose understood immediately. 'Three sandwiches – Mike, Pop and you? Now, which sauce?'

'Ah, tomato please.'

Back in the kitchen she applied the sauce liberally. Then, wrapping each sandwich individually, she laid them on the counter top. Taking a thick pencil, she wrote on each bag. As she did so she spoke out loud. 'M for Mike. P for Pop. BB for Billy Brown.' With that she put them all into a large brown-paper bag and closed the top. 'Hurry back, Billy, or they'll get cold.'

I ran all the way back to the yard. Mike and Pops were already in the shed with three steaming cups of tea on the bench. I handed Mike the bag.

'What did Rose say?' he asked. Although I remembered the cheeky bugger comment, I thought better of it.

'Nothing, Mr Mike. She gave me a cup of tea.'

'Good,' he laughed. 'That'll be on my bill next time I'm in there.'

The sandwich was the best I'd had in ages, although I did feel a pang of guilt while I was devouring it, thinking about Mum's cheese sandwich, ignored in its bag. Both Mike and Pops thought it hilariously funny when the mustard in the sandwich caused my eyes to water, but I wiped them with the freshly laundered hankie Mum had put in my pocket.

Mike noticed it. 'That'll be your mother again, eh, Billy?'

'Yes, Mr Mike. She always makes sure I have a clean hankie with me.'

He nodded, not saying a word. Sitting on my box, eating my sausage sandwich with these two men made me feel so grown-up. The stove was nice and warm and life felt good – until I spotted Jessie, that is. She was under the bench with her eyes riveted to my every movement.

'Mr Mike,' I whispered, trying to catch his attention without exciting the dog. 'Mr Mike.'

'What's the matter, Billy? You've gone as white as a sheet!'

'Mr Mike,' I repeated, indicating with a faint nod that he should look under the bench.

'Oh, is that all. Old Jessie?'

'But Mr Mike, she's not on her chain.'

'No, Billy. She's free to wander when the yard's open. It's only when it's closed or I'm in one of the sheds that I put her chain on. She's been taught to be aggressive when her chain is on, or when the yard's shut. She won't hurt you. She's only after your sandwich.'

Looking up in my direction, she showed me the whites of her eyes. She didn't seem as fierce as she had been, but I was still wary. Slowly I stretched out my hand, offering her my last piece of sausage sandwich. Mike's voice came over my shoulder.

'Good girl, Jessie. Gently.' The terrifying jaws opened just wide enough to take the treat. It was gone without chewing. She came a little closer. 'Let her sniff you, Billy.'

It wasn't a case of letting her, she was going to anyway, I thought, because I was sitting down on my box and her head was almost level with mine.

'Good girl,' I said, just as Mike had done. Feeling braver, I stroked her huge head. She stood still, allowing me to stroke her for a few moments before lying down in front of the stove. Giving a huge sigh of relief, I continued breathing.

'Well, you're a surprise, Billy. She normally takes much longer to make friends with people.'

Breakfast over, we all went back to work. From where I was stood on my box I could now see out across the yard. As I tied my bundles, people came and went, some buying timber or building materials, some selling scrap metal to Mike who weighed it on giant scales with a nice brass plate engraved 'Avery'. The prices were chalked up outside the weighing shed on a black board. Brass, copper, lead, iron and steel all had a scrap value.

I noticed that several older boys came in with scrap metal and, when I asked about it, Pop explained that they picked it up from the bombsites. Although it wasn't really legal, the police were too busy to patrol the thousands of sites in the area.

One hour passed and lunchtime came. No sooner had I sat down on my box when Jessie appeared and sat near me, eager to share whatever I had. I gave her some of my cheese sandwich as I was still quite full from the breakfast one, but saved my biscuits for the afternoon.

'Pops?' I asked. 'Is it OK if I pop out for five minutes?'

'Sure, but be quick. Mike usually has a short nap in his van after lunch unless a customer comes in, so just hurry.'

As fast as I could I went through the passage again and straight to the butcher.

'And what can I get for you, young man?' the butcher enquired.

'A big bone please, if you've got one.'

'How big?'

'Very big, please.'

From a large steel bin the butcher produced an enormous beef bone. 'How's this one for size?' he asked.

'That's just right, thank you.'

'Jolly good. That'll be three pence please.'

'Oh, I'm sorry. I didn't know you had to pay for bones.'

'I'm afraid so, young man. We get a good price from the bone man.' I remembered seeing the van collecting the bins of bones, but never thought there would be any money in them.

'I'm very sorry, sir, but I didn't bring any money with me. It's only for old Jessie, Big Mike's dog.'

'What are you doing with Big Mike?' the butcher enquired.

'I'm Billy Brown. I'm the new Saturday Boy.'

'Well then, Billy Brown, you give this to Jessie with my compliments. There's no charge – and make sure you tell Big Mike. OK?' I hadn't even noticed that he had already put some paper round the huge bone while we'd been talking. Picking it up off the counter, I thanked him for his kindness and headed back, surprised at the weight of it.

Back at the yard, Pop laughed at the size of the enormous bone. 'That'll keep the old girl happy 'til Christmas,' he joked. I went over to the stove where

Jessie was still lying. After a few sniffs she seized the huge bone in her jaws and walked out with it. The disappointment at not seeing her enjoy it must have been written all over my face.

'Well, if you had a nice treat, would you want to share it or let everyone else watch you eat it?' Pop said. And although I didn't like it, I understood his logic, and pictured Jessie in some secret den in the corner of the yard enjoying her treat.

The afternoon passed quite quickly. Two builders came in and bought an RSJ, which Mike cut to length with the acetylene torch. I was fascinated as I watched bright sparks of molten metal fly everywhere as he cut through the thick steel.

'Don't look at the cutting tip, Billy,' Pop warned me. 'It's too bright to look at without goggles and can cause arc eye.'

'Arc eye? What's that?' I asked.

'It's an injury to the eyes from bright lights. Just don't look, OK?' We went back to the firewood while the three men loaded the steel beam, two at one end and Mike at the other.

At four thirty, Mike came over. 'That's it, Billy. Time to go home. Here's your money.' Taking the half-crown I said, 'Thank you. Shall I come again next Saturday?'

'You'd better, or I'll come and get you.' For a moment he scared me. Then I saw the twinkle in his eye.

'I'll be here, Mr Mike. At eight thirty sharp.'

As I went to leave he stopped me. 'Wait a minute.' He rummaged in the back of his van, returning with a small parcel. 'Here, Billy, give this to your mum with my compliments.'

I didn't need to ask about the contents of the parcel as it was just like the one I had taken to Rose at the café.

'I'll tell her. And thank you.' Walking back, I held the coin in my hand all the way home. I was very tired but so pleased with myself, a proper Saturday Boy!

On the third Saturday Mike asked if I wanted to do a delivery with him. The thought of going out in his van filled me with excitement. We loaded ten trays of kindling in the van before setting off. I felt so grown-up, riding in the van with Big Mike.

'Where are we going, Mr Mike?' I enquired.

'We're off to Acre Lane first, then Brixton Hill near the Clifton Cinema. You know that?'

'Of course I do. I know all the cinemas, Mr Mike.'

'I thought you might. Do you like the film shows?'

'Oh yes. They're smashing. Last week Mum and Dad took me to see *The Sea Hawk* with Errol Flynn. It was really good. He's ever so brave and daring.'

Mike laughed out loud. 'I can see why you'd like that. You're a bit of a pirate yourself.' I took this as a huge compliment; being compared to my hero Errol Flynn was just brilliant!

Arriving at the first shop and unloading, Mike carried in six trays of bundles. Jones's oil shop was stacked floor to ceiling with everything a home might need.

Brooms and brushes hung from the wooden boarded ceiling, one wall was shelved out with pigeon holes containing huge bars of carbolic soap, tins of boot polish, scrubbing brushes, boxes of matches in three different sizes, hanks of washing line, tins of paint and tools, and there were open-top barrels filled with dog biscuits and chicken feed. The walls and floor were made of old tongue-and-groove pine, and the whole place hadn't been painted for years. Walking into the shop was like entering a giant wooden box filled with amazing and useful things. Throughout the entire shop was the pervading smell of paraffin oil, which was sold by the pint or the gallon depending on how much you needed. During the war every house had a paraffin lantern or two and a heater, just in case the electricity was cut off, either by bombing or, more usually, due to power cuts to save energy. Mr Jones also sold cooking oil, methylated spirits and car engine oil (when available). I liked the smell almost as much as the smell of marzipan.

'Billy, stack the bundles on that shelf over there while I see Mr Jones.'

I set to unloading the trays, piling up the bundles like logs on end. While I was doing this, Mrs Bentham from flat 238 came in with Janet, her daughter, and stopped dead in her tracks when she saw me. Mrs Bentham worked part-time at Woolies with my mum. In the winter I would stay at her flat after school and play with Janet until Mum got home from work.

'Billy Brown, what on earth are you up to?'

'I've got a job,' I announced proudly. 'I'm the Saturday Boy.'

'Are you indeed. Well, you need better gloves,' she said, looking down at my cut-off mittens. I couldn't really see anything wrong with them.

'They're fine,' I reassured her. 'I need me fingers free to tie the slip knots, you see.'

'I need *my* fingers free,' she corrected me. 'So, you're doing our firewood?'

'Yes, I am,' I assured her.

'And does your mum know?'

'Of course – and Dad. They said it would teach me the value of money.'

She gave me one of those 'hmmm, I wonder' looks.

'You're awfully dirty, Billy.'

I turned round to see Janet. 'It's the work, Janet. You can't stay clean in this job.' I liked Janet. She was my age and very pretty, and always dressed nicely with her hair brushed and tied with a ribbon.

'Honestly, Billy, I don't know what will become of you.' God, she was starting to sound like her mum.

'I'll tell you what will become of him,' barked Mike as he strode back into the shop, with his boots still going galloup, galloup, galloup. 'He'll either become a millionaire or be hung for piracy. Ah, good lad,' and with that, he picked up the six empty trays and walked out, still slopping his great unlaced boots.

'Who was that awful man?' Mrs Bentham asked.

'That's Big Mike, he's me boss. I must be going. Bye, Janet, see you later.'

I followed Mike out to the van, smiling. Of course I

knew I should have said he was 'my' boss, but it was much more fun to see Mrs Bentham's nose turn up at 'me'. I was pleased Janet had been with her to see me really working.

As we drove up Brixton Hill, I noticed Mike was having trouble changing gear.

'What's up, Mr Mike?'

'Second gear's gone on this bloody old van so I have to go from first to third and it's not easy uphill.'

It's not easy in those boots either, I thought to myself. I had to turn away and look out of the window so he wouldn't see me grinning.

The second delivery was much like the first. I stacked while Mike chatted and collected some cash. As I replaced the sale card on the top of the newly stacked bundles I noticed the prices: 'Sixpence a bundle or three for one shilling.' On the drive back to the yard I worked out that I was tying at least one hundred bundles every Saturday for two and six, which the oil shops would sell for two pounds ten. I didn't realise it but, at that moment, I understood the principles of supply and demand, profit and loss.

During my stay at Mike's yard I had already got a nice little sideline going. At the end of the day I would shovel all the wood ash raked from the pot-bellied stove and put it through an old metal sieve I'd found in one of the sheds. This separated the ash from the old nails and bolts in it. The remaining clean ash would normally fill two of Mike's large brown-paper bags. On

Sunday morning I would take them over to the allotments where the gardeners were eager to buy them for sixpence a bag, using the ash as fertiliser for their tomatoes and chrysanthemums. I now had a demand for this, as there were one hundred allotments in the flats and they were all potential customers. Pop would soon complain that I kept the stove burning too hot, but in fact, all I was interested in was making lots of wood ash!

'Listen, Billy. It's a piece of cake. Just be there at five thirty. Help put away the barrows and stock, and get five shillings on Saturday night.'

I'd known Tommy all my life because we'd grown up in the same block of flats. Since he was older than me he was not in my little group of pals, but he always said hello when he saw me in Brixton market where he had an after-school job helping one of the stallholders clear away at night. He was going away for a week, but needed someone to fill in for him to protect his nice job.

'Look, come down on Saturday and I'll show you the ropes. OK?' I agreed, so long as Mum said it was OK. Once she knew it would only be for one week she agreed to let me do it, especially as it was coming up to Christmas and an extra five bob would come in handy. Lots of the older boys and girls had Saturday jobs in Brixton market. The girls worked for Woolworths, Marks and Spencer and the fashion shops, while the lads worked for various stalls in the market. The pay was good and so were the extras. In the market you soon learnt who was who, what they could supply and for how much. Extras were important because of the rationing, whether they were food, clothing or other essentials, so the market was the centre of Brixton life, and indeed for most of south London. With three major shopping arcades, over two hundred outside stalls, plus department and retail stores, it was a shopping mecca.

On the next Saturday I left the yard dead on four thirty. I had to carry my bags of ash home to the pram shed first before I could head to the market. We were to meet at the entrance to Granville Arcade and Market Row. Crossing Coldharbour Lane from Somerleyton Road, I entered the Arcade at the opposite end to the one where Tommy was waiting. Even though it was now four thirty, the market was still packed with shoppers. The first thing I noticed was the noise level, from the stallholders shouting their wares and friends calling to each other, all topped off with music blaring from the two record shops.

'Here you go ladies, last of the oranges, two bob a scoop!' The stallholders sold fruit and veg at knockdown prices on Saturday afternoon just to get rid of everything, shouting above each other for the last sales of the week. Traders all over the market would be trying to make a sale: 'That's it, Mrs, buy two pairs of shoes and I'll throw in a nice pair of slippers, any colour you like.' 'Buy ten yards of curtain material and get the lining free.' 'Box of twelve cakes, two shillings, last of them loaves sixpence each.' Every kind of smell filled my nose, from sawdust in the butcher's shop, leather, bread, fruit, flowers and spices to the soused herrings in the huge wooden barrels outside the delicatessen.

I finally made my way through the crowds to where Tommy was waiting for me at the far end of the arcade. 'Right, this way.' I followed him to the stall where he worked.

'This is Billy Brown, Mr Robinson.'

The man turned round to meet me. He was in his early fifties, short and stout with thinning hair under a flat cap. His cheeks were well rounded and rosy from always being out in the open air. I couldn't help but notice how his short, podgy fingers were ingrained with the dirt of serving vegetables for so many years. Once you'd got a stall in Brixton market, it was for life. Many stalls had been handed down for three of four generations, and each one was a goldmine.

'You honest?' he asked abruptly.

'Yes, sir, I work for Big Mike during the day.'

'Ah, Big Mike Gallagher. Eh, well that's good enough for me, Billy. Tommy will show you what to do.' With that he began to untie his leather money apron, which most market traders wore. The apron had three long pockets across the front for money. The front one held coins, while the back two held notes. 'I'll be in the Canterbury if you need me.' He made his way to the Canterbury Arms pub. Tommy could see I was curious.

'He goes there every night for a pint of Guinness and a smoke before he goes home. He'll be back in about an hour unless he meets a pal or two and they start talking about the gee-gees.'

'What's the gee-gees?' I asked.

He looked me up and down. 'You know, the horses, racing. Mr Robinson likes nothing better than a little flutter on the gee-gees. Now, help me pull this stall out.'

Once we'd kicked the day's rubbish out of the way I found the market stall quite easy to manoeuvre, even still loaded. The large iron-shod wheels crunched over the cobbled market streets. Steering was done by the wooden front wheels, which had long iron handles attached at the hub. The straight shafts joined across the front, allowing room for two people to pull a loaded cart quite easily.

We turned into the row by the fire station and stopped at the third railway arch along. The gate was open and other traders were packing up for the night. Tommy seemed to know them all and was greeted like a long-lost friend.

'Hello, Tommy boy, who's this you got wiv ya?'

For a second I smiled to myself; if Mrs Bentham could hear these men talk she'd have a fit!

'This is Billy Brown, George. He's doing my job for the next week.'

'Is he, by God? How old is he?' Before Tommy could answer, I spoke up.

'Old enough to work for Big Mike,' I said. It hadn't taken long for me to realise that being a friend of Big Mike was going to be very useful.

'Big Mike, is it? So, you must be his new Saturday Boy?'

'That's right, I am.'

George came over. 'You know what happened to his last Saturday boy, I take it?' Before I could answer he continued, 'He ate him and gave the bones to Jessie!' The men in the arches thought this was hilarious and all joined in the laughter.

'Thanks very much, George,' I addressed him in my most commanding voice. 'I'll mention it next time I see him.'

'Now look, Billy, I was only joking.'

'That's OK, George. So was I.'

The other traders were now howling with laughter. 'You're not as green as you're cabbage-looking, are you, lad?' George clenched his fist but just gave me a gentle push to the chin. 'You'll be alright with us.' As he withdrew his fist I read the word ARMY tattooed across the knuckles of his right hand and NAVY across his left. Noticing my curiosity, George held up both clenched fists under his chin and said proudly, 'Army-Navy Joint Welterweight Boxing Champion, un-defeated, not even by old Adolf.' He crouched into a fighter's stance and threw a few punches, just missing my ears. He was so fast I was spellbound.

'So, Billy, what d'ya think? Wanna go a few rounds?'

I regained my composure. 'No thanks, George, but if you like I'll bring Big Mike next Saturday. I'm sure he'll take you on!'

George stroked his chin thoughtfully. 'Maybe, when he's down to eight stone seven pounds, just maybe.'

As we all went back to our market stalls, I heard the other men talking to George. 'That's a cheeky little bugger,' one offered.

'So he may be, but he's got spirit and I like that.' Without saying any more, George went back to moving hundredweight sacks of potatoes as if they were filled with ping-pong balls.

The railway arch we were in was partitioned off to allow for three lock-ups down each side. Tommy opened the middle one and got busy unloading the stall. 'Fruit on the right, veg on the left. Any crap leave outside.'

'What's crap?'

'You know, Billy, rotten stuff.'

'Oh, right.'

We sorted and stacked the produce. Out of about thirty boxes we had six full boxes of rotten stuff.

'Where does all this go, Tommy?'

'Put it just outside the arch by the wall,' Tommy said. 'The old girls will be along soon. Go and get the hose by the door.' I wanted to know about the old girls, but Tommy was busy going through a crate of oranges for mouldy ones. Returning with the hose, I was instructed to half-fill an open-topped, forty-gallon drum. There was already some water in it so it didn't take long.

'Now, tip these in carefully.' Tommy handed me the half-crate of good oranges.

'What for?' I asked.

'Jesus, Billy, is everything a bloody question with you?'

'I just like to know, that's all.'

'It's Saturday night. These oranges are old stock, so we keep them a bit fresh by putting them in water until Monday morning, see?'

'Sure Tommy, now I know.' I watched as the oranges plopped into the water, then bobbed to the surface, all shiny-skinned.

As I rewound the hose onto its drum by the front door, two old ladies were sorting through all the stuff we chucked out. The 'old girls', as Tommy called them. Standing just inside the arch I witnessed this little spectacle.

'Sad, ain't it?' George was beside me. 'Every night, it's the same. All these old dears come and collect anything they can cut and use. It saves them on their war widow's pension.'

'But these two are too old to be war widows,' I said.

'Not this war, the last one. The First World War.'

I looked again and one lady saw me. 'Hello luv, got any good tomatoes left?'

'Over here, Billy.' George handed me half a box of ripe, juicy tomatoes. The minute I put them out, the ladies descended on them as if they were gold coins.

'Thanks, darlin'. What's your name?'

'It's Billy Brown, ma'am.'

'Well, Billy Brown, you're a good, kind-hearted boy and God will watch over you.' They carried on sorting while Tommy and I stripped the stall, finally folding up the fake green grass cover the fruit was displayed on.

The last job was to brush the barrow off, leaving it clean for Monday morning.

'What shall I do with all these empty crates, Tommy?'

'Chuck 'em out with the rubbish. The market cleaners clear all that after seven o'clock.'

'But they're all wooden. Don't you keep them?'

'No, you think we're going to send orange boxes back to Spain for a refill?'

Looking at all these wooden boxes set my mind into supply-and-demand mode.

'So, I can take them if I want?'

'For Christ's sake, Billy, you can clear the whole bloody market if you want. It'll save the cleaners a lot of work. But what do you want with a load of old boxes anyway?' Before I could explain Mr Robinson came back from the pub.

'Ah, good boys, that's it. Oranges in soak, Tommy?'

'Yes, Mr Robinson. Billy did 'em.'

'That's it, then. Lock up and fuck off!'

I was a little surprised by Mr Robinson's swearing, especially the F-word. I'd only said it once and Mum had scrubbed my mouth out with a bar of soap. Behind his back, Tommy mimed a gesture of tipping a glass to his lips and making his legs go wobbly. From this I gathered Mr Robinson might have had more than one pint of Guinness that evening.

Mr Robinson handed five shillings to Tommy and gave me two. 'See you at the stall Monday, five thirty. Yes?'

'Yes please, Mr Robinson. I'll be there.' He waved goodbye and tottered off home.

'You did OK. Two bob for an hour's work. He either likes you or he's pissed. Well, I'm off to the Prince of Wales. See you in a week.'

I stood there staring at all the wooden boxes.

'Here you go, Billy.' Turning around, I saw George offering me a wooden tomato box filled to the top with ripe fruit. I stared in amazement. The box looked like something from the church's Harvest Festival celebrations. Oranges, apples, pears, plums, tomatoes and a marrow filled it to overflowing. 'Thank you, George. Mum will be delighted.'

'That's OK. Most of it will be going off by Monday.' I looked into the box again and knew he was lying. It all looked perfectly good to me but I didn't say anything. As I walked out into the market I turned back. 'George?'

'What?'

'Didn't you have any bananas?' I couldn't help grinning from ear to ear.

'What, for the bloody cheeky monkey?' He aimed a rotten apple at me, which I easily avoided.

'See you Monday night, George.'

'Not if I see you first, Billy Brown!'

Mum was speechless when I told her about my first trip to the market. She couldn't stop saying, 'And he gave you all this, are you sure?'

'Honest, Mum!' I told her all about George and his tattoos and the old ladies. 'You must always remember,

Billy, that there's always someone worse off than you. Now, let's see . . .' and she began to unpack the box. In the bottom were six large green cooking apples. Picking one out, she turned it around in her fingers and sniffed it.

'Here, smell it.' I sniffed as directed.

'It's an apple, Mum.'

'Ah, not just any apple, these are Bramley apples, the best for apple pies. I'll make three with these.'

'Mum, we can't eat three big pies,' I protested.

'I know that. One's for us, one's for old Mrs Dawson on the second floor and one is for you to take to your nice Mr George next Monday. Kindness brings its own rewards, Billy.'

'I know, you're always telling me.'

'Here, have a pear. It's time for *Dick Barton*.' As nobody had a TV in 1949, our entertainment was the radio. At seven o'clock each night it was the detective series *Dick Barton, Special Agent*, with his sidekick, Snowy. At least fifteen million people listened to it every night, only to be left with a cliff-hanger ending to make us tune in again for the next episode.

The following Monday I arrived early for the market with my go-kart. Dad had made it for me from some old pram wheels, a plank and a large sturdy wooden box. It was steered by a length of rope attached to each side of the front axle. Parking it in the railway arch, I went off to find Mr Robinson. The same little pantomime ensued. 'I'll be in the Canterbury Arms if you need me. See you in an hour.'

Clearing the rubbish from under the stall, I pulled it

out into the market. As I turned into Station Road for the arches, George came alongside me pulling his stall. Shifting nearer to me, he seized the corner of my handle. 'Come on, I'll give you a pull.' He now pulled his stall one-handed. It was only the brilliantly simple design of these stalls that allowed him to do so.

Reaching the arches, he first pulled his stall in and then mine. Thanking him, I went to my go-kart where, under a cloth in the box, was the fresh apple pie with a doily over it.

'Here, George,' I offered up the pie. 'Mum said "kindness brings its own rewards".'

He took the pie from me and removed the paper doily cover.

'Well I'm blowed. Look at this!'

The other traders gathered round. On top of the pie Mum had cut some scrap pastry into a boxing-glove shape.

'Did you ever see such a pie?' he said. They all agreed. 'You must thank your mum, Billy. She's a very kind person.'

'So are you, George, but she wants her plate back. She's not that kind!' He laughed, and once again the ARMY fist nudged my cheek.

It didn't take long to empty the stall and I didn't have to soak any oranges. Once everything was put away and swept out I set to, stacking and packing boxes onto my go-kart. The traders were most curious until I told them it was all for firewood. The tomato boxes were the best, as they stacked inside each other. Apple boxes fitted inside the orange crates and in no time at all I was loaded. George gave me a piece of thin rope to tie it all down and was surprised when I showed him my slip knot. Mr Robinson arrived to close up, checking the lock-up first and then the market stall. He nodded his approval. 'Well done, lad, see you tomorrow.' He didn't seem to notice me pulling a kart-load of boxes behind me.

From inside the arch George shouted, 'Billy, don't forget to thank your mum for the pie.'

'Don't forget the plate,' I shouted back.

For the rest of the week the scenario was the same. Market stall, then boxes. George and his fellow traders saved all their empty tomato boxes for me so the kart was quickly filled each day. On the very last night George gave me another Harvest Festival fruit box for Mum, this time with a box of dates on top for me. On the lid it said EAT ME. Well, I was certainly going to do that. The empty EAT ME boxes were a great thing to have. About ten inches long and three inches wide, they had a wooden top and bottom. The ends were rounded to allow the stiff cardboard sides to run in one piece, fixed with a few staples. We children would strip off the paper cover and use them as pencil cases. The girls always covered theirs in coloured paper with their names on. I just drew a skull and cross bones in the middle and a swastika at each end with a black crayon. I didn't need to put my name on mine as everyone knew who it belonged to.

I thanked them all for being so kind, especially

George. He laughed out loud when I told him that although I was very grateful, he wouldn't be getting another pie.

Dragging the kart home was tiring, but I didn't care. I had a pram shed full of boxes, a box of fruit for Mum and two bright half-crowns in my pocket. I couldn't stop smiling.

Mum was surprised at me being up so early on a Sunday morning. I wanted to be out straight away but she insisted we all sit down and have breakfast first. Sunday was the only day we were all together, so breakfast was a fry-up with egg, fried bread, potatoes, tomatoes, sometimes mushrooms and, on rare occasions, a sausage or bacon. All this was followed by toast and marmalade. We never ran out of marmalade as Alf Bentham, Janet's dad, was a crane driver on the London docks and had given Mum a damaged case of Seville oranges, perfect for marmalade. It had taken her a while to save up her sugar ration coupons but, as mums always seem to do, she'd managed it.

I almost choked on my breakfast, I ate it so quickly. 'Can I go now, please?'

Dad looked up from his *News of the World*. 'What's your rush, Billy?'

'I can't tell you. It's a surprise.'

'Oh, off you go then,' Mum said. 'Back at one sharp for lunch – and don't get into trouble!'

I flew down the stairs and across to the pram sheds. Unlocking ours, I surveyed the boxes. Under some sacking I had hidden my trusty axe. I had rescued it from a bombsite several weeks earlier while on one of my brick-collecting trips – I sold them to the allotment owners for their paths. Without further hesitation I set about the boxes. Bits flew in all directions, but I soon learnt the best way to get reasonable sticks from each box. The orange crates were the hardest because they had a thick board at each end to stiffen them. In just over an hour I had filled six tomato boxes with kindling and was now ready for phase two. Loading the filled boxes onto my cart, I set off for the first block of flats.

Pressing the doorbell to flat No. 1, I waited until it was opened by a man who was holding the *News of the World*. Obviously this was the preferred reading matter of the male population on a Sunday morning. 'What do you want?'

'Please, sir. I'm selling firewood so I can buy Christmas presents.' I offered up one of the filled boxes. He glanced in. 'How much?'

'Only sixpence a box.'

'OK. I'll have two.' Leaning against his doorway, he read his paper while I went to get another box, stunned and delighted by my immediate success. After paying me one shilling he rang the other two bells on the floor before I could do so. Two ladies in aprons answered and, once he'd explained what I was selling, they bought two more boxes of kindling. It took me only one more floor to sell the other two boxes.

Back at the shed I cut up more wood – and my thumb. It began to bleed quite a lot, but I didn't have time to worry about that. I have a business to run, I thought and, smiling, I wrapped it in one of Mum's pristine hankies to stop the blood dripping onto the wood.

I was soon on the road with another four boxes. Back at the first block, I decided not to climb all the stairs but just do the ground-floor flats. The first two said no thanks, and my enthusiasm started to wane. I pushed the bell at the third flat and waited. Beryl Prentis opened the door. She was older than me by a year, and thought I was the devil. She was one of the prettiest girls in the whole of the four hundred flats. Her blonde hair was pulled back in a pony tail tied with a yellow ribbon, her smart white cotton dress held with a yellow belt. The only thing out of place were her pink ballet shoes. She saw me looking and glanced down at herself, then back at me.

'Billy Brown, if you don't go away I'll call my mother.'

'I'm selling firewood,' I announced.

'Go away. Mother!'

Mrs Prentis came to the door. 'Whatever is the matter, Beryl?'

'It's that Billy Brown from over Ashford House. I've told him to go away but he won't.' Mrs Prentis squeezed past her daughter. She was rather a large lady and, from the look of her apron, was right in the middle of cooking Sunday lunch. 'Now then, my lad. What's all this commotion about?' With her arms folded across her ample bosom, she awaited my reply.

'Sorry, Mrs Prentis. I'm only selling firewood so I can buy my Christmas presents.' I held up a box. 'They're only sixpence each.' She looked me up and down. I was wearing the same old clothes that I wore to the yard: after all, I *was* working!

'How many have you got?'

'Well, I've got four with me.'

'And they're sixpence each?'

'Yes, Mrs.'

'Then I'll have all four. Beryl, get my purse.'

'But, Mum,' said Beryl, 'it's Billy Brown. I bet it's all stolen.'

'Don't be stupid, girl. It's all market boxes, isn't it, Billy?' It was more of a question than a statement. 'That's right, Mrs. Fresh today,' I added, to support the market theme. Beryl returned with the purse as I got the last box to the door.

'Beryl, give him two shillings.' She started to protest at the humiliation of having to give me money. 'It might be a good idea if *you* did something for your Christmas money, young lady.' Beryl knew when she was beaten, and handed over a two-shilling coin.

'Thank you very much, Beryl,' I said, rubbing it in. 'I'll be around again next week, if that's alright, Mrs Prentis?'

'You'll be very welcome, Billy. Mr Prentis doesn't do wood on account of his back.'

What firewood had to do with Mr Prentis's back I had no idea, but I'd be calling next Sunday, if only to annoy Beryl. 'Say goodbye, Beryl.' Mrs Prentis wedged her way past her daughter and disappeared into her kitchen.

In a voice that would melt your heart Beryl said, 'Goodbye, Billy Brown, and thank you so much for calling,' all the while making faces and giving me the V sign.

I put my hand in my pocket and pulled out my fistful of silver coins, showing them to her. Smiling mischievously, I made her even madder by saying in a posh voice, 'Goodbye, Miss Prentis. It's been wonderful doing business with you. I do hope I'll see you at Sunday School this afternoon.' I thought Beryl was going to explode as I ran out of her block. The slamming door resonated up the open stairs like a bomb.

I nearly ran into Alf Austin, one of the caretakers to the flats, coming back from the pub. 'What are you up to, you little sod?'

'Nothing, Mr Austin, honest. Have you got the time?' Eyeing me suspiciously, he pulled out a silver pocket watch from his waistcoat. Flipping open the lid he informed me it was one fifteen.

'Oh bugger, I'm late for lunch. Mum will kill me.'

'If she doesn't, I will, the day I catch you redhanded!' He wandered off, grumbling about bloody kids.

I grabbed my kart and headed home. 'You're late. It's in the oven. Wash your hands and hurry up.'

I sat down at the table, avoiding eye contact with Dad or my older brother, Bob. Being seven years my senior with a part-time job assembling racing cycles for a shop in Herne Hill, he looked down on my limited money-making schemes.

'You're in trouble,' he smirked.

'Be quiet, or so will you be,' Dad retorted. One word from him and we were both silenced. Mum put my steaming dinner in front of me, giving it a generous coating of thick Oxo gravy. As I lifted my first mouthful of roast potatoes she grabbed my wrist, nearly taking my eye out with the fork. 'Billy, whatever have you done to your hand?' The blood-stained hankie was still around my thumb.

'Oh, it's alright, Mum. I cut it with my axe.'

'Axe, what axe . . . ?' Her sentence trailed off at the sight of my blood.

'Well, you see, Mum . . .' I wasn't allowed to finish the sentence. She took me off into the kitchen, still holding my wrist. I tried again to tell her about the firewood business.

'Shut up and sit down, young man.' Realising she was in no mood for an argument, I sat on the kitchen chair while she unwrapped my thumb. At the sight of the cut she called out, 'Jack, can you come here, love.' Dad came in straight away and held my thumb up for inspection. 'He'll need stitches,' she advised.

'No, I don't think so. It's long, but not too deep. If we bandage it tight he'll be fine in a week or two.'

'Ooh. Can I stay off school, then?' I asked, as they both said, 'Shut up, Billy!'

Mum poured some Dettol disinfectant into a bowl and added warm water. Dipping a wad of cotton wool into the solution, she started to clean the wound. At the first touch I flinched. It stung like hell. By the time she'd finished I had tears in my eyes. She put her arm around my shoulders. 'Billy Brown. What am I going to do with you?' Drying my eyes with the corner of her apron, she applied Germolene to the cut. 'You could

51

have taken your thumb off. Then where would you be?'
That silly question again, I thought. Soon the thumb
was neatly bandaged up and secured with a bow, tied
with the split ends. I was marched back to the table to
finish my lunch which was still hot, thanks to a second
layer of gravy.

I had my lunch, plus apple pie and custard, eating in
silence, only now noticing how my thumb was throb-
bing. As if sensing my discomfort, Mum appeared with
half an aspirin and a glass of milk.

'Now, young man, you can sit with me and tell us all
about this axe business.'

We sat on the sofa and I related my story. 'You went
ringing on doors on a Sunday morning selling firewood? Oh, the shame of it!'

'Wait a minute, Eileen, he wasn't making trouble
for a change because he was occupied in honest labour!'

'But he nearly cut his thumb off!'

'An accident. I'm sure he didn't mean to do it on
purpose.'

'No, Dad, of course I didn't.'

'Well, Billy, did you sell any firewood?' he asked,
half smiling. I put my good hand in my pocket and
showed him the fistful of silver coins. 'I sold ten boxes
at sixpence a box!' I announced casually. The three of
them stared incredulously at the money. Dad sat back
in his armchair and reached for a cigarette. 'Well I
never!' he exclaimed.

'That's going in the post office, young man,' said
Mum, taking the money from me, 'and we'll hear no
more about it.'

'But Mum, I've got more orders for next Sunday.'

Dad almost choked on his cigarette, but I'm sure he was smiling at me.

2

Thank You, Mr Hitler

Brixton did not escape a visit or two from Goering's Luftwaffe. It mainly targeted the railway and some open ground where the US army was billeted, but the planes were either in too much of a hurry to get back to their French airfields and safety, or their aim was pretty poor.

At the back of our flats on Shakespeare Road were the railway marshalling yards of Loughborough Junction and Herne Hill, vast stretches of line for assembling goods trains. Although hit a few times, the yards were never put out of action. However, adjoining roads were hit again and again, especially the Barrington Road area. Row upon row of houses had been hit by high explosives and incendiary bombs. There was hardly a house not damaged. Most residents had been moved out several years earlier, and everywhere was overgrown and derelict.

It was now a wonderland and a constant source of adventure and profit for me. The playground and swings at the flats were great, but the bombsites were irresistible adventure and danger to all us boys. From exploring bombed-out houses to rafting across disused water tanks and flooded factory basements, nothing could keep us away. Few sites were fenced off and policing was nothing more than the odd policeman on the beat. Whole gangs of us from the Guinness Trust flats would often go to the Barrington Road sites just to cause mischief and play soldiers or pirates amongst the ruins. Always, we stuck to the sacred code of 'No Girls Allowed', although occasionally some of the braver ones, like Brenda or Sally, would attempt to trail along behind us to pick armfuls of golden rod, lupins and buddleia which had self-seeded all over the bombsites.

Jim, Derek and I were always up for an adventure, although some of the others in our group were not as keen. Kevin, a Scottish lad with ginger hair and protruding ears, who would always be telling us 'but it's breaking the law, I'm not going in there', inevitably ended up sitting on the wall outside the houses as our lookout.

We were all at school together: Sussex Road Primary School was just a five-minute walk from the flats, an old Victorian red-brick rambling pile of a school. The two stone porticos simply announced 'Boys' and 'Girls'. I don't remember too much about my early school years there but then I don't remember too much about any of my school years. I do remember my nose and the trouble it caused, though. Running into school one cold winter's morning, I slipped on the snow-laden granite steps. Unfortunately the step my face struck was not cushioned by snow and I broke my nose. The poor teacher was confronted by a screaming Billy Brown, covered in blood. I was duly dispatched to

King's College Hospital in a white Daimler ambulance with our English teacher, a nice lady who comforted me all the way there with, 'Now, my lad, are *you* going to be in trouble,' which was very reassuring as you can imagine.

Once at King's, a surgeon was summoned, resplendent in his white gown, hat and short wellingtons. After close inspection he held my nose with the edge of both palms and with a deft twist and pull, reset it perfectly. Sixty years on I am still indebted to him.

The outcome of my accident was a team of workmen descending on our school. In the next few weeks they cut grooves in every granite stair both inside and outside the building. My broken nose would make sure that no other child would slip again. I was the talk of the school.

All my pals in my class thought my two black eyes were hilarious, especially Jim, one of my closest friends. Although not very tall, what he lacked in height he more than made up for with his cheek and brilliant sense of humour. His teeth protruded slightly and gave him a permanent grin, emphasised by his spiky crew-cut blond hair. In all the years we were friends, I never knew anyone to get the better of him. He had all the fun of a young Charlie Chaplin, always coming out on top. Derek, on the other hand, was smarter than the both of us. A stocky lad with a square jaw and ready smile, his jet-black hair was always Brylcreemed by his mum every morning with a neat side parting. He was the best artist in the whole school and could draw any aircraft from the Battle of Britain in detail. Even at his young age, he knew he wanted to the join the RAF as soon as he was old enough.

We were the three musketeers, always to be found together, either in the playground at school or in the flats. United against our common enemy, boys from outside the flats – or girls! The fourth musketeer was a surprise to all three of us. To say Anthony was different to the rest of us was an understatement. Where we were all noisy and brash, he was quiet and studious, forever with a book in his hand. Quite tubby, with slicked-back hair, he was a target for bullies from the first day he joined our school. It wasn't just his studious manner, it was his glasses. His eyesight was so poor that he had to wear the thickest glasses available from the National Health. They were like the bottom of glass milk bottles and a constant target for jokes and pranks. The three musketeers made him the fourth and we took on the role of his protector. None of us liked bullies or being bullied and, besides, Anthony knew the answers to all our homework questions. The four of us would be in the same class at school for the next six years, all going on to Effra Road School at the age of eight.

Anthony never came on our bombsite expeditions, preferring to sit in the playground with his nose in a book. I always liked to find an old book or two to take back to him and, on one occasion, took him back the complete works of Shakespeare as a joke. But the joke was on me because he was absolutely delighted with it – and even offered to pay me for it, which I declined.

One bombsite expedition was quite profitable. Taking my trusty go-kart one day, I walked the half a mile to

Barrington Road. Stopping at the third house down I surveyed the front-garden wall, which had been demolished by the bomb blast that had also destroyed the house. The impact of the bomb as it struck the pavement had caused most of the bricks to separate, and so they were easy to load into my kart. Mr Green wanted two hundred bricks to do the paths on his allotment with and he was paying me one and six per load. This would be the last load as I could only move fifty bricks in the kart. Putting the last few bricks in, I straightened up to survey my booty.

'Now you can put them all back, Billy Brown.' I had no need to turn around. I knew the voice quite well. PC Collins stood there with his thumbs tucked into his tunic top pockets, his big black boots slightly apart to balance his not inconsiderable body. His helmet looked too small above his round chubby face. Small beads of sweat shone on his forehead from the exertion of pounding the beat. His moustache was the biggest at his station.

'But Constable Collins,' I protested. 'They're just rubbish.'

'Oh no, they're not. Once in that kart, they're loot. And looters will be shot. Now put 'em all back!' Still with his thumbs in his tunic pocket, he swayed gently back and forth, watching me unload the kart. 'Now, off you go – and don't let me catch you again or I may have to speak to your father.' Although I couldn't be sure, I thought he was smiling to himself.

Just my luck to be caught by Constable Collins, I thought. He lived in our flats and his son was in my class at school. It didn't help that he was also on the allotment committee with my dad. I turned around several times as I dragged my empty kart off, but he was still standing there watching me.

I reached the corner and pulled the kart into the first house still standing. Half of the house was gone, but a lean-to garage with only one of the doors on was still OK. Pulling the kart inside, I sat on its now empty box and surveyed my hideaway. The sun shone through the missing slates in the roof allowing light in. The place was full of old tins of dried paint, half a broken ladder, old doors piled against one end and a ragged tarpaulin over more rubbish in one corner. I had a good look round.

There was nothing of use until I looked under the tarpaulin. I couldn't believe my eyes. Pulling the sheet off created clouds of dust and cobwebs that had been undisturbed for years. Stepping back I surveyed my prize, allowing the dust to settle. I grabbed the handle, pulled it into the middle of the floor and walked around it. The huge old carriage pram was from a time long gone when rich families would wheel their infants out on a Sunday stroll to take the air and socialise. The pram was a fine piece of engineering and was built in exactly the same manner as old horse-drawn carriages. The carriage was suspended on leather straps attached to springs on the frame and axles giving it superb suspension, absorbing all the bumps so as not to bounce the baby. The spoked wheels had solid tyres so they hadn't gone flat, and the wide mock-ivory handle was still in one piece. I raised the collapsible hood and it fell to pieces. The canvas had perished years ago. This was a minor thing. Held by two rusty wing nuts, I soon had it off and discarded. The plastic-covered padding inside was worn and faded but still sound. I estimated roughly that I could move one hundred bricks at a time in my new transport.

At least half an hour had passed since I had entered the garage, so, covering up my find, I took my kart back to the corner to check for PC Collins. Good, he'd moved on, I thought, and I quickly reloaded my bricks and headed for home. As soon as they were stacked on Mr Green's allotment and my kart was back in its shed, I was off to get the pram. Back at the garage you could have heard my sighs of relief from the flats, such was my joy at finding my prize exactly where I'd left it. Although, if no one had been here in over seven years, why would they come back now?

Once out on the pavement I really got to appreciate my new form of transport. It was absolutely huge. Never mind one hundred bricks, I thought, this would carry at least ten boxes of firewood at a time, maybe more. I headed up Sussex Road almost effortlessly, with one wheel squeaking to keep me company. Two of my school pals passed me by.

'How's the baby, Billy? You don't look old enough to be a dad.'

'Sod off, the pair of you. How's your sister, Arthur?'

'Shut up, you bloody sod!'

Everyone in the flats knew about Arthur's sister. One of the older girls had heard her mum and Arthur's mum talking about how she was at least three months

60

gone, and that they'd had to move the wedding forward. In the Guinness Trust flats, nothing stayed a secret for very long.

Arriving at the pram shed, I set to stripping out the padded lining which came away quite easily, leaving the inside bare except for traces of old brown fish glue. The inside bottom was stepped down to allow two young children to sit opposite each other with their feet in the well. Rummaging in the shed, I soon found an offcut of plywood from one of Dad's projects. It fitted over the well quite snugly, giving the pram a flat floor ideal for brick-stacking. Fetching the filled watering can from Dad's allotment, I washed the whole thing down with a brush and my hankie. The black enamel with cream stripes gleamed back at me as if to say thank you. After years of neglect there was hardly a scratch on it. When Mum finally saw it she couldn't resist using one of her many sayings. 'Just look at that quality, Billy. As I'm always saying, you get what you pay for.'

My next trip to the Barrington Road area was to further my earning power considerably. Working in Big Mike's yard had taught me about scrap metal and the desirability of the non-ferrous type, as displayed on his price board. Having hidden my transport in the old garage again, I began my quest with a vengeance. It took me several houses to find one untouched, but there it all was. The incendiary bombing had set fire to several rows of houses, which had been virtually left to burn out. Most were gutted and the roofs burnt away. Inside, the copper cable glinted back at me, the lead sheathing having been melted away by the intensity of the fire. It took about twenty minutes to roll up a ball of copper wire the size of a small melon. Tucking it under the front hedge, I went back inside and collected what lead pipe had survived the inferno. The kitchen sink was easily smashed with a piece of old iron tubing to allow me to remove the lead waste pipe and brass waste trap. The toilet-flush pipe was a little more difficult, however, and I made a mental note to bring Dad's hacksaw next time.

One of my treasures proved invaluable. At the corner of Acre Lane was an ex-WD shop selling anything and everything the War Department didn't need any more. The stock was bought unseen at auctions run by the War Department. Sold in huge wooden crates with just a government number on them, the buyer simply took a gamble that he could make a profit on the contents.

Inside the shop, items were always stacked everywhere. Boots, webbing, tunics, tins of grease, shackles of every size, rope, tents, two- and ten-gallon petrol cans, pick axes, pointed shovels and ammunition boxes. There was enough to start your own war. The owner already looked keen, dressed in camouflage trousers, desert boots and a string vest with a tank corps leather waistcoat and a khaki woolly hat. He only had one name. Tosh. It was all he was ever called.

From Tosh's shop I had bought a folding trench spade for two bob, which would come in handy if I ever had to dig a trench in a confined space, and my army jack-knife, which Mum didn't know about, for one and six. It had two different-sized screwdriver blades that made short work of brass door handles. It was far too dangerous to try to get onto the roof for the lead flashing, although on a few occasions I had tried. A beam giving way and crashing into the basement on one attempt had taught me the error of my ways!

The trick was to look outside the house into the overgrown gardens, where the bombed roofs had been blown, often with their lead flashings still intact. A few well-aimed blows with my trusty axe reduced the nine-inch wide lead to movable pieces.

Recovering the pram, I shoved the scrap metal in the well before covering it with the plyboard sheet. A layer of bricks on top, and I was off. My beautiful black chariot coped with the load effortlessly. First stop, the allotment, for brick deliveries; second stop, Big Mike's yard.

The first time I took the pram to the yard they had a great time at my expense.

'So, you're doing baby-walking now, Billy? I suppose it'll be dogs and cats next, eh?'

It was a different story when I showed Big Mike the scrap metal.

'Well, well, breaking out, are we? I heard about the firewood.' He gave me a look that expected an explanation.

'Oh, I'm not selling it to the oil shops,' I said.

He roared with laughter. 'You bloody better not or I'll have your guts for garters! Now, let's have all this lot out.' He methodically separated the metals. He weighed the lead first, then the brass and the copper. 'That's three and six I owe you. Have you got change for a pound note?' Offering the green bank note, he waited. I looked at the one-pound note, then back at him.

'I haven't any money.'

'Will you take an IOU?'

I thought for a moment. 'No thank you, Mr Mike. I'm cash only, but I'll go round to the shop and change it for you.' Roaring with laughter, he found three and six in his pocket and paid me.

'That's what I like to hear, Billy, a cash-only man. I've started to get some of these cheques recently and they're a bloody nuisance; have to keep going to the bank. You stick with good, honest cash. Now listen to your friend Mike. I know where this metal comes from, and that's fine by me, but when you see lorries working, stay away. OK?'

'Yes, Mr Mike. Thank you.'

'Oh. And while you're on your expeditions, if you find anything,' he said, tapping the pram, 'too big for your transport, you let me know. I'll see you're alright.'

'What sort of big stuff do you mean, Mr Mike?' He gestured around the yard at RSJs, old machinery and galvanised water tanks, gates and railings.

'Me stock-in-trade, Billy, me stock-in-trade.'

'Oh, I get it.'

'Good lad. As I said to that lady in the oil shop, you'll go far, now didn't I?'

'I don't think she'd approve, Mr Mike.'

'No, thinking on it I don't think she would, but always live your life, Billy, not someone else's.'

'Is that one of them proverbs?'

'Well, I suppose you could call it that.'

'Oh, good. I'll tell it to Mum. She can add it to her collection.'

He laughed again. 'Jesus, Billy, you're a real caution and that's the truth.'

I had no idea what he meant but as he was laughing so much I took it as a compliment.

Mrs Kingdom owned and ran the sweet shop next to Sussex Road School. It was so small that only three or four children could get in at any one time. The reason was simple. It had been converted from the front room of her cottage. Apart from the attraction of her penny ice lollies, which she made from fruit squash and water, she would buy any items that we found on the bomb-sites. China, glass, brassware, pictures, anything she could make a nice little profit on. In the past I had taken her a blue china wash bowl and jug, the only item left intact following a direct hit on a house, and still inside there years on. I also sold her some nice horse brasses (ones that were too good for scrap), old books and other items. She always bought whatever I found and, after paying me, would give me a penny bar of Cadbury's milk chocolate and tell me to help myself to a penny lolly from the fridge.

'You're a good boy, Billy,' she would say. 'You know how old Mrs Kingdom likes these pretty things.'

Old Mrs Kingdom, my arse, I thought. She was a

female Fagin! All the boys visiting the bombsites knew her, but she paid promptly and never asked too many questions.

One summer day I was on the Barrington Road site with Derek. We had taken my pram just in case. Somehow we had managed to get into the garden of a large house, which had taken a direct hit from a three-hundred-pound bomb destined for the railway yard. The house was now a large overgrown crater covered in buddleia bushes and golden rod. In a corner of the walled garden was a potting shed which had fallen over sideways. We both agreed it was worth investigating; as it was still overgrown with brambles we knew no one had been there before us. It took quite an effort to get to it and we were both cut and scratched by the time we had cleared a path to the lopsided door.

The contents were useless. A pair of hedge shears, rusted solid; a roll of perished rubber garden hose and some old rotten gloves covered in spiders' webs were all that was left. The shed, being at an angle, was quite dangerous to be in but something had caught my eye out of the small window at the back. The sunlight was dancing on something white and shiny. Calling Derek over, I made him have a look.

'It's an old washing machine or something,' he said. 'But I'm not going back there, I've been scratched enough for one day.'

'OK, I'll go. You keep a look out.'

The collapsed boards were rotten at the bottom so it was fairly easy to kick a few out. Crawling through the gap, I squinted at the whiteness glaring back at me. The overgrown brambles and the bright sun still made it impossible to see what was there.

Pulling the sleeves of my jumper over my hands and closing my eyes for safety, I forced my way through until, reaching something solid, I stopped and opened my eyes. The Greek God Zeus stared back at me with unseeing eyes.

'Bloody hell!' I exclaimed, my heart pounding. 'You nearly scared me to death.' Zeus didn't answer but Derek did, poking his head out of the hole.

'What is it?'

'Come here and have a look.'

'Bloody hell,' he repeated. 'Old Ma Kingdom will surely want this. Who is it?' The statue was made of white marble and stood about three feet high. It was on a brick plinth and on the base was carved the word *Zeus*. It was obvious that when the bomb exploded it had blown the potting shed over, covering the path to the back corner of the garden and the statue. By the size of the crater I would not have thought anyone inside the house would have survived.

'Find a tyre,' I yelled.

'What for?'

'Just go and find one and be quick.'

Derek went off while I uncovered Zeus. He was totally undamaged. A bit of careful rocking soon dislodged the old cement holding him on his brick plinth. Derek returned with a bald lorry tyre. We put the tyre flat by the base, rocked and slid the statue until, with a final shove, it dropped onto the rubber. It took both of us to steady it as it bounced up, but it was down in one piece. Like every schoolboy I had watched the dray men delivering barrels of beer, which they dropped from the lorry onto an old tyre, never breaking one. Being far too heavy for us to lift, we spent the next half an hour clearing the other pathway to get the pram in.

'How are we going to get him into the pram? We can't lift him.'

'Don't worry, Derek, I'll show you.' Laying the pram on its side, we rolled Zeus into it. Then both of us stood on the wheels, gripped the top of the pram and flipped it upright. On the third attempt the baby was in the pram!

'You clever bugger, Billy. Where did you learn that?'

'At Big Mike's yard. It's how he gets old car engines in the wheelbarrow without having to pick them up. Now, give us your jumper.' I started to pull mine off.

'What for?'

'To cover up the baby, stupid!'

The wonderful pram transported Zeus without a hitch. We passed very few people and arrived at Ma Kingdom's shop safe, but exhausted. The shop bell jangled as we went in.

'Hello, Billy. Who's this then?' she asked.

'This is my pal, Derek. He's been helping me.'

'Oh, that's fine then. What have you got for me?'

'You'll have to come outside, Ma.'

'I'll have to do what?'

'Come outside. It's too big to get in.' Opening the flap on the counter, she forced her way out. I'd never realised how fat she was, only ever having seen her from the waist up behind the counter. Once outside I lifted up the edge of my jumper. She slammed it back down. 'Round the side gate. Now!' She hurried back through the shop. I could hear her shouting someone's name. Several bolts were shot back on the other side of the solid gate.

'In here, Billy, and be quick about it!' We trundled the baby into her backyard past the empty Tizer crates and R. White's lemonade bottles, which you could get twopence for so long as they had their stoppers.

'Reginald! Get your lazy arse out here.' Ma's son came out to the yard. He was even fatter. If they were ever in the shop together they'd have to call the fire brigade to get them out again, I thought.

Ma handed us back our jumpers and began examining the baby.

'Very nice, Billy, very nice indeed. Reginald, get it out. And mind you don't chip it!' With a grunt he lifted out the statue, placing it upright in the yard. Poor old Zeus didn't look at all happy in amongst all those crates of empties, having spent his formative years in his garden location.

'Can I go now, Ma?'

'Oh, for goodness' sake, Reginald, go, go.' He disappeared back indoors. Whoever is making his trousers must be on a nice little earner, I thought.

'Right boys, how much?' Derek looked blank. I stepped forward.

'Look, Ma, you've always played fair, so you tell me.' Stroking her chin, she eyed Zeus, who eyed her back.

'Five bob. How's that?' She'd never paid me five bob

for anything before and I was a bit taken aback. She must have taken my hesitation for a refusal. 'Each, of course.'

'Done, and a box of chocolates for our mums.'

'You cheeky little devil,' but she smiled. 'It's a done deal, Billy.'

'A done deal, Ma.' We shook hands but I didn't spit on my palm this time, in case she did!

'Go round to the shop and I'll pay you.'

We pushed the empty pram out and she re-bolted the gate. Once more the shop bell announced our presence. She scooped four half-crowns out of the wooden block with the holes which she used as a till. 'Two for you, and two for you.' We both pocketed our ill-gotten gains. Now for the box of chocolates. She found us the two smallest boxes in the shop. Cadbury's Milk Tray, with one single layer.

'There you go, boys. That old statue will brighten up my garden nicely.'

I didn't bother saying, 'What garden?' But I did ask for twopenny bars of chocolate and twopenny ice lollies.

'Cor blimey, Billy, you'll want shares in me shop next!' Handing over the penny bars, she told us to help ourselves to lollies.

'Thanks, Ma. See you again.'

'Any time, Billy, any time.'

Several weeks later, I was on my way home with a pram full of scrap from Barrington Road, when I stopped outside The Lodge for a breather. The Lodge was a grand, late-Georgian three-storey house, now derelict and boarded up, whose side wall bordered our flats. A sound coming from the rear of the house attracted my attention. Someone was knocking. Since there were no vans or lorries outside, I guessed it wasn't workmen, so decided to investigate.

Hiding my transport behind the front hedge, I made my way to the back of the house. A bottom panel had been knocked out of one of the French doors to the garden ages ago, so access was easy for a small boy. Crawling through, I allowed a minute or two for my eyes to become accustomed to the gloom. The remnants of an oak parquet floor were littered everywhere, the majority already having been removed. The marble fireplace had also suffered the same fate, leaving a huge blackened hole in the wall. The strange thing was the grand piano, still here but minus its keyboard lid. Some keys had been smashed and the brass pedals were gone, but it still stood there as if waiting for the maestro to return. The noise, however, was still coming from somewhere below me. Just off the main hall I found the entrance to the cellar half open. Opening the door as silently as I could I stared down, being immediately grateful that I hadn't rushed in. The stairs were gone. Peering into the darkness I recognised the noise-maker. It was Jim. He had his back to me and was trying to dislodge some floor bricks with an iron bar. He was making so much noise that he was totally oblivious to any I may have made.

Drawing in a big breath and using the deepest adult voice I could manage, I slammed back the door shouting, 'Hey. You there! What do you think you're doing?'

When he spun around, his face was a picture of terror until he recognised me.

'Jesus, Billy, I nearly pissed myself! What the hell are you doing here?'

'Me? You daft bugger! The whole flats could have heard you banging. What are you doing? Digging for gold?'

'Exactly.'

'What?'

'Come down here, Billy, and I'll show you, but watch the last rung of the ladder.'

'Why?'

'It isn't there, that's why.'

Someone had placed a section of an old wooden ladder to gain access to the cellar, and light was getting in through a filthy half-window high up in the wall overlooking the back garden. I climbed down, carefully avoiding the missing rung.

'So, where's this gold then?' I asked, half smiling.

'You'll laugh on the other side of your face, Billy Brown, when I find the hidden treasure.'

'Oh, so it's hidden treasure now, is it? You've been watching too many pirate films, Jim. It's affecting your brain.'

'Listen, my grandad was telling me that when the Blitz began, people thought Hitler was coming.'

'Right, so did they expect him to bring us a box of treasure?'

He was getting cross now. 'Now listen, smart-arse.

Grandad said rich people buried all their treasures in big tin trunks in fields, barns and their cellars so the Nazis wouldn't get it, see? Cellars – and this is a rich person's cellar!'

'They couldn't get it down here,' I offered.

'Why not?'

Pointing to the corner where the ladder was, I said, 'Because there's no bloody stairs!' I couldn't hold back the laughter any more. 'Wait 'til I tell them about Jungle Jim, Treasure Hunter!'

He waited for me to finish and, gesturing with his iron bar, announced, 'Oh no, big gob, then what's this?'

I stopped laughing and looked at the spot where he'd been digging.

'A load of these bricks were missing,' he continued, now holding my full attention. 'I've managed to get a few more out and look what I've found.' Moving closer, even I could make out the corner of a metal lid.

'Could be the drains,' I offered.

'Wouldn't cover them up – and anyway, they're over there.' Once more he pointed with his iron bar. I hadn't noticed the rest of the cellar, my attention being taken with Jim's activities. One whole wall was covered with old wooden slatted shelving, holding an assortment of jars, bottles and cardboard boxes.

'What's all this stuff?' I asked.

'Crap. Ancient food and drink, all crap. Here, I'll show you.' Picking up a large jar with something brown and murky inside, he smashed it against a wall. The room was filled with acrid fumes.

'Pickled onions,' he announced. 'Loads of them. You wouldn't want those with your fish and chips, Billy. I just wish I had a spade.'

'I've got one.'

'What?'

'Yeah, I've got one in the pram.'

'Well, bugger off and get it then so I can dig up the treasure.'

'So *we* can dig up the treasure, Jim. It's my spade, after all.'

'OK, OK. Half-shares, just bloody hurry up though, will you?'

I quickly found my ex-army folding spade hidden in the bottom of the pram with my axe and Dad's hacksaw. Back in the basement, Jim watched in amazement as I unfolded the spade's blade.

'That's bloody marvellous, Billy. Do you want to sell it?'

'No, sorry, Jim. This one was really hard to find (I pictured in my mind the crate full of them in Tosh's ex-army shop), but I know a man with one arm who's got one that he can't use any more. He might sell it for half a crown.'

'Get it for me, Billy, and I'll give you three bob.'

'OK. I'll do me best, Jim,' I assured him, again visualising the crate full at Tosh's for two shillings each. 'Now let's get this treasure.' With the sharp pointed spade it was easy to shift more loose bricks and dirt, uncovering even more of the treasure chest's lid.

'It's painted grey,' I observed.

'Well, they wouldn't have had some fancy brass-bound pirate chest, would they?' retorted Jim. 'They'd have used any solid tin trunk they had before Adolf's stormtroopers arrived.'

I could see Jim's logic and carried on digging. 'This is odd!' I announced. 'This lid is stuck to something down one side.'

''Ere, give us a look.' Jim peered into the small excavation.

'There's writing here.' Pulling his jacket sleeve over his hand, he rubbed the loose dirt from the lid. A hand-painted message read, 'Ein Weihnachtsgeschenk vom Drittes Reich'. We later found out it meant, 'A Christmas present from the Third Reich'. Neither of us could understand the writing, but we both recognised the numbers stamped on our treasure chest: 250 kilos.

We froze in fear as we suddenly realised that what we were crouching over was a 250-kilogram unexploded bomb.

'Don't move,' I whispered.

Jim looked at me as if I was stark raving mad. 'Don't move! I'm not bloody well waiting for old Hitler to get his own back on us for winning the war. It's been here for eight years without going off, so I'm off.'

'Well go slowly, for God's sake. We've disturbed it enough already.' I waited while he climbed the old ladder, and looking up as he went I could see the sky through the three floors and the roof.

'It came right through their house and buried itself

in the cellar. It must have been a dud.' Passing my spade out to him, I clambered up into the hallway.

'We can't leave it, Jim,' I said.

'Well, it won't fit in your pram and I don't think you can scrap it at Big Mike's,' he retorted, 'and I'm not bloody moving it anywhere.'

'No, I mean we should tell someone.'

'Oh sure, and get ourselves into big trouble for being in here!'

I thought for a while. 'I've got it.'

'Well, you can keep it. I'm off.'

'No, Jim. Find me some chalk.'

'What?'

'Some chalk. I'll leave a message.'

'What you gonna say, Billy? Sorry, Mr Hitler, it didn't go off! Better luck next time.'

'Jim, don't mess around. It could still go off; especially with the knocking around we've just given it.'

'Here, this should do.'

He'd found a large piece of plaster cornice that had fallen from the ceiling. Taking it, I managed to write on the top of the grand piano: 'DANGER – 250 KILO BOMB IN CELLAR!'

'Well, I hope whoever finds that doesn't recognise your crappy handwriting.'

'I already know who's gonna find it.'

'What? How can you know?'

'PC Collins will. I'll tell him.' Jim throws his arms wide and looks up to heaven.

'We'll both go to prison, you daft sod.'

'No, we won't. Now let's get out of here.'

Back at the flats we parted company, after swearing the usual vow of secrecy. Once my pram was put away I returned to the front gate and climbed onto the wall. The clock said ten minutes past six. Mum would already be home, but PC Collins wouldn't. I knew his shift finished at six o'clock and it took him about fifteen minutes to walk from the police station to home.

Bang on time he turned the corner, still in uniform.

'One day, Billy Brown, you'll fall off that wall, then where will you be?' He must have been chatting to Mrs Thompsit, I thought.

'Yes, Mr Collins,' I answered.

'And what mischief have you been up to today, then? I didn't see you round Barrington Road way. I suppose there's nothing left to nick, eh?'

'No, Mr Collins. I'm staying away from old houses, especially after all the goings-on today!'

'Oh – and what goings-on might they be, now?'

'At The Lodge, Mr Collins. You know, the old lodge; bangings and crashes all afternoon.'

'Were there now, lad? Well maybe I'll just go and take a look before it gets too dark. You wait here.'

I sat on the wall, knowing what he was going to find and feeling sorry for having to do this to him before his tea. Within five minutes he was running back to the gate.

'Bomb, Billy. Bloody great bomb.' Rushing into the phone box, he dialled 999.

'Bomb, Sergeant. Two hundred and fifty kilos. How do I know? It's written on the bloody grand piano. No,

Sergeant, I haven't been in the Canterbury Arms on my way home. It's a bloody unexploded bomb! Yes, Sergeant, I'll be there.' Hanging up the phone, he ordered me to tell the superintendent to send all three caretakers to him outside The Lodge with torches. 'And if he argues, tell him I'll arrest him under the Home Defence Act. OK?'

'Yes, Mr Collins, under the Home Defence Act.'

The superintendent didn't believe me. 'Billy Brown, if this is one of your pranks to make me look stupid again, I shall tell your mum.'

'It's a two-hundred-and-fifty kilo bomb.'

'A what?'

'A two-hundred-and-fifty kilo bomb in the cellar of the old lodge.'

'Oh my God. If that goes off it'll take half the flats with it.' Picking up his phone he started dialling, the caretakers being the only ones in four hundred flats to have telephones.

By seven thirty when Dad got home, the flats and neighbouring streets were in full evacuation mode. I met him outside the gate carrying two blankets.

'We're going to Sussex Road School. Mum's there with Bob already.' We hurried past the barriers. The Lodge was ablaze with lights, police, fire brigade and the army bomb-disposal team. I noticed PC Collins with his thumbs hooked into the top pockets of his tunic. He was talking to a man with a notebook. He would be in the next day's paper. 'LOCAL BOBBY SAVES 400 LIVES!' I wanted to stay and watch, but Dad hurried us to the school. Mum was already helping ladies to hand out sandwiches and mugs of tea from the Salvation Army van. I heard one lady say, 'Just like the war, Marge, ain't it lovely. It's brilliant.' There were hundreds of people in the school hall and room, but I soon found Beryl.

'Isn't this exciting, Beryl.'

'No, it's not, Billy! I don't want to sleep with all these smelly people.'

'Don't worry. You can come under my blanket,' offered Jim, and added to me, 'Bloody hell, Billy, I think they got your message alright.'

'Shut up, Jim.'

'What message? What have you two been up to now?'

'Oh, just a message to PC Collins, thanking him for saving us all.' Beryl eyed me suspiciously.

'You sent a message to PC Collins, Billy?'

'Well, sort of.' Jim and I dissolved into laughter.

'We could have all been blown to bits and here's you two laughing!'

'Don't worry, Beryl,' said Jimmy. 'It was a two-hundred-and-fifty kilo dud!' We both stopped laughing, silenced by his stupid admission.

Beryl glared at us suspiciously. 'And how do you two know it was a two-hundred-and-fifty kilo dud?'

3

Broken Clowns

'Ah Mum, do I have to go?'

'Yes, you do, Billy. I'm not leaving you home to get up to I don't know what!'

'But, Mum . . .'

'Stop whining. You're going and that's that, young man.' There it was again, the 'young man' bit. I might as well resign myself to my fate. I was going to have to stay at Woolworths for the Christmas school holidays because there was no one to look after me at home.

The following Monday I was up and dressed early, with a clean shirt and tidy clothes. 'Polish your shoes, Billy, they're filthy . . . and don't get shoe polish on your new socks. And be quick about it. I can't afford to be late.'

Taking the wooden shoe-cleaning box that Dad had made, I went out on the landing. While I was brushing the polish on, Mr Morris came out of flat 244. 'Well, there's a sight I never thought I'd see. You cleaning your own shoes!' His sarcasm was lost on an eight-and-a-half-year-old.

'I've got to stay at Woolworths for the holidays,' I informed him in a voice that sounded more like I was going to be hung, drawn and quartered and then shot at dawn.

'Which Woolworths, Billy?' he enquired with mock kindness.

'Walworth Road, near East Street, where Mum works,' I told him, perking up a bit at his interest in my welfare.

'Well then, I'll be sure to avoid it for the next three weeks, and God help them all when you get there!' And with that he went off to work, shaking his head.

'Billy, you ready yet?'

'Coming, Mum.' A final spit on each shiny toe and a quick rub with the soft cloth brought them up a treat.

We were soon on the No. 45 bus for East Street market. 'Now, listen carefully, Billy,' Mum began as we bounced over the tar blocks at the tram intersection at Loughborough Junction. 'Mr King is only allowing you to stay as a great favour to me. None of the other children are allowed, so you must be really special. Mr Norris, the storeroom manager, has agreed to keep an eye on you for me, so be polite and mind your manners.'

Arriving at our stop, we waited for the traffic lights to change before crossing to Woolworths. Looking across the road, I could see the store with its red sign and F. W. Woolworth & Co Ltd in gold letters. The windows were all dressed for Christmas with toys and gifts of every type, with a huge real fir tree with lights and tinsel. Crossing over, we stopped for a moment so I could admire the tree. It went from floor to ceiling, but what really caught my eye was a large teddy bear standing upright on a golden box. It was dressed in red trousers, a shirt and bow tie with a red waistcoat, toy watch and chain. It also had a full black tailcoat with a top hat and a gold-tipped cane.

Turning to Mum, I began to say something but she quickly interrupted. 'Yes, Billy, it's the teddy I've been dressing in the evenings. Can you read the sign?' With her help I managed it. 'Christmas Raffle. One shilling a ticket. All proceeds go to the Orphans' Home.'

'You understand, don't you, Billy?'

Even though I said yes, I didn't really. I had watched her working on Big Ted, as we had named him, for the past few weeks, deftly cutting and sewing old scraps of material from her work-basket to produce this most wonderful outfit for Big Ted. Dad had made the top hat, cane, watch and chain from odds and ends.

I walked into Woolworths, devastated that Big Ted was not for me. It was bad enough I had to stay here for three weeks of my holidays, but to have to pass Big Ted every morning was more than I could bear! Following Mum up the staff stairs was like being led up the gallows to be hung.

'Come on, Billy, just get a move on or you'll make me late. Now behave!' Mum opened the door to the Ladies' Staff Room. The noise level nearly knocked me over. Dozens of young women were stood around chatting and getting ready for the shop floor. Some were in just their slips or petticoats, changing into their work dresses, adjusting suspenders, fluffing up their new hairstyles, putting on fresh lipstick. I stood and stared, mouth open.

'Billy, sit over there for a minute,' said Mum. I sat on

a metal fold-up chair against the wall while she got into her work clothes. Later she explained that all the girls who worked on the food counters had to wear regulation over-dresses, while the non-food girls could just wear a large apron, which covered nearly all the front of them. Several of the younger ones had machined their aprons to give them a more daring neckline. The food ladies wore a hat or hairnet, depending on status. Mum had a hairnet.

There were as many as thirty girls working at Woolworths. Every counter had at least two tills, sometimes three, and most counters were double-sided, allowing sales from both sides and both ends. An alleyway in between allowed the girls to move up and down to serve. Woolworths sold everything, from sweets and toys to bootlaces and reels of cotton. You knew you could get it all at Woolworths. No town was complete without one!

Taking my hand, Mum towed me off to the stockroom, my ears still ringing with the girls' chatter. 'Oh, no Doreen, give me your Ronald Coleman any day!' 'But Maisie, you know what they say about that Errol Flynn!' They all burst out laughing when she made a gesture with her arm, which I didn't understand. Over the next few weeks I would learn more about boyfriends, husbands, fashion, film and singing stars than in all my previous years put together.

'This 'im, Eileen?'

'Yes, Ted, this is Billy. Billy, say hello to Mr Norris.'

He looked a kind man; his hair was almost gone and

he wore spectacles that he constantly had to push back along his nose. His moustache was trimmed and neat. The breast pocket on his brown warehouse coat was crammed full of pencils and the new biros.

'Hello, Mr Norris,' I said, offering my hand as Mum had taught me. As he took it I noticed his wristwatch had a leather cover over the face with an army crest on it in the shape of a winged dragon.

'It's the Buffs, lad, Royal East Kent Regimental Sergeant Norris at your service!' He shook my hand. During my stay, he would tell me stories of El Alamein 1942 and the Anzio campaign in Italy. 'OK, Eileen, he'll be safe with me.'

'Bye-bye, Billy. See you at tea,' and with a wave she was gone. I suddenly felt very alone.

'Right, lad, I've just the place for you.' Mr Norris showed me to a huge bay window seat above the shop front, looking out onto the Walworth Road. He had put a fold-up metal chair by the window on which were some colouring books, pencils and crayons. I looked up at him, not quite understanding.

'For you, lad, from the damaged and returns shelf. Now, you just amuse yourself while I get on, OK?' He marched off to the main stockroom through an archway. I could hear him giving orders for boxes to be lifted and put on trolleys by the delivery lift. I could hear the fold-back gates being opened and closed and the lift bell tinging each time it descended.

Turning back to my window, I gazed out at the passing trams, thinking about Big Ted sitting below me in the front window. Oh well, I thought, shrugging my shoulders, it's all for one of Mum's good causes, but I was still badly disappointed.

I had been so engrossed in the colouring books that I hadn't noticed anyone come in. Half turning, I nearly jumped out of my skin. The man had a brown warehouse coat on like Mr Norris, but there the similarity ended. This coat would have made a tent for Mr Norris and me. He was in his early twenties and was almost as big as Big Mike from the yard, although he didn't have Big Mike's belly. His hair was cropped short and he had really dark bushy eyebrows like two furry caterpillars crawling across his forehead. He seemed to be grinning and smiling at the same time. He pointed to the picture I was colouring with a huge hand.

'Bus, bus, it's a bus, ain't it? Eh?'

I didn't know what to make of him. He sort of scared me, but I didn't know why.

'Ah, there you are, Tom. You know you're not supposed to be in here.' Tom stood up, holding his huge hands together, still smiling.

'It's a bus, Mr Norris, ain't it?' Looking over my shoulder, Mr Norris agreed with him.

'Yes, Tom, it's a red bus.'

Mr Norris stood directly in front of him. 'Tom,' he seemed to be speaking slowly. 'Tom, this is Billy. We're going to look after him for a while. Now, say hello.'

Tom's voice made me jump. It was so loud and booming. 'Hello, Billy.'

'Tell him your name.'

'My name's Tom.'

'Tell Billy what you do, Tom.'

'I do what Mr Norris tells me to.'

'That's it, Tom. Now off you go. There's a good lad.'

Tom returned to the stockroom, his giant body filling the arch on his way out.

Mr Norris sat on the window seat facing me. 'I know he's a bit of a shock sometimes, Billy, but he's quite harmless. He wouldn't hurt a fly. He's not too bright but he's the strongest man you'll ever meet, so we gave him a job shifting stock and clearing up. He shouldn't bother you, but if he talks to you just keep it simple and slow, do you understand?'

'Yes, sir. Mum said Grandad went a bit simple when he came back from the First World War, but he had loads of medals!'

'Well, Billy, your grandad and Tom may have much in common.' Placing his hand on my shoulder, he gave it a gentle squeeze.

'Soon be teatime.' Standing back up straight, he saluted me. 'Steady the Buffs!'

I saluted him back as he marched off again to Tom and his stockroom.

At the sound of a bell downstairs, half the girls went to tea. As I listened to them coming up the stairs, the door opened and several of them came in.

'Hello, Billy. You must be Eileen's boy.'

'Yes, Mrs or Miss,' I said, not knowing how to address them both at once.

'Here you go, Billy. Two sugars.' The first girl put down a cup of tea.

'Don't forget the bun, Jean.'

'As if I would, Josie.'

Opening the white paper bag, I found my favourite iced bun.

'Your mum is on second tea this week, Billy, so she said we were to look after you.'

The two girls were absolutely gorgeous, and I thought they could have been film stars like Betty Grable. They both had similar hairstyles to the Hollywood star.

'I'm Jean.'

'And I'm Josie,' they both chimed, almost simultaneously. They were, of course, sisters. We all sat and drank our tea. Jean told me how lucky I was to have such a wonderful mum.

'Any problems and your mum's the one to go to.' Josie couldn't say enough good things about her. The bell rang again, announcing second tea. The two got up to go.

'Oops, nearly forgot.' Jean reached in her pocket, pulling out a small white paper bag similar to the one the bun came in.

'There you go, Billy, compliments of Woolies.' Jean leant over, pinching my cheek. 'Ooh, you're such a cutie.' I blushed all the way down to my toes.

'Jean, leave the poor boy alone!' scolded her sister. 'You'll have to wait at least ten years!' Then they both went off laughing, and I realised I was starting to enjoy my enforced incarceration!

Then Mum arrived with some of the more mature ladies.

'OK, Billy?'

'Yes, Mum. It's smashing here.'

She gave me a knowing smile. 'That wouldn't have anything to do with Jean and Josie, would it?' Once again I blushed all the way down to my toes.

'Leave the poor boy alone.' I was introduced to Eaddie Peel, a jolly lady with glasses. 'Now Billy, what do you want for lunch? You can't be in the canteen, so I'll bring it out to you.' She then proceeded to recite the entire day's menu. I looked at Mum, who gave me a nod of approval.

'Can I have the fish and chips please?'

'Good choice, Billy. And for pudding?' I looked at Mum again. Mrs Peel stopped me.

'Don't worry, Billy. It's all with the compliments of Woolies, so have the ice cream.'

'Yes please, Mrs Peel, and thank you.'

'It's my pleasure, young man.' For once the 'young man' bit didn't sound like I was in trouble!

The rest of the day was just great. The bag Jean had given me was full of broken-up bits of toffee, not still in its slab form, so it was easy to eat. I went to the stockroom and offered some to Tom and Mr Norris. He took a piece but said Tom wasn't to have too much sugar so he didn't get any, but he still said thank you three or four times.

By the end of the day I was so full of food and treats I thought I'd go bang! I had mastered the bell signals, so I knew when to expect Mum and when the younger girls would be up. I almost wished I was back at school to tell all my mates about Jean and Josie. Before I left for the day Mrs Peel gave me a big bag of broken biscuits to take home. There were so many that Mum let me put them into small bags, which I sold to my pals for one penny a bag. This was repeated nearly every day of my stay. I was becoming very popular in the playground of the flats at about six thirty each evening!

I had been at Woolies for over a week and had got into the routine of calling it Woolies, not Woolworths. Each morning before opening time Mr Norris made adjustments to a chart in the window by Big Ted, showing how much money had been raised so far. It was like a giant cardboard thermometer, and he raised the pointer each day. The donations initially came in quite slowly but, as Christmas drew near, the level went up faster. It was in ten-pound markers and the pointer was already between forty and fifty pounds. One of the girls had told me that one man had bought five pounds worth of tickets, which was more than their entire week's wages!

One morning Mr Norris came in with a brightly coloured box.

'There you go, Billy.'

The lid on the box showed a circus ring with white horses and clowns on the cover. The lid had a tear in it. I looked up at Mr Norris and he winked at me.

'Damaged-goods shelf!' We both smiled and no more was said. Unpacking the box revealed a red plastic circus ring with twelve white plastic clowns in different poses, some even with hoops in their hands, two white horses and a ringmaster in red, white and black. The hands of the clowns, were designed to snap onto the hands of the other clowns, so that the variations were limitless. I sat on the floor, delighted with my new toy. Clowns stood on top of each other, two on a horse, three on a horse. I was oblivious to all else. It was the best toy I'd ever had!

I didn't hear him coming until it was too late. Tom picked me up effortlessly and held me high in the air. I stared straight into his eyes, terrified.

'Put me down, Tom. I'll tell Mr Norris.' His grinning only served to scare me more. Then he did something which made the hair all over my body stand up on end. He laughed, not a happy laugh, but the laugh of a simple man, long, loud and booming.

'Haaa, haaa, haaa,' he wouldn't stop. By now I was shouting for him to stop, but he wouldn't. Carrying me into the stockroom still laughing, he lifted me into the baling machine. This large box-like device made from huge wooden stays and iron straps was used to compress cardboard packaging before it was held with a steel band. I was crying and screaming as he lowered the lid on top of me. And still he laughed. He engaged the power button and held the compression lever in his huge hand. I was convinced I was going to be crushed to death.

'TOM!' The command stopped him dead. He stood rigid, releasing the lever. He turned away as I sunk to the floor of the baler.

It seemed like hours, but within seconds the power was off and I was free. I fell into Mr Norris's arms.

'No one heard me, no one heard me,' was all I could say.

'Christmas carols, Billy, bloody Christmas carols. They've got them on the tannoy system so loud down there you can hardly hear yourself think.'

'He was going to crush me!' I cried.

'No Billy, he couldn't do that. The lid doesn't come down until you remove the safety pin. Tom wouldn't know how.'

We walked back to my window where he sat me down.

'Now listen, Billy. I know Tom scared you but he didn't mean to. He's not well, but I'm sure he meant you no harm. He was just playing. Now I need you to be a big boy over this. You mustn't say a word to anyone or Tom will be in serious trouble and will probably lose his job. He's got a wife and two kiddies to support, so it's not too easy for him to get another job. Do you understand?'

I nodded. 'But he won't do it again, will he?'

Mr Norris put his arm around me. 'No, Billy, I'll make sure he doesn't. It'll be our secret, OK?' Wiping my eyes with his hankie, he offered his hand. Still sniffing back the tears, I spat on mine and offered it to him. Smiling back he spat on his palm and shook my hand.

'You're a good boy, Billy Brown. I'd have had you in my regiment any day.' I swelled with pride.

'Steady the Buffs,' I said with a shaky voice.

'Steady the Buffs,' he repeated, and I vowed never to

tell a soul of the day that poor Tom nearly crushed me to death.

I dried my eyes on one of Mum's white hankies and, blowing my nose, turned back to my new toy. Mr Norris must have seen the look of horror on my face.

'What is it, Billy?' he asked with genuine concern. I could hardly get the words out.

'My . . . my clowns,' I stammered. We both looked down on the floor. Unbeknown to me, Tom had trodden on them when he picked me up and had broken most of them. They lay in disarray, some with arms and legs missing, some completely in half. The ringmaster had lost his whip arm and a horse one leg. I sat on the floor looking at the carnage and started to cry. Mr Norris crouched down beside me. 'Never mind, Billy. It's only broken clowns,' and began picking up all the pieces.

When it came time to go home that day Mum asked me why my eyes were so red.

'I got a bit tired and rubbed them,' I lied.

'Well, it'll be an early night for you, young man. Now, where's my coat and hat?' She went off to fetch them, leaving me alone. Someone grabbed my arm and I nearly fainted.

'It's OK, Billy, it's only me.'

'Oh, Mr Norris, you scared me.'

'Sorry, Billy, but I wanted to catch you before your Mum took you home. Here.' He offered me a brown-paper parcel tied with string. I didn't need to ask its contents. I knew.

'From the damaged and returns shelf?' I said.

'Exactly!' he replied. Then, standing to attention, he saluted me. 'Goodnight, soldier!'

'Good night, Sergeant,' I replied, returning his salute. We both smiled at each other.

'What's all that about, Ted?'

'Just saying goodnight to your little soldier, Eileen,' he said as he turned and marched back to his stockroom.

A few days later it was Christmas Eve. All the girls were in party hats and the whole store was covered in decorations. By nine fifty the store was packed, as was the pavement outside. A tombola box had been set up in the main window to raffle Big Ted. Mr King, the manager, and Mr Clarke, the assistant manager, were on either side to supervise fair play. A little girl had been picked from the crowd to do the actual draw. As the time drew near the crowd began the countdown. Ten-nine-eight . . . it was absolutely fantastic. To think that all these people wanted the teddy bear that my mum had dressed. I felt so proud of her. Seven-six-five-four. Mr King gave the tombola one last turn, then opened the lid. Three-two-one! The crowd roared.

Standing on a box in her pink winter coat and hat, the little girl took out a ticket and handed it to Mr King. Mr Norris had set up a microphone connected to the tannoy system and an outside speaker. 'And the winner is . . .' He hesitated a moment for maximum effect. 'Number three seven six.'

Hundreds of people checked their raffle tickets. Just for a moment he thought the lucky winner may not be in the crowd. Then a huge cheer went up over on the East Street side of the crowd. 'Me, me, it's me!' a lady was pushing her way through the throng of shoppers, followed by her husband carrying a little boy of about five. The crowd parted like the Red Sea, and she was shown into the store followed by her family. For a moment they disappeared, then, seconds later, they reappeared in the window. The crowd cheered and clapped the winner. After making a big performance of checking her ticket, Mr King announced: 'The Winner – Mrs Margaret Mills.' The little girl in pink presented her with Big Ted and, in return, received a Cadbury's Chocolate Christmas Selection Box, to the delight of the crowd.

Holding Big Ted aloft, she let the crowd cheer before offering him to her son. They waited while he took off his gloves, which were joined by a length of elastic passing up one sleeve and down the other to stop him losing them. He needed no encouragement. Seizing the bear, he clutched it to his chest. The crowd cheered even harder. Over the tannoy, Mr King announced that Woolworth's Annual Christmas Charity Raffle had raised one hundred and twelve pounds and nine shillings for the orphans of the Borough of Southwark. A rapturous round of applause broke out and people nodded their approval to each other.

The rest of the day was all mince pies and Christmas lunch. Mr King had managed to get several joints of beef from a supplier as a thank you, and all the girls had a good roast lunch, albeit in two shifts. The store closed early at four o'clock but it took a while to leave, what with everybody saying their goodbyes and Merry Christmases.

Jean and Josie found me and gave me a huge kiss on either cheek, leaving a print of lipstick on both. The pair had party hats on and now some of the store's tinsel around their shoulders. It had been like a giant party. Mr King thanked my mum and gave her a Christmas box of biscuits. He was then dragged off to the nearest pub by all the young Woolies girls for a Christmas drink. As my mum and I left I saw Mr Norris in the store window rolling up the microphone cable. He looked up when I tapped on the window. Standing to attention, I saluted him through the glass. He returned my salute followed by a goodbye wave. Mum waited for me to catch up.

'You're a funny one sometimes, Billy,' she said. She ruffled my hair with her woolly gloves still on.

'Only sometimes, Mum?' I asked, smiling. She offered me her arm as we walked up the road for the No. 45 bus and home.

The rest of Christmas Eve was a bit of an anti-climax. I helped Mum prepare the veg for Christmas dinner as she always did it the night before, so that she could be with us on Christmas morning. At about eight o'clock that night we all went across to the clubhouse for Christmas carols with the Salvation Army band. Mum, of course, was in the clubhouse kitchen doing the teas and mince pies for everyone. By the time we all got back home it was nearly midnight and I had no problem falling asleep, even with the thought of Father Christmas dancing in my head. I slipped quickly into the land of nod.

On Christmas morning I awoke to the biggest surprise I could ever have imagined. Sitting on the end of my bed was a teddy bear wearing red trousers with a gold stripe, a white shirt, a waistcoat with gold watch and chain, a red bow tie and a full black tailcoat, finished off with a black top hat and a black cane with a gold top. Mum had worked on him secretly after I'd gone to bed nearly every night for a month. I instantly named him Little Ted.

Mum worked for another four years at Walworth Road, during which time I had so many good times with the Woolies girls. Apart from school holidays, there were many charabanc outings to Southend and Margate, to the circus at Olympia and Christmas ice shows at Wembley. For a while, at least, Woolies was like my extended family. Then Mum transferred to the Brixton branch to be closer to home, but it was never the same for me. With the advent of single checkouts, staff cuts were inevitable and she was finally made redundant after fifteen years' service. She would always be a part of Woolies, as Woolies would always be a part of her.

4

New Friends, All Shapes and Sizes

'You, boy, come here.'

I froze. I was standing on the pram's board, picking some apples off a tree. I was on my way back home, loaded with scrap metal in the well of the pram, and had stopped off at the old US army site to pick Mum some fruit. All the old Nissen huts and buildings had long gone and it was now a sort of unofficial lorry park. But the mature fruit trees from gardens planted way back were still there.

'Yes, you, boy. Come here.'

I turned to the sound of the voice but could see no one. It was then that I noticed a stick waving above the back hedge of one of the adjoining gardens.

'That's it. Over here,' the voice said. 'Come to the gate.' I climbed down from the pram and went over to the close-boarded gate. As I arrived it opened inwards and there, stood before me, was the smallest man I'd ever seen. I stared in utter amazement. He had the smallest long trousers on, a purple shirt with a black satin waistcoat and slippers smaller than mine.

'Didn't your mother tell you it's rude to stare, boy!' the little man said.

'Yes, sir. I'm very sorry but I've never seen a . . .'

He cut me off abruptly. '. . . a midget. That's right, boy. I'm a midget, but I didn't call you over to pass the time of day discussing my height, or lack of it. Here, fill this basket with good apples and I'll give you sixpence.'

It was more of a command than a request, so I took his wicker basket and went back to the tree with my mind reeling. While I filled the basket I wondered to myself, a midget, a real midget, in Brixton. What's he doing here?

With the basket now full of good apples, I returned and knocked on the gate.

'Come in, come in. Put the basket by the back step. Samson will get it.'

'Excuse me sir, but did you say Samson?'

'Of course I did, boy. You're not deaf, are you?'

'No, sir.'

He seemed very short-tempered with me. Going to the back step, he tapped on the glass door pane with his cane. 'Samson. Get out here now.' Once again I stared open-mouthed as a huge man with enormous muscles was coming through the door wearing just a vest, black braces and trousers.

'What's all the fuss about, General? This boy causin' you trouble?' He advanced towards me and I stood behind the General, although I was actually taller than him.

'Not at all, not at all. Do you want some apples?'

'Apples, what kind of apples?'

The General looked skyward with an exaggerated gesture. 'That kind,' he said, pointing to the filled basket with his cane. 'Go and get a basket and tell the princess.'

'The princess?' I repeated from behind him.

'Do you have to repeat everything I say, boy?'

'No, General, but . . . a princess?'

Samson came out with his basket, followed by the most beautiful young woman I'd ever seen. Her voice sounded almost musical. Her accent was foreign, but from where I didn't know. She too had a basket.

'Hello, little boy. Will you fill my basket too?' Her long white satin caftan swirled in the breeze. She was like one of the girls in the Douglas Fairbanks movies. I had no idea how to address a princess so I simply said, 'Yes, Your Majesty.' Samson roared with laughter.

'Be quiet!' the General commanded. Taking a step back he held his long cane to one side and, with the other hand, made a sweeping gesture towards the princess. In his loudest voice, which was still a bit squeaky, he announced, 'May I present the equestrian sensation of the age, The Princess Tatiana!' And with that he bowed low.

'And if you're not a horse, she's not interested,' added Samson.

'So uncouth,' retorted the princess. 'And who do we have here, then?' she asked, extending her basket.

Taking it I answered a bit shakily, 'I'm Billy Brown, Your Majesty.'

She knelt down to my level. 'Well, Billy Brown of Brixton Town, you fill my basket with good apples and give Samson all the rotten ones and you can call me

Miss Tatiana. I'll go and make some tea for us all. Now, off you go.'

Once more I scaled the tree in a daze. The General, Samson, a princess. My pals would never believe me, not ever!

By the time I had returned with the two filled baskets, tea was ready. In a corner of the garden was an old wooden gazebo in a tired state. Some of the trellis was missing, as were a few wooden shingles on the roof. But the table was laid with a white linen cloth, china teacups and saucers, side plates with a small fork and, in the centre, a glass cake stand with a thick Victoria sponge cake. I put the fruit down as the princess beckoned me over. 'Here you are, Billy, you sit by me.' I sat as if in a dream.

From the basement doorway came yet another squeaky voice. 'Samson, you lazy brute, come and get the tray.' I watched as the strongman collected the tray with matching teapot, milk and slops jug. It wasn't until he moved clear of the steps that I could see the tiny lady, Mrs General, was climbing the stairs very gingerly, holding on to a wooden handrail that had been fixed low down for her. Finally reaching the gazebo, she managed to get onto her wicker chair after a great deal of huffing and puffing.

It was only then that I noticed that her chair, and the General's, had about three inches sawn off the legs! Wrapping her brightly coloured shawl around her shoulders, she turned to me.

'Now, little monkey, who are you?'

The princess intervened before I could speak. 'He's

not a little monkey. He's Billy Brown from Brixton Town.'

'Well, Billy Brown, you could be a monkey the way you went up that tree. I was watching you from my window.'

'Oh yes, ma'am. I'm really good at climbing trees.'

'Maybe you should join us at the circus,' she said, and in that moment the penny dropped like a one-ton weight.

'Ah, you're all from the circus,' I said incredulously.

'Well, we're not from the freak show,' snapped the General.

'Rupert, he's only a boy. Don't be so grumpy! Princess, pour the tea please.'

'Of course, Mitsi.'

So they were actually Rupert and Mitsi. Over tea they told me that they'd been in America for the *Wizard of Oz* film and with Barnum and Bailey's famous circus. Now they were appearing in London with Chipperfields Circus. The General was the Second Ringmaster and also appeared as General Tom Thumb, the original having died in America. Samson came from Manchester and had been a champion bodybuilder, and the princess really was a princess from the Ukraine, where she said almost everyone was a prince or princess from some ancient dynasty or other. They all lived together in this huge terraced house with other theatricals. At the time there were many theatrical people in digs in Brixton. At the turn of the last century it was so famous for this that Sir Arthur Conan Doyle wrote about

Brixton Water Lane and its theatrical lodgings in one of his famous Sherlock Holmes mysteries.

'More cake, Billy?'

'No thank you, Miss Tatiana. I've had two bits already.'

'Pieces,' squeaked the General.

'Be quiet,' said Mitsi. As she leant forward to put her cup on the tray, her gold chain swung forward revealing the medal attached to it. Noticing me looking, she held it in her tiny hand to show me.

'That's the President of France,' she informed me with pride. 'Rupert and I both have one. It's one of the circus world's highest accolades.'

'It's lovely, ma'am,' I said. She settled back in her chair with her eyes closed still holding her medal. 'Ah, magical times,' she sighed, 'magical times.'

'Well, I must be going. Mum will be home soon.'

'That's a good boy, Billy, always respect your parents.'

Suddenly the General leapt to his feet and, with a deft twist to the handle of his stick, withdrew the rapier-like blade concealed within. 'And if you don't, Billy Brown, I'll run you through.' With that he made several slashing movements towards me.

'General!' admonished the princess. 'You're scaring the boy.'

I stood as tall as I could. 'I wasn't scared,' I said, lying. The General replaced the blade. 'Always expect the unexpected,' he advised.

There's another one for Mum, I thought.

The General shook hands to say goodbye after he had paid me one and six for the three baskets of apples.

My hand was bigger than his, but his grip was firm and strong. What I didn't know was that he and his wife were in their mid-sixties, an amazing age for midgets. Samson bid farewell with a wave. The princess knelt down to me again, placing both hands on my shoulders.

'Goodbye, Billy Brown of Brixton town.' She leant forward and kissed me on both cheeks in the Continental manner. I turned to Mitsi to say goodbye but the princess held a finger to my lips.

'Shush, Billy, she's asleep.' The tiny lady was sound asleep wrapped in her coloured shawl, still holding her gold medal.

The princess saw me to the gate. 'Do come again, Billy. We're nearly always here during the day, except for Saturday matinees.'

'Thank you, Miss Tatiana. I'd like that very much.' Pushing the pram back, my mind was still spinning. Who's going to believe me? I wondered. Who?

'Honest, Mum, I'm not lying. Two midgets, a strongman and a beautiful princess.'

'Billy, I don't know where you get all this nonsense from, I really don't. Now go and play while I wash all these apples.' I trudged back to my bedroom. I knew no one would believe me, not even Mum!

Dad came home from work and we all sat down for dinner.

'So, how is everyone?' he asked.

'Well, Billy has excelled himself in the storytelling department today!'

'OK, and what fib has he come up with this time?'

Before I could answer, Mum continued. 'Well, it would appear that he's had afternoon tea with two midgets, Samson, a strongman and a Russian princess!' she said, smiling.

'She's from Ukrania,' I corrected.

'Billy, you're such a little liar!'

'Hold on a minute, Eileen.' Dad had stopped half-way through his favourite toad in the hole. 'Do you mean the General and his wife?'

I sprayed half-chewed toad all over the tablecloth.

'Billy Brown, you little pig.'

I couldn't believe it. Dad actually knew the General and Mitsi. 'But Mum, that's them, the ones I've been telling you about since I got home.'

She looked at Dad with one of her quizzical looks usually reserved for me. 'Jack?'

'They live down Short Loughborough Road, near the old US army site. I only know them because they sometimes get on my bus. He always carries a long black cane.'

'It's a sword stick. He showed me.'

'Billy, a sword stick indeed! Who do you think he is – the Scarlet Pimpernel?'

'It *is* a sword stick,' announced Dad calmly. 'I admired it once and he told me that he carried it after being knocked over and humiliated by some young lads several years ago.'

'Well I never, Billy, the company you keep.'

'Tell me about the others, Billy,' Dad continued, so

I repeated the whole story again. At the end he sat back in his chair.

'Well, Billy, I'd say you're very honoured. What boy gets to meet a real princess?'

'See, Mum, I wasn't lying.'

'Never mind "see Mum". Maybe this time you're telling the truth, but I shouldn't wonder that it'll be Queen Mary herself you'll be having tea with next!' Gathering up the dishes, she went off to the kitchen.

'Thanks, Dad. I never thought anyone would believe me.'

'I'll give you a tip, Billy. Next time, ask for a photo!' His wink made me smile.

'Good idea, Dad, I'll do that.'

Hurrying home from school, I turned the corner and stopped dead at the wonderful sight before me; the coal cart had stopped outside my block, drawn by two of the biggest black horses I had ever seen. As I approached them, they towered above me. Tim the coalman was busy scooping up piles of recently deposited horse muck.

'Can I have that please, mister?'

He gave me an enquiring look.

'Have what, lad?'

'That,' I said, pointing to the horse muck on the roadway. 'You always scoop it up into your sack. Can I have it instead?'

'What do you want with horse muck, lad?'

'It's for the allotments, for the roses.'

'Oh, I get you. How much do you want?'

'How much?' I looked towards the two huge cart-horses standing waiting. 'Can they do it to order?' I asked.

Roaring with laughter, he crouched down to my level. 'I wish they could, lad! I'd get them to crap in the yard before we leave each day, save meself a lot of trouble. What's your name?'

'Billy Brown, sir.'

'Well, Billy Brown. You can call me Tim. Now come and meet Wellington and Napoleon.' The two black horses were gigantic, towering above me, re-splendent in their polished black leather and brass harnesses.

'Which is which?' I enquired.

'Wellington is the one with the white blaze on his forehead.' Tim pointed it out. 'And Napoleon has furry feet!' Looking from one horse to the other, I saw what he meant. Wellington's hide was smooth satin black all the way to his hooves, while Napoleon had long fluffy hair covering his.

Napoleon leant down and sniffed me, his head as big as my body, and I took a step back. 'Whoa, boy,' Tim reassured him, and gently stroked his flank. 'Always around horses, Billy, no sudden movements, nice and slow so you don't startle 'em. Now, try again, at the front so he can see you past his blinkers.'

Tim held my hand up for Napoleon to sniff me. I stood stock still, waiting for his huge mouth to open and chomp off my fingers like four pink carrots. I was surprised when the wonderful creature simply sniffed the palm of my hand, his nostrils flaring.

'Now, gently rub his nose and talk to him.'

'What shall I say?'

'Anything, just keep it soft.'

So I had my first conversation with a horse, albeit one-sided.

'Whoa boy, good boy. Don't bite my fingers off.' As I continued gently rubbing and talking I was suddenly aware of Wellington's head next to me. Offering my other hand, he began to sniff then nuzzled to let me rub his nose.

'Well, I'm buggered,' exclaimed Tim. 'How long have you been around horses, Billy?'

'I haven't,' I replied honestly. 'These are the first ones I've ever touched, except for the donkeys on Margate beach.'

'If you're telling me the truth, then I'd say you're a natural.'

'A natural what?'

'A natural with horses, lad. It's a gift. They sense immediately, you know.'

Glancing over at Napoleon, Tim was amazed. 'Look, Billy.'

Still gently rubbing their noses, I looked to where Tim was nodding. This great carthorse, which could have trampled me to death in an instant, had his eyes closed.

'What's he doing?' I asked.

'He's bloody well sleeping, that's what he's doing. He's dozing off. I would never have believed it if I hadn't seen it with me own eyes. You better stop, or we might have to lift them both onto the cart and you and me will have to pull it back to the yard.'

For a minute I thought he was being serious. Then I realised it would take a lot more than us two to lift one of these horses, let alone pull the cart!

''Ere, hold yer hands out.' I held out both hands as instructed and Tim put some horse nuts into each one from a bag behind the driving seat. Offering them to my new friends, I was surprised how gently they scooped up the treat, leaving my hand wet and sticky. Wiping them on my trousers, I patted their noses. 'Good boys, good boys.' Napoleon blew warm breath through his nose onto me.

Tim had removed his cap and was scratching his head with coal-blackened fingers.

'Now, Billy, horse muck, before I get on. How much do you want?'

I quickly calculated how many bucketfuls it would take to fill a coal sack.

'A sackful, if that's possible.'

'You can have a cartload if you want. The yard is always full of the stuff.' I imagined just what Mr Austin the caretaker would say if I had a cartload of horse muck dropped off to all the allotments.

'A sackful would be really good, Tim. Can I have one a week, please?'

'Your dad must have a lot of roses,' he said, giving me one of those knowing looks grown-ups are good at. 'Sack of dung, once a week, by the allotments, so long as you leave the empty sack, OK?'

'OK, Tim,' I said, pleased.

'And how many sacks of coal?'

'What?' The look on my face started him off laughing again.

'Only kidding you, but don't forget. Anyone wants coal, you let me know, OK?'

'Of course, Tim – and thank you.' Turning back to the horses I repeated, 'And thank you, thank you.'

With a 'hup, hey, hup, giddy up', the cart trundled off to Tim's next delivery.

Brilliant. I was in the horse-muck business. I couldn't wait until the weekend when the allotment owners were about. That evening I asked Dad if he would put a notice on the allotment noticeboard in the clubhouse. 'Will I what?' he exclaimed.

'You know, Dad, to let the gardeners know I'm selling horse muck.'

'Ah, that's what the smell is, Billy,' said Mum, dishing out the pudding – rhubarb and custard, my favourite! 'You stink of horses.'

I related my meeting with Tim, the coalman. When I got to the part where Napoleon fell asleep, Mum couldn't keep quiet any longer. 'Honestly, Billy. You never cease to amaze me. Next you'll be telling us not only is he delivering coal, but horse muck too.'

'That's it, Mum, once a week. A sackful.'

'What? I'm not having horse muck delivered. What would the neighbours say?'

'No, Mum, he's going to drop it off at Dad's allotment for me.'

'You seem to have it all worked out,' Dad observed. 'How much are you thinking of charging?'

'Oh, Jack, don't encourage him. It's bad enough the neighbours giving me orders for his firewood, without horse muck as well.'

'Sixpence a bucketful.'

'Not one of my buckets, young man.'

'No, Mum, I've already got a few from the bombsites.' Oops. The minute I mentioned bombsites, I knew I was in trouble.

'What have I told you, Billy? Stay off those bombsites, they're too dangerous. Jack, you tell him.'

Dad supported her. 'Billy, what have your mum and I told you? No bombsites!'

'Yes, Dad,' I replied, remembering that he'd just ordered a hundred bricks for the paths on his allotment!

'Your horse muck is free, Dad, as much as you want!'

He thought about it for a moment, watching his cigarette smoke curling upward and picturing his roses winning first prize, with some help from good old Mother Nature!

'I'll fence you off a small corner of the allotment behind the dahlias. But make a mess and I'll take it back, OK?'

'Thanks, Dad, I'll be really good, you'll see.'

'That's what Hitler said in 1936,' added my brother Bob.

I ignored him. I was already working out what I'd be able to store in my new outside warehouse.

*

It was half-term, and I was out and about in the flats. Approaching one block through the allotments, I spied the baker's horse and cart pulled up.

'What's her name?'

Mr Price decided to humour me. 'If it's any of your business, it's Maisie.'

Exploiting my new-found skill, I offered her my hand to smell then gently rubbed her nose, all the while serenading her with, 'Good girl, Maisie, pretty girl.' The dapple-grey blew through her nose.

'Sod me, old Tim was right. You must be Billy!'

'How do you know my name?' I asked.

'Oh, it's all over the yard about you! Tim couldn't stop telling us about how you nearly put Napoleon to sleep.' As he chatted he continued loading his big wicker basket full of loaves, bread rolls and cakes. 'Here.' He offered me a plain bread roll.

'No thank you, sir. I've had breakfast.'

'It's not for you, silly, it's for the horse. Here, this is for you.' I didn't refuse the doughnut. 'Thank you, sir, very much.'

He held back the treat. 'You sure you've only just had your breakfast? Now break up the roll for Maisie. I'll be back in a tick.'

Holding the doughnut in my mouth, I broke up the roll and gave it to Maisie, who made a real show of enjoying it.

'What are you doing with that 'orse, Billy? Have you just nicked that doughnut?'

The doughnut was still in my mouth, so I removed it.

''Course not, Jim,' I informed my pal, 'as if I would.'

'You would if you could eh, Billy? 'Ere, give us 'arf.' I broke the doughnut, giving him the half with the least jam in it.

'Thanks, Billy.'

For a while there was only the sound of two boys and a horse chewing.

'So, what are you doing with the baker's horse, then?' I duly explained that I was a natural with horses, and that he should show me some respect.

'Horses? You, Billy? The only thing you've got in common with 'em is you can both fart good,' he said, laughing.

I remembered the incident he was talking about. After one of Mum's super steak and onion pies I had terrible wind for days, much to the amusement of my classmates, but not Mr Beard, our teacher, who had removed me from the class until I could control my bowels, whatever they were! It had, of course, gone round the school like wild fire and, at playtime, I was greeted by 'smelly Billy Brown with his pants hanging down'. I was only upset when the girls joined in, especially Beryl.

'Hey, Billy,' Jimmy said. 'Do you want to hear her fart?' I'd never heard a horse fart before and thought it might be an interesting thing to know about. Jimmy was off to the apple tree, which overhung the end wall, some fifty yards away. He returned a few minutes later with a jumper full of unripe green apples and immediately set to feeding Maisie, who ate as fast as he could feed them to her.

'What if Mr Price comes back?' I asked.

'Don't you know anything, Billy? He's always up there for at least half an hour. He sees that redhead in the middle flat, her with the husband still serving in Berlin.'

'What does he see her for? Does she have a lot of bread, then?'

'Honest, Billy. Sometimes I wonder about you! It's not bread she's after. She just wants his sausage roll,' he said with a knowing smile. Before I could enquire further about her bakery requirements, Jim made a circle with his thumb and finger and then poked the finger from his other hand through it in a rude gesture.

'Get it now? It's his sausage she's after?'

'Oh, I get it.'

'Thank God for that. I thought I might have to draw you pictures! My mum told my aunt there'll be hell to pay when her husband gets home. He's with the Intelligence Corps, so it shouldn't take him long to find out what she's been up to.'

'I bet she doesn't pay for her bread,' I said. Jim laughed.

'Yeah, I bet she doesn't.'

Before long, the last apple had disappeared into Maisie's mouth.

'How long?' I asked. As if to answer my curiosity Maisie's tummy began to rumble.

'Not very long, but I can't wait around to see. I said I'd help Anthony fix his bike. He's been reading a book on it but he still can't get the wheel off, stupid sod. Anyway, I'm off. Watch standing too close to that 'orse. She can't 'alf piss!'

After watching him go I turned back to Maisie, gently rubbing her nose. She seemed very contented, full of bread roll and apples. It was then that I noticed the rumblings from her tummy were getting louder.

Mr Price arrived back with a bright red face, his tie undone and an empty basket. 'Everything OK, Billy? She been good?' As if on cue Maisie spread her legs a little and began to relieve herself.

'Oh, for God's sake,' Mr Price raged. 'I've never had a horse piss so much as this one. Mind your feet, Billy.'

I skipped out of the way before the spreading pool of steaming yellow liquid could reach me.

'Thank God she's not farting, too. That's even worse! Well, I'm off now. Thanks for keeping an eye on her, Billy. She likes to raid the allotments, given half a chance.'

Climbing onto his seat, he gave her the 'giddy up girl' routine. Whether it was the sudden movement or her indignation at the light flicks of his whip on her rump, I'll never know, but she began to fart. At first just wafting woofs of gas, but they steadily increased to gale force ten and smelly.

'You feed her anything while I was gone?' Mr Price shouted back from his seat.

'Only the bread roll,' I yelled back, trying not to

laugh. As he pulled further away, I could hear him. 'Oh, for God's sake, Maisie, I swear you're the smelliest horse I've ever 'ad!'

5

The West Indies Comes to Brixton

'What's going on down your road, Ray?'

I'd bumped into one of my school pals on my way down Somerleyton Road to the market. For some reason he always wore black plimsolls. Only a few months later they would save his life when he touched the new electrified train line with an iron bar, receiving a massive six-hundred-volt electric shock.

'Haven't you heard, Billy? Loads of people are being moved to the new flats on Tulse Hill.'

'You going?'

'Afraid not, mate. We didn't get chosen. I wish we had. Nearly the whole street's getting rehoused. Those new flats have got it all: playgrounds, lawns, flower-beds, even their own laundry! I don't think Grandad put our name down. Most of the street can't wait to leave.' He wiped his runny nose on the cuff of his school jacket. There was never a time when Ray didn't have a runny nose.

'Have you seen all the black people?' he asked.

'What black people? I've seen the one in school, if that's who you mean.'

'No, not Joshua, there's hundreds of 'em.'

'Where?'

'In my road. Somerleyton Road. Come with me and see for yourself!'

As we walked down the road, every removal van for miles must have been there. The pavements were covered with sofas, chests of drawers, boxes, prams, bicycles, you name it. 'It's been going on for weeks, Billy.'

A little girl was sitting on a pile of suitcases swinging her legs and holding her dolly. The heels of her button-down white shoes made a drumming noise on the big leather case. 'Sally, for goodness' sake, will you stop that!' complained her dad, still loading boxes into an empty Sunlight Laundry van. 'You'll drive me nuts.'

Her mum arrived with all the household linen bundled up into three big sheets tied at the top, like huge Christmas puddings ready for the steamer. 'Oh, leave her, Charlie, she's being really good.' It was as if Adolf was coming to bomb us again and everyone had been told to evacuate.

We carried on down the street. 'Here you are, I told you so.' Ray indicated as we stopped outside a three-storey terraced house. There must have been at least a dozen black people going in and out with suitcases and brightly coloured bags. What I found odd was that the men were quite smartly dressed, some with their jackets off and most wearing coloured trilby hats, while the women were in brightly coloured dresses, some in hats and others with coloured scarves tied around their heads.

A council lorry was discharging its load of assorted furniture onto the pavement, where it was seized upon and taken into several different dwellings. Ray stopped an old man carrying a bag of shopping on his way back from the market.

'Grandad, what's going on?'

The old man put down his bag and sat on a front wall surveying the scene. 'Buses. That's it. Bloody buses and the Tube, the bloody Tube. They're here to drive 'em, Ray, to drive 'em.'

'Where have they all come from?'

Ray's grandad waved his arm in the air in a sweeping motion. 'The West Indies.'

'Where's that?' I asked, not wanting to be left out.

'Jamaica, Trinidad, Barbados, St Lucia, you know, the Empire.'

I didn't tell him that the only Empire I was interested in was the Empire cinema!

'There was a big advertising thing over there, and now they're all over here. There's hundreds of 'em. You coming home, Ray?'

He picked up his grandad's shopping, wiping his nose with his free arm. 'See you, Billy.'

'See you, Ray. Goodbye, Ray's grandad.'

The old boy held his arm up but didn't turn back.

'Look out. Man coming through.' The man's accent was so thick I could hardly understand any of his words. He had folded his jacket over the iron balustrade leading down to the basement flat. He still had his tie on but it was undone, as was his shirt, with sleeves rolled up, showing off his toned muscles. I couldn't help smiling as both he and his companion still had their trilby hats on. It was the first time I'd seen a man wearing black and white two-tone brogue shoes. His companion was more stockily built, with a neat goatee beard. He was wearing a dark purple waistcoat, even in the heat. I quickly moved out of the way to allow the two new arrivals to carry a large double mattress past me, into the basement flat. After some exertion they got it round the awkward turn at the bottom and disappeared. A few moments later, they re-emerged to sit on the low wall which Ray's grandad had warmed up for them.

'Man, dat's hot work! Where can you get a beer, man?' I looked behind me but there was no man there. 'Yeah you, man.'

'Me, sir?'

' "Sir!" Me like dat. Yeah you, man.'

'I'm not a man. I'm a boy.'

'What's your name, man?' There it was again.

'Billy Brown, sir.'

'Well, Billy Brown sir, where can me get some cold beers?'

I thought for a minute. 'There's the George, the Prince of Wales and the Atlantic.'

'Dat's two men and an ocean, man.'

'No, no. They're pubs, you know, bars.'

'Ah, dat's what we need. Will you go and get some beers for us?'

'I can't. I'm not allowed in. But I can go to the off-licence.'

'De what licence?'

'It's where you get beer when the pub is shut. They sell it in bottles.'

'Oh, dat will do fine.' The first man offered me a one-pound note. 'Here man, go get two beers, and one for yourself.'

'I'm not allowed beer. Dad only lets me have a sip of his at Christmas.'

'Well, man, you get what you want, but right now we need two beers.'

His companion clapped him on the shoulder. 'Ain't dat de trufe, Horace!'

Horace. I'd never known anyone called Horace.

'Haven't you got anything smaller?' I asked.

'Smaller dan what?'

'The pound note. Beers only cost a shilling a bottle.'

'Sorry man, we only got deese.' He fanned out some one-pound notes.

I grabbed them shut. 'Put your cash away, it might get nicked.'

'Nicked?' they chimed in unison.

'Yes, nicked, stolen, you know.'

'Hey, hey, dis boy, he's just dynamite.' Enjoying his broad smile, something caught my eye.

'What's that?' I asked, pointing to his teeth.

'What, dis?' He tapped the side of the tooth in question. 'Solid gold man, solid gold. Cost me a for-tune. Here, take a look.' Holding back his lip, he showed me the gold tooth. It was the size of a small nugget. During my association with the early West Indian community I would come to realise that gold teeth were a status symbol. The more you had, the wealthier you were.

'Here, take the pound. We tink you won't nick de money.'

So off I went on my first errand for our visitors from the Empire.

'Two beers and a lemonade, please.'

'How old are you, sonny?' the assistant enquired.

'Oh, they're not for me. They're for two men from the Empire.'

'Oh, that must be Jake and Dave.'

'No, it's for Horace and his friend.'

'There's no Horace at the Empire.'

'No, our Empire overseas. The black people for the buses. Round in Somerleyton Road. They're very thirsty. They've come a long way.'

'If they haven't had a beer since leaving the West Indies I should think they would be, lad. What beer do you want?'

Suddenly remembering Dad called it brown ale, I ordered two.

He looked at me as if I was pulling his leg. 'Fremlins or Watneys?'

'The first one.'

'Right. Two Fremlins and a lemonade. That's two and six.' I handed him the pound note.

'Robbed a bank, have we?'

'No, sir. It's from Horace.' He decided not to pursue it further, placing the bottles in a paper carrier bag on the counter. He passed them to me along with a large amount of change, which I put straight in my pocket. 'Ain't you gonna count it?'

'Do I need to, sir?' I looked him straight in the eye like Big Mike said to do.

'No, lad, it's all there.'

'That's what I thought. Thank you.'

I went back to Horace and his companion, the bottles clinking away in the bag. 'There you go. Two beers.'

They took the dark bottles out and unscrewed the tops. The effect of their shaky journey was immediately evident as the beer frothed and bubbled from the neck of the bottle. Both men clamped their mouths over the tops to save wasting the beer. 'Jesus, man, what is dis stuff?'

'Brown ale. Fremlins Brown Ale.'

'But it's warm, man. Where's de ice?'

'Ice? We don't have ice in the beer, only in Mum's gin and lime. If you want ice you have to go to the ice man in the market.'

'What sort of country have we come to, warm beer and no ice!'

'Got any glasses?' I enquired.

'Sure, we got glasses.'

'Well go and get two big glasses.' In a flash Horace was back with the glasses. 'Here.' I took his bottle and carefully poured half in each glass, tipping it so the beer ran slowly down the glass to stop it frothing, just as I had seen Dad do. I then topped up the two glasses with lemonade.

'Try that,' I said. They both took a large swig.

'Hey man, dat's a bit better. What's it called?'

'That's a shandy. Dad lets me have one with Christmas lunch.'

'A chandie. Dat's not bad, man.'

'No, a "shandy", with a *sh* sound.'

'OK, man, with a "sh".' I got their change from my pocket and handed it over.

'What's all dis, man?'

'It's your change from the one-pound note. I told you it was a lot of money.'

'Well, Billy, man. I t'ink you could be invaluable to us. Do you live near here?'

'In the Guinness Buildings at the top, but I pass here at about five o'clock every night on my way to the market. You can't miss me. I'll be pushing a pram.'

'You got children already?'

'No, of course not. I go to the market for firewood. You know, to light the coal.'

'Where do we get dis coal stuff from?'

'Tim comes round twice a week with Wellington and Napoleon.'

'Are dey pubs, too?'

'No, they're the horses that pull the coal cart. Don't you know anything?'

Horace leant forward. 'Between the two of us, we know less than each other.'

'Yeh man, ain't dat de trufe!' They clinked glasses and drained the contents.

'Well, Billy, man, it's been very good to chat, but we best get the bed put together or we'll all be on de floor for de night. We sure will look out for you.'

As I wandered off I called back, 'Save the bottles, there's twopence on each of them,' and got a friendly wave before they disappeared back into the house.

The next evening, as I passed on my way back to the market, they were both sitting on the wall with a shandy each. 'Evening, Billy, man. Dat's de biggest pram I ever seen.'

'I know, Horace. Smashing, ain't it? What's your name?' I enquired of his friend. 'I forgot to ask yesterday.'

'Toby, man. You can call me Toby. It's short for Tobias but Toby is just fine, man.' I still didn't understand all this 'man' business, but I was getting used to it.

'Billy, where can we buy some chickens?'

'Chickens? What kind of chickens?'

'De kind dat lays eggs, of course.'

'Oh, that kind. I'm not sure, but be here in an hour and I might have found out.'

'We'll sure be here, man.' They clinked glasses. 'We sure will.'

I made enquiries at Max's meat store in the market. 'Chickens, is it? Well, chickens are scarce 'cos of rationing, but I might be able to do chicks. How many do you want?'

'I'll let you know tomorrow evening, if that's OK?'

'Sure Billy, just give me a few days' notice.'

'Oh, and how much will they be, Max?'

'Sixpence each or five bob a dozen.' I repeated the price out loud.

'That's it, Billy. See you tomorrow, maybe.'

*

With the pram loaded with wooden boxes, I stopped in to see Horace and Toby. They were now sitting astride the wall facing each other, playing drafts.

'Who's winning?'

'Toby is,' said Horace. 'I already owe him three bob, man.'

'You play your drafts for money?'

'Yeah, man. Makes it worth de effort. What's the chicken situation?'

'Ah well, there are no chickens 'cos of the rationing.'

They both looked very disappointed.

'But I can get you chicks.'

'Dat's it, Billy, chicks is good, but we don't want any males 'cos dey don't lay eggs.'

'Dey sure don't,' observed Toby, who moved a draught while Horace was looking at me.

'What's de cost, man?'

'Six bob a dozen.'

'We'll have a dozen each. Dat's two dozen female chicks.'

I extended my open palm. 'Money up front, please.'

'Up front?'

'Yeah, now, so I can pay for them. I don't have twelve shillings.' I did, in my money box, but I wasn't going to tell them that.

'Dat's OK, Billy, man,' and he counted out twelve shillings from the change I'd given him the day before.

'I'll let you know tomorrow sometime about a delivery date, OK?'

'Dat's a date, Billy! Here, do you want the empties?'

Horace handed over six beer bottles and two lemon-
ades.

'I only got you two and one.'

'Dat's for sure, but we found the offie.'

'You're catching on fast, you two.'

'Well, we t'ought dat a little celebration was in
order. We gotta new friend, and we start our bus-
driver training Monday morning.'

'That's brilliant. Maybe you'll be on the 45s!' I
wedged the eight empties down the side of the pram,
neck first. 'See you tomorrow, man!' I said smiling.

They both look surprised. 'You catch on fast too,
man!'

Max the meat man wasn't too happy about only female
chicks. 'It's not easy to sex 'em, see, when they're so
small, but I'll see what I can do. You're lucky. I've just
had a load come out of the incubator on my farm so I'll
have them here for tomorrow. See you the same time?'

'I'll be here with the ten bob, Max.'

'Just don't be late. West Ham are playing Millwall
tomorrow night so I'll want to be off a bit sharpish.'
Max was a West Ham United fan and had the crossed
hammers insignia tattooed on his arm.

'Up the 'ammers, Max,' I chanted at him.

'Up the 'ammers, Billy.' He went off happy and I
went back to box-collecting.

I couldn't wait for the next evening to come and was
constantly told off in school for not paying attention.
Bang on time I arrived at Max's. 'Here you are, Billy.
Just be very gentle with them. After all, they're just

babies. Here.' He handed me a small bag. 'Chick feed, very small. You can get some more at Jones's.'

I remembered all the barrels of assorted feed in the oil shop.

'Thanks, Max. Here's your ten bob.' After carefully counting the mound of change I'd given him, he got a cardboard box from the back of the butchers, placing it on the chopping block.

'Well, have a look.' There were tiny chirpings coming from the box. As I opened the lid and let the light in, the chirpings got much louder.

'They're so lovely and fluffy.' The little yellow bundles were packed in so closely they looked like tennis balls. Max picked one out and handed it to me. It was warm and snuggled in my cupped hands. I gazed down in wonder at this tiny miracle.

'Twelve months' time – lunch!' he said.

'Max, you're horrible!'

'Fact of life, Billy. Look at their mums.' He gestured to the half a dozen or so scrawny chickens still on display. Returning my chick to join her sisters, I closed the lid. I hadn't got so many boxes tonight so there was plenty of room for the chicks. The trip back to Horace and Toby was made as slowly as possible as if the pram were full of eggs, which, give or take a few days, it almost was.

My new black friends were delighted. 'Dey's just de t'ing, Billy. Come in and see deir new home.'

I followed them inside where they showed me part of the back kitchen, with a corner cut off by two planks nailed together. In the corner was an old soup bowl filled with water. The faded lino had been covered with wood chips. Placing the box of chicks inside the enclosure, Horace opened the lid.

'Give us a hand, man.'

I didn't need any persuading and helped lift the twelve chicks out to freedom. Once the box was removed, Horace scattered some of the chick feed onto the wood chippings. It didn't take long before they were all pecking away to their hearts' content. Standing up, I banged my head on a large light bulb which was really hot.

'Sod that,' I remarked, rubbing my head. 'It's a bit low, isn't it?'

'For de chicks, Billy. Dey have to be kept warm.' I looked at the yellow bundles bathed in the bright light. Then I remembered their mums hanging upside down in Max's window.

'Well, chickies. Have a good year.' I left with my two bob profit and a nice memory of the chicks.

'You want what?' I asked, in shock.

'A big knife, Billy, not like your mum's but much bigger.' In a flash my mind went back to the twelve chicks I'd delivered the week before.

'Not for the chicks, Horace?'

He laughed out loud. 'No, man, well, not yet anyway.' He smiled at me again, his eyes full of mischief.

'Well, what's it for, then?'

'For the jungle.'

'What jungle? We don't have any jungles here,

Horace. Maybe where you come from, yes, but not here in dear old Blighty.'

'No? Follow me, Billy Brown.' He led me through the old kitchen where the chicks were pecking happily under their permanent sunshine, to the back garden.

'No jungle in England, man? Den what ya call dat?'

The whole of the sixty-foot back garden was a mass of buddleia, golden rod and lupins, with brambles six feet high, all the way to the back door. It hadn't been touched for years.

'If dat's not a jungle, den I don't know what is.'

'I see what you mean, Horace. Big knife. I'll do my best.'

I had a good look around Tosh's ex-army shop.

'D'ya want any more ally cook pots?' he asked before I could even open my mouth. I had bought about a dozen aluminium cook pots from him cheaply because they were too big for domestic cookers. Big Mike hadn't scrapped them for the metal, but had doubled my money and sent them home to Ireland, for what I'll never know.

'Not today, Tosh. I need a really big knife.'

'Who you gonna kill, Billy?'

'What? No, it's for clearing brambles,' I reassured him.

'Well, you're in luck.' He rummaged behind the counter where he kept what he called the good stuff.

'There you go. US army, jungle issue, 1944, only issued to US marines serving in the Pacific theatre.'

'What theatre?' I asked, thinking of the Empress Theatre in Brixton.

'It's a term we military men use, you know, the theatre of war.'

'Oh, of course. I can see it now.' I couldn't, of course, but I knew from past experience that if I didn't say so Tosh would go on and on. I had once asked him about D-Day and he told me about it from start to finish, even though he wasn't there but at a supply depot in Woolwich!

He withdrew the huge knife from its canvas sheath, the blade still wrapped in protective waxed paper. 'Unused,' he announced. 'Absolutely mint condition, should be a collector's item, very rare.'

'How many you got, Tosh?'

'Five hundred,' he blurted out, caught by his own stupidity.

'Oh, that rare! How much?' Back from his imaginary campaign in the jungle he sheathed the machete and thought for a moment.

'How many we talking about, you little sod?'

'Well, only one to start with.'

'Bloody one!' he exploded.

'To start with, Tosh, but I think a lot may follow.'

'What's a lot, you little bugger?' In my mind I visualised flogging them in Somerleyton Road, Geneva Terrace, Sussex Gardens.

'I dunno, Tosh, maybe fifty or sixty, who knows? So long as they're cheap, these rare items.'

He waved the machete at me, still in its sheath. 'One day, Billy Brown, one day.'

'Yes, I know, but not today. How much?'

'Four and six each. Five for a quid.' As I was trying

to add it all up in my head, he intervened. 'Buy five, save two bob,' we both said together.

'You're getting better, Billy.'

'Right, I'll have one for four bob now, with possible orders for more soon.'

'How soon?'

I thought of Horace and all his friends, all with their own personal jungles. 'I think, possibly, tomorrow.'

'OK, you can have one for four shillings as a sample.'

I paid Tosh while he put the machete in a new sandbag sack, tied up with string. 'In case you bump into the Old Bill,' he said.

Right, let's see if this is what Horace wants, I thought, hurrying back to his house, hoping I hadn't wasted my four shillings. Horace wasn't just pleased. He was absolutely delighted. Peeling off the wax paper, he looked along the blade's edge. 'Dis is just de ticket, Billy, just de ticket! How much?' The way he was going on about it I thought he'd pay anything.

'Six bob each or four for a pound, but I don't know how many my mate's got left,' I lied, imagining what Tosh's stack of five hundred looked like.

'I'll have this one and four more.'

'They all for you?' I asked, amazed at his order.

'Well, I'll keep another for cutting up de dried fish and meat. And the occasional chicken,' he added, with a rascally smile. 'When can you deliver, Billy?'

Horace was pleased and so was I. A two bob profit, with more to come.

Tosh was delighted with my first order for five machetes coming so quickly. He couldn't wait to put them in another sandbag sack. As he counted out the one pound in coins on his old glass-topped counter, my eye was drawn to a brass object on one of the shelves. 'What's that, Tosh?'

'Hang on a minute,' he said, finishing counting out my money. He rang it up in his old-fashioned National Brass till, accompanied by bells, clangs and clicks as the ancient mechanism did its job. 'Now, what's what, Billy?'

Pointing, I indicated what had caught my eye. 'That round brass tin. What is it?' The article was the size of a tin of boot polish but deeper, with a brass ring attached.

'Ah no, Billy, that's not for you. That's for a connoisseur of militaria.'

'A what?'

'The blokes who collect this stuff.'

'Oh, one of them. Well, I'm one of those conno . . . conno, whatever it is.'

'Connoisseurs, Billy.'

'That's it. Give us a look.' Taking if from the shelf, he placed the item on the counter as if it was the crown jewels. 'There,' he said with unabashed pride.

'What is it?'

He was stunned. 'What is it, what is it, you ignorant little sod? I'll show you what it is.' Picking it up, he flipped open the lid and put it back down. Red, black and gold spun before my eyes, slowly coming to a stop.

'Wow, it's a compass, Tosh.'

'Yes, indeed, but not just any old compass.' He pointed a dirty broken fingernail at the serial number under the initials WD. From a shelf he got down a grubby dog-eared War Department manifest with the cover missing. Licking the dirty finger, he flicked through the page numbers until he found what he was looking for. He spun the book around and stabbed at a line with the same finger. 'Read,' he commanded, dramatically. The writing was very small. From somewhere he produced a chipped magnifying glass without its frame. 'Read, Billy.'

'Item. Magnetic Compass. Brass. Officer Issue No. 77670471. Crimea Pattern.'

'Wow. How much?'

'Not for sale.' I gazed at the compass, then reread the catalogue reference. The Crimea War.

It must be worth a fortune, I thought.

Tosh closed the manifest and returned it to its shelf.

'The Crimea,' I said, almost reverently.

'Exactly, Billy Brown, and not for the likes of you. Feel the weight of it.'

Picking up the object of my desire, I held it in both hands as if it were the Holy Grail itself.

'Sell it to me, Tosh. Please?'

'Out of the question.' The compass was still open in my hands.

'It's broken,' I pleaded.

'What?' He snatched it back, checking the glass bezel and turning it over several times. 'No it's not, you crafty little bugger!'

'Yes it is. It doesn't point north!'

'What bloody rubbish!'

'Here, look.' Placing the open compass back on the counter, we watched it spin and settle.

'See, I told you so!'

'See, I told you so,' he mimicked. 'Clever little sod! We'll see, we'll see.'

He had a cardboard box filled with small cheap tin compasses for map-reading. Putting the whole box next to the Crimea compass, they all pointed north but the Crimea one was not having any of it, deciding that south-west was just as good!

'Well, I'm buggered! How come I missed that? And how the hell do you know which way is north?'

'Stockwell Tube Station,' I stated with confidence.

'What the f . . . are you on about?' There was a hesitation mid-sentence and I knew the F-word he was going to use but I didn't tell him so.

'Stockwell Tube, the Northern Line: runs south from Morden to High Barnet in the north. So that's in that direction.' I pointed towards his back wall. The Crimea compass was pointing to the army water bottles which I indicated, hanging on a side wall.

'Well, it doesn't matter, it's still rare.'

'It's rare, but broken rare.'

'Still not for sale.'

'I'll give you five bob.'

'Haah!'

'Six bob.'

'Never. I'd rather sell my soul to Adolf!'

Taking all the money from both pockets, I laid it on the counter and added it up. Tosh folded his arms with an air of superiority and sniffed at the coins with disdain. 'You're wasting your time, Billy Brown.'

I finished counting all the coins, having put them in order of value to make it easier. 'Seven shillings, three-pence and a halfpenny.'

'Done!' he exclaimed, scooping up the money before I could argue. The ringing bells, clinks, clanks and clonks signalled my hard-earned cash was now in Tosh's till. I closed the compass with care, noticing how the lid shut tight with a gentle click.

Holding up the compass towards him, I repeated: 'Item. Magnetic Compass. Brass. Officer Issue No. 77670471. Crimea Pattern.' It always surprised me that I could remember stuff like that, but never anything from school lessons.

'That's it, Billy,' he leant on the counter, coming down to my level. 'Did I ever tell you about the terrible fever hospital at Scutari?'

Quickly I put the compass in my pocket where it just fitted. The nice weight of it, snug against my thigh.

'Well, thanks, Tosh. It's been a pleasure doing business with you. I must be off. Mum will be wondering where I've got to!'

As I headed out the door he called, 'It was one of the Crimea's grimmest places . . . maybe another time . . .'

The shop bell sounded like the one Mr Belcher rang at school. I'd rather listen to Tosh than Mr Belcher any day, but I was off home with my treasure, bought for the princely sum of seven shillings, threepence halfpenny!

A good group of my pals were in the playground when I got back to the flats. Pushing my way through to the middle, I watched for a minute or so while two of them finished their game of marbles. Once Jim had lost his best fiery alley it was all over.

'Oh, bugger,' he exclaimed.

'I'll tell Mummy you swore,' threatened his sister.

'Oh, sod off, Susan. You're a pain in the arse!' Jim had a great collection of swear words and knew how to use them. Susan sulked off with a final, 'I'm telling Mummy on you.'

'Tell her, smell her, lock her in the cellar,' came his reply. I wished I'd thought of that.

'Want to see something really good?' I asked. The boys crowded round.

'What you got now, Billy? Show us.' The last time it'd been one of Tosh's one-shilling jack knives which I had swapped for a two-and-sixpence *Buffalo Bill* annual.

Slowly I pulled the compass from my pocket. 'Wow, look at that! It's smashing! What is it?'

'You dummies. Don't you know history when you see it?' I opened the lid and the compass spun, then settled.

'It's busted.'

'No, it's not, Kevin Bradley (we all called him Clever Kevin because he was a know-it-all). 'It just needs adjusting.'

'What's that on the lid?'

I took a deep breath 'Item. Magnetic Compass. Brass. Officer Issue No. 77670471. Crimea Pattern.' Hushed whispers went around the group.

Jimmy was the first to speak up. 'I'll give you me new football for it.'

'It's not for swapping. I'm keeping it.'

'I've got two and six in my money box,' another offered.

'Sorry, lads. This is a no-sale item.'

'Billy Brown, everything you've ever had you've sold!' Sod it. Beryl Prentis. Moving quickly out of her path, my pals let her through.

'What's that lump of junk?' she demanded to know, indicating my prized possession.

'It's a compass, Beryl.' I didn't really know why I liked her. At every given opportunity she would try to make my life a misery, from telling me off for walking on top of the pram sheds and commenting on how scruffy my shoes always were, to forever asking me what I was up to whenever she saw me out with the pram and telling me I'd come to no good. But still, I liked her. Stretching out her hand, she gave her command.

'Give it to me.'

'Not bloody likely. You'll smash it.'

'Of course I won't, you stupid boy.'

'Cross your heart and hope to die?'

Going through the routine we all held sacred, Beryl mimicked me. 'Cross my heart and hope to die. There, satisfied?' Once more, she extended her hand.

'No, sod off,' I said, reasserting my standing with my pals.

'Billy Brown, you said . . .'

'I said nothing, only cross your heart and hope to die.'

'Oooh, you're an impossible boy!' I took this as high praise indeed!

'This could have been used by Florence Nightingale,' I ventured. 'She was in the Crimea.' I clutched at the only name I could remember from Mr Bryant's history lesson on heroes of the Crimea.

'She was a nurse, you fool.'

For a moment I was floored. 'But she'd still need to find her way around.' Again, muted support from the lads.

''Course she would. Wouldn't want to get lost,' someone added.

'You really are a bunch of dimwits. She was in a hospital all the time, not travelling from the South Pole every day. Now give me a look.' Once more, the spotlessly clean hand extended towards me.

I was almost beaten, but not quite. 'Give us a kiss and you can hold it.'

'What! Kiss you? I'd rather kiss Jimmy!'

'Alright by me,' came the reply from the back.

Suddenly support arrived that surprised even me. The other girls, who were envious of Beryl, began chanting, 'Beryl's scared of Billy! Beryl's scared of Billy!' Soon it was picked up by the lads. 'Beryl's scared of Billy!'

'Alright, alright. I'll kiss you,' she shouted.

The playground fell silent. Monty had defeated Rommel, the Russians had held Stalingrad, Dunkirk had turned into D-Day and now Beryl Prentis was actually going to kiss Billy Brown. The entire group held its breath.

'On the cheek, only on one cheek.'

'Oh, swizz, no deal.'

'Don't do it, Billy.'

In my best posh voice I silenced them. 'That would be very nice, Miss Prentis.'

'Oh no, he's gonna do it.'

Whether she saw something in my face or not, I didn't know. 'You're up to something!' It was more of a statement than a question.

'Now what could I be up to? It's only a kiss on the cheek, Beryl.'

Before the chant could start again she ordered, 'Hands behind your back, no touching!' Quickly the compass was returned to my pocket and, with hands clasped behind my back, turning my head I offered my cheek. I watched her with one eye as she came closer. She really was quite pretty. She pouted her lips and closed her eyes just before making contact with the allotted spot. At the last split second I faced forwards, and kissed her full on the lips as hard as I could. Her eyes flew open but our lips stayed together for a millisecond longer. Stepping back, she wiped her mouth furiously with the back of her hand.

'You cheat, Billy Brown. You rotten cheat!'

One of Mum's sayings flashed into my head. 'Stolen fruits taste better, Beryl!' I said. Everyone was laughing and cheering me.

Still wiping her mouth as if she had kissed a dog's bottom, she threatened, 'I shall tell my mother.' The minute she uttered those words, she wished she could take them back.

'Tell her, smell her, lock her in the cellar!'

Beryl gritted her teeth.

'I hate you, Billy Brown, I hate you!' As they continued chanting, I offered her my compass.

'For the kiss. I made a deal.' Once again silence fell. Coming closer, she took my treasure. Her expression changed so fast it was frightening. Now the cat had the mouse.

'Please don't smash it, Beryl. It cost me seven shillings, threepence and a halfpenny.' The murmurs of approval from my mates continued. Turning it over in her hands, I was sure she was going to drop it. Beryl was now back in full control. Coming very close, she gave me a look I didn't understand. Pressing the compass back in my hands she kissed me on the cheek very gently.

'I too stand by a deal,' she said. Stunned, I just stood there holding my compass like the village idiot.

'Billy Brown loves Beryl! Billy Brown loves Beryl!' I hardly heard them. As she walked back to her girlfriends, she turned round and looked at me victoriously and smiled. The grin which replaced my look of astonishment nearly broke my jaw. I could still feel her lips on my cheek. Suddenly I knew why it was special. The last kiss had been given freely, not stolen.

Sod 'em, let 'em chant, I thought. I had just remembered Mum's other favourite saying: 'Sticks and stones . . .'

I kept my treasured compass for nearly forty years, never once thinking to sell it. Sadly it was lost in a house move in 1990. Even then, all that time later, I was heartbroken at its loss. It had held so many treasured memories.

6

Variety, the Spice of Life

'Saturday night,' my dad had announced, 'we're all going to see the new review at the Camberwell Palace. Arthur gave me four tickets for fixing the roller shutters to his arches.' Mum had asked who was in it but Dad had simply replied, 'Don't know, don't care. We're going.'

And so, the following Saturday evening, just before seven o'clock, we were stood outside the entrance to the Camberwell Palace Theatre at Camberwell Green, having just got off the No. 45 bus. My brother and I gaped wide-eyed at the billing posters displayed on each side of the theatre entrance. Each poster was eight feet high with the photos and names of the artists appearing that night. Keppel and Betty, exotic comedy dance duo, Anne Shelton, the Forces Sweetheart, Joan Rhodes, the world's strongest woman and, top of the bill, Max Miller, 'The Original Cheeky Chappie'.

Although all of these were top-line acts, they weren't what had grabbed our attention. What did was the centre of the billboard which declared, in bold letters, 'Never before shown outside of the West End, direct from the Windmill Theatre, Living Tableaux of Famous Women in History'. Now, for those readers who have led a more sheltered life, 'living tableaux' was a polite phrase for nudie shows. My brother and I couldn't wait to get in.

'Jack,' said my mother. 'Do you really think this is suitable for the boys?'

We both stopped dead and looked at my father with the best puppy-dog eyes we could muster.

'Don't worry, Eileen,' he reassured her. 'I hear the girls are mostly covered up and not allowed to move. I'm sure it will be alright.'

The sigh of relief from my brother and me could have been heard all the way back to Brixton.

It was then that I noticed the crowd entering the theatre. A large percentage were young men in the eighteen-to-thirty age group dressed in their Saturday-night best; smart pressed slacks with a sharp crease, freshly laundered white shirt with fly-out collars, sports jackets and, to complete the look, a pair of the latest brown suede shoes.

As we approached, the doorman checking tickets stopped us.

'Just a moment, sir,' he addressed my father. 'You do know this show's a bit risqué, don't you? How old are these lads?'

'George?' Mum enquired, peering from under his gold-braided cap. 'Is that you?'

'Cor blimey, Eileen, the boys are a bit young!'

'Is Eaddie in there?' she enquired, half smiling. 'And the boys?'

'OK, OK, just get in quick and make the boys sit up tall.'

Unhooking the red braided barrier rope he allowed us into the theatre and having glanced at the tickets, gave us directions to our seats: 'Straight on, front stalls.'

'Who was that, dear?' my dad enquired.

'That's Eaddie Peel's husband, the canteen manageress at Woolies.'

'Enjoy the show, all of you,' said George, winking at me and my brother.

I nearly fell down the aisle steps with surprise. Mum caught us both by the arm, drawing us close to her. 'OK. So you've got into a grown-up show. Just be quiet and behave.'

'Yes, Mum,' we both chorused.

The pretty usherette with the Lana Turner hairdo showed us to our seats in the fourth row of the stalls. Mum went in first, followed by me, my brother and Dad at the end of the row. From Mum's bag, which she called her portmanteau, she produced a packet of Smiths crisps, an apple and a small bar of Cadbury's Dairy Milk chocolate for all four of us. What magical and marvellous ladies mums are, to anticipate a small boy's every need!

'Don't scoff the lot in one go, Billy. I know what you're like. If you're good, I'll buy you an ice cream during the intermission. So, save half your chocolate for later.' Mums are also brilliant at staggering out a young boy's eager consumption of treats, especially where crisps, apples and chocolate are concerned.

'Yes, Mum,' I replied. 'I was going to save the chocolate for the second half.'

'Shush, Billy, the show's about to start.'

The lights dimmed and the orchestra struck up the overture. I felt so grown-up. What a story I would have for my pals at school on Monday morning, I thought to myself.

The first act, Keppel and Betty, were very well known. Two men, in Egyptian costumes, wearing hobnail boots, danced on a big tin sheet, liberally sprinkled with sand. This they would add to from two tin shakers, causing their hobnail boots to make shushing noises as they danced back and forth like Egyptians. There was rather a rude song around at the time set to the same music, and many of the men in the front row of the stalls were singing it. Keppel and Betty were either oblivious to this or ignored it, carrying on with their act no matter what. I thought the whole thing was hilarious. Their act was absolutely brilliant, and I learnt the rest of the words to the rude song. I looked at Mum, who had tears of laughter running down her face which she quickly wiped away.

Anne Shelton came on next and the lads in the front row went wild. Apart from the fact that she could belt out a good song and had entertained our troops all over the world, she had other attributes as well; two, in fact. She was endowed with rather large breasts, which she happily displayed to her advantage. My uncle Mike had once described them as 'two puppies in a pet shop window waiting for a home'.

She glided across the stage in a black velvet ball gown which, of course, made her pale skin stand out even more. With her blonde hair and bright red lips, she was every lad's favourite pin-up. She finished her act with a medley of all the favourite songs from the war years. I am still not sure to this day whether it was this final triumph of song, or the very low bows she took at the end of her performance, that brought the entire house to its feet. I was carried away with the intoxication of the moment and cheered as loud as I could whilst Mum, Dad and my brother applauded until their hands hurt. Several times Miss Shelton was called back to take another bow, always accompanied by wolf whistles from all the lads down the front. This was turning out to be one of the best nights of my life. I'd forgotten all about my crisps.

Two more acts followed, the first a juggler on a unicycle who I said I thought was better than Miss Shelton (to which my brother told me to shut up), followed by a dance troop of high-kicking girls, all of whom I thought were beautiful. Though when Mum commented that, 'The third from the left had legs like tree trunks,' I nearly choked on my apple for laughing. The intermission came and Dad bought us all ice creams from the girl with the tray. I loved to see them as they always picked a pretty girl to sell from the tray. I supposed ugly girls wouldn't be good for trade. I always marvelled at the light on the tray, especially effective in the dark of the cinema. Where did the power come from? Dad had explained that it was batteries, but I still didn't really get it. I just loved to see these angels with their frozen chests and their beautiful faces lit from below, a beacon beckoning me to buy their ice creams.

Following the intermission, during which my mum had spent most of her time wiping drips of ice cream off my previously spotless shirt, the lights dimmed and the orchestra played a selection from the overture to Fingal's Cave by Mendelssohn.

As the curtains opened for the second half there were audible gasps from the men in the audience, accompanied by oohs and ahs from the ladies. There, in the centre of the stage, on a raised plinth, was a naked young woman, so beautiful she took my breath away. I nudged my mum.

'Mum, Mum, she's got no clothes on,' I whispered.

'Shut up, Billy,' she hissed back.

The naked woman was holding a large earthenware pot on her shoulder, causing her breasts to rise majestically. Thin white diaphanous material was strategically placed to obscure most of her lower body except for one leg, naked to the thigh. I don't think anyone in the audience had noticed the man on the side of the stage. He now stepped forward, wearing a black beret, artist's smock and sandals. Gesturing to the immobile figure, he announced to the audience, 'Aphrodite at the Well.' For a moment there was stunned silence. Then, by what seemed to be a prearranged signal, the whole audience went mad, clapping, cheering, shouting, waving and whistling. All the while, the girl did not move or bat an eyelid. The curtains closed but the noise did not abate. Cheering and applause was now replaced by a chorus of, 'Did you see that?' 'She was gorgeous.' 'You could almost see her . . .'

The orchestra struck up again and total silence fell,

none of the male theatregoers wishing to delay their next lesson in art. Helen of Troy and Venus Rising from the Waves followed. Each time the applause and cheers grew louder. I was quite enjoying looking at the girls, but this was soon interrupted by Mum telling me off for tearing the little bag of salt in half from the Smiths crisps, and spilling the whole lot down my new long trousers. Some of the salt was quickly absorbed by the ice cream blobs deposited earlier.

The final tableau was The Three Graces, involving all three of the stunning girls wearing very little, which encouraged the young lads in the front rows to shout even louder. I looked at my dad, who was clapping enthusiastically. Still, none of the girls moved so much as a curl on her head.

In later life, I would learn that the then Lord Chancellor had decreed that, so long as the nude female body remained still and was displayed as art upon the stage and not for titillation of a sexual nature, the show could go on. The cast-iron rule was that the girls must not move. At earlier shows at the Windmill Theatre in Soho, mice had been thrown onto the stage as a joke, causing the girls to shriek and run away. The show was a sell-out for weeks afterwards.

The curtains finally closed on The Three Graces, and the men in the audience reverted to mumbling amongst themselves. 'Well, what did you think of that, then?' 'I wouldn't say no to any of them!' 'They wouldn't ask you!' And, 'Might as well go to the pub now.'

After their foray into the world of art, the audience

now seemed restless and noisy. The orchestra struck up a rousing Sousa march and we all settled back into our seats in anticipation of the next act. The curtains drew back once more, accompanied by a fanfare of trumpets. Everyone's eyes were drawn to the centre of the stage where, rising from the floor, was an Amazon goddess, wrapped in a glittering gold cloak. I stared with my mouth open. The dais she was on stopped rising at about ten feet above the stage so we could all get a view of the eighth wonder of the world – Joan Rhodes – the world's strongest woman. Along with the whole audience, I was spellbound.

Slowly, she unclipped her cape and let it fall to the floor. There were gasps of astonishment from the crowd and looks of disbelief from most of the women. Dressed in a copy of the outfit worn by the comic-strip character Wonder Woman, she stood at least six feet tall. The spotlight struck her and the fanfares played again. From her cascading curly blonde hair to her strapless sequinned bodice with pinched waist and silver belt, down to her red spangled knee-high boots, she was the most fabulous thing I had ever seen. It was like the character from the page had been brought to life before my very eyes.

As the lights danced over her, and more fanfares blared out, the stage began to revolve while Miss Rhodes went through her posing routine. The spotlights hit her costume and coloured lights spun off in all directions. She was like the glitterball at the Wimbledon Palais. England had seen bodybuilders before, but nothing like Miss Rhodes. She had muscles where muscles shouldn't be, especially on a lady. The crowd was ecstatic.

She stopped flexing and came down to the front of the stage for the main part of her act. Selecting a large iron bar, she bent it around her neck with ease into the shape of a horseshoe. There followed several more bar-bending feats, including some in her teeth, all the time being cheered and applauded by an ever more enthusiastic crowd.

Finally, she selected two of the fattest men from the front row that she could find. They were sat on chairs to either side of her. A wooden yoke was placed on her shoulders and each end was attached by chains to the two chairs. By now Miss Rhodes was in a squatting position. The drums began to roll, building to a crescendo. Spotlights played over her, sending more tiny beams of light all around the theatre. The world's strongest woman gave an almighty heave and stood upright. Both men were lifted clear of the floor. Their combined weight easily exceeded thirty stone. More fanfares blared and the searchlights swirled as she stood motionless for a few seconds.

After what seemed to be an eternity Miss Rhodes dropped the men to the floor with a bang, emphasising to the audience their tremendous weight. For a few seconds she seemed exhausted, then, straightening up, she threw both arms into the spotlight in a triumphant gesture. The whole theatre erupted. No one had ever seen anything like it.

Following several well-earned bows, she shook hands with her two portly assistants and ushered them back to their seats. Making motions for the audience to quieten down, she waited until she had our full attention. Once more moving to centre stage, she took up the microphone.

'Now,' she boomed. 'I want ten strong men from the audience.' Without waiting for volunteers she began pointing into the crowd. 'Yes, you sir, with the red jumper on – and you, sir, you look big and strong.' Then, pointing in our direction: 'Oh, and definitely you, the handsome man on the end.' I turned to my left in shock. She'd picked out my dad! He got up and headed towards the stage.

I turned to my right. 'Mum, what's he doing?' I asked, concerned that he might embarrass us all. In reassurance, mum took my hand and gently patted it.

'Don't you worry about your dad, Billy, he may even surprise you!'

'Surprise me, Mum? I don't understand.'

'Shush,' she whispered, as she gestured towards the stage.

By now Miss Rhodes had all ten men lined up on the stage in a row facing the audience. Starting at one end, she walked down the line giving each one a number and asking their name. When she came to my dad, she turned to the crowd.

'Oh, oh, ladies. And here we have number seven. What's your name, handsome?' In a clear voice my father announced, 'Jack Brown.' Cheers and wolf whistles broke out. 'Steady, ladies,' she called. 'Let's see what he's made of first!' She continued up the line, numbering the last three.

They were all big men, including a red-headed Irishman called Patrick who was huge with a great beer belly, fast becoming the crowd's favourite. An assistant wheeled on a sparkly trolley from which he and Miss Rhodes produced a stack of London telephone directories. Each man was given one and Miss Rhodes took one herself. Still with the microphone in her hand, she announced that the object of the challenge was to tear the London telephone directory in half, indicating with the microphone the direction of the tear across the book. Turning once more to the audience, she urged them to cheer for their favourite contestant.

Placing the mike down, she readied herself. A gong sounded from the orchestra pit as the signal to begin. For a split second the audience was silent. Then everyone cheered for their favourite. 'Go on, Tommy!', 'Go on, Patrick!', 'Show her, Jack!' No one cheered for Miss Rhodes, who was at the front of the stage steadily ripping her directory into two neat halves.

The gong sounded again and the men duly stopped. Some were sweating profusely. Others were gulping in air to regain their composure. Miss Rhodes, ever the showman, held her two separate halves aloft in the spotlight, accompanied by the now compulsory fanfare. Once again, the audience went wild with applause.

She quietened them down and turned to the ten men, mike in hand. 'Now, let's see what these fine men have done.'

The first few had only managed to start a tear in the side of the pages. Number five was almost halfway across and received a rousing cheer. Number six, the

Irish giant, was covered in sweat and was bright red in the face. Most of his directory had been demolished, but it was still in one piece. The crowd cheered and cheered.

Miss Rhodes now stood at my father's side. It was only then that I realised I had not been watching him, being riveted to centre stage and Wonder Woman. My father stood expressionless with his hands behind his back.

'It's OK, handsome,' she teased. 'We can't all be heroes.'

I looked up at my mum, willing Dad to have at least made a respectable dent in his directory. She must have sensed my trepidation for she looked straight at me and, squeezing my hand, gave me a knowing wink. I looked back at the stage as my father brought both hands from behind his back. Each hand held one half of the London telephone directory. The whole of the Camberwell Palace audience was silent in disbelief.

Quickly Miss Rhodes took the two halves and held them aloft. 'At last,' she shouted, 'a real man!'

The crowd went crazy. First one, then another, shouted my dad's name. 'Jack, Jack, Jack.'

Within seconds most of the audience had joined in. It was just like West Ham United scoring the winning goal!

Miss Rhodes allowed the audience adoration to continue a while longer, then quietened us all down. Continuing down the line, but finding no more successes, she called for a round of applause for all the contestants. Mum squeezed my hand again. 'Bit of a surprise, your dad, eh, Billy?'

'But, Mum,' I started, 'how did he do it?'

'You'll have to ask him, dear,' she said. 'Now, watch the show.'

The world's strongest woman had not finished yet. After removing the remnants of the directories, each man was given a standard six-inch nail and a bright yellow duster. Accompanied by a drum roll, Miss Rhodes wrapped her nail in the cloth and began to grunt and grimace as she attempted to bend the nail with her bare hands. Now the crowd got behind her, cheering her on. 'Come on, Joan, you can do it,' a rather stout lady in the front was shouting.

We were soon all carried along on the wave of excitement and I too began shouting for Wonder Woman. She stood up straight, wiping her brow and, handing her bright yellow duster to number five, asked him to open it and hold it up. The crowd applauded loudly as the six-inch nail, bent into a perfect horse-shoe, was held up for all to see. Taking the bent nail, she handed it to a young man in the front row, blowing him a kiss and affording him a fine view of her encased bosoms. Allowing a respectable time for her well-earned applause to die down, Miss Rhodes announced it was the turn of the ten good men.

At the sound of the gong the stage was filled with much grunting and puffing, accompanied by the supporting cheers and encouragement from the audience. This time I watched my father closely. Several men were attempting to bend their nail over their knee, one man even behind his neck. My father had his high up on his chest, affording him muscular leverage with his arms. Holding his elbows close to his body, he bent and pushed at the same time. I also saw that he twisted the cloth against the nail in alternate directions. He would explain to me later that the friction caused the nail to heat up slightly. Watching him, I realised he was doing exactly as Miss Rhodes had done.

With all the cheering going on, the ten missed the first gong and the percussionist had to beat it for several seconds until they had all stopped. Once again Miss Rhodes moved along the line, unwrapping each contestant's nail. Number two had managed a slight curve to his, numbers three and four had fared slightly better and the red-haired giant got a great ovation by bending his nail to a right angle. Approaching my dad, she wagged her finger at him as if to say, don't be a naughty boy. The crowd loved it and some had already started the 'Jack' chant.

Dad offered up his bright yellow cloth. As he did so something fell to the floor. Bending down, the world's strongest woman picked up one half of a standard six-inch nail. This time there was no stunned silence, only cheers, applause and cries of 'Jack, Jack, Jack'. Miss Rhodes slowly unwrapped the other half of the nail before holding both pieces up to the ecstatic crowd for inspection.

All this time, my father stood impassively, with no hint of a smile or smirk on his face. It took what seemed like an eternity to get a semblance of order. The last three men weren't even looked at. What was the point? Miss Rhodes took my father's arm and led him to the front of the stage, the audience still cheering wildly.

'Ladies and gentlemen,' she began, 'I give you the winner and strongest man of the night: Jack.' The crowd was on its feet, stamping and shouting, along with my brother, myself and my mum, who, with tears in her eyes, was glowing with pride. I felt so proud. My dad was a hero.

As we watched, my dad took the two halves of the nail from Miss Rhodes and, leaning down, offered them to a pretty young lady in the front row, just as Miss Rhodes had done earlier. There was a rush as half a dozen young ladies, all eager for the amazing souvenir, leapt to the front of the stage. Luckily, the one chosen got there first and claimed her treasure – two halves of a standard six-inch nail. Taking hold of his arm, Miss Rhodes guided my dad to the side steps. If she was surprised she didn't show it, for under his jacket my father had biceps like two cannon balls. For what Miss Rhodes did not know, and what my mother obviously did, was that before taking a job as a maintenance foreman Dad had been a blacksmith and had spent twelve years hammering hot metal, bending and breaking six-inch nails as a party piece!

Making his way back to his seat took a while as members of the audience, wanting to show their appreciation, shook his hand and patted him on the back. When he eventually got to us, he squeezed past my brother and me and kissed my mum. Once more, the crowd roared its approval. It couldn't have been better if he'd been the winning gladiator at the Colosseum.

Miss Rhodes, to her credit, allowed the crowd its moment of hero-worship. Waving to her assistant, she asked for another nail and cloth. The crowd fell silent. Her assistant took the mike and said, 'Miss Rhodes will now attempt to break a standard six-inch nail.' The drum roll began. This time she wasn't playing around. Her pride and fame were at stake. My father looked a little embarrassed as she flexed and applied her incredible muscles. The crowd held its breath. After much bending, twisting and straining she stood up, at which point the assistant came forward and unwrapped the bright yellow cloth. After first showing it to the front row, he announced with great gusto, 'Two halves.'

My father was on his feet first, followed by the whole audience. With feet stamping they chanted 'Joan, Joan, Joan'. Regaining her composure, the world's strongest woman blew my dad a kiss. She may have been equalled but she hadn't been beaten. The crowd loved it and she took several bows and curtain calls. My brother was shaking my dad's hand. I thought this was the thing to do and offered my own.

Dad took it with a 'Thanks, Billy. You enjoying yourself?' I couldn't say a thing, but nodded enthusiastically. I was nine years old and my father was a hero.

The top of the bill was Max Miller, 'The Original Cheeky Chappie'. Max was one of the top entertainers of the day, always wearing a very sharp suit, trilby hat and wide tie covered in red and gold sequins. Very similar to a traditional clown's outfit. His opening line was, 'D'ya like the suit? Not too flash, is it?' The whole audience was laughing. He had them in the palm of his hand. He was quickly into his patter with jokes and innuendos, some near the mark and some downright rude. As an adults-only show, he could get away with anything and the audience roared with laughter.

'That Joan Rhodes,' he said, leaning over the audience from the front of the stage as if to share some secret with only those in the front row (but allowing everyone to hear), 'she's got some muscles, eh?' He indicated his biceps – 'two bigguns here!' Then indicated his thighs – 'two very bigguns here!' Then, with an exaggerated rolling motion of his hands down his chest – 'and two very . . . well, need I say more!' By now the whole house was in the throes of laughter. 'And that Jack, where are you, Jack?'

My father raised his arm and the crowd cheered. 'Imagine what Jack could do to a flasher,' and he made the motion of snapping something in half. The crowd loved it and I loved Max Miller. To think, the greatest comedian of the day knew my dad! I was starting to glow like my mum!

The act continued amidst shock from the ladies and howling laughter from the men. For his finale, Max Miller came to the front of the stage and announced a little ditty to sum up. The orchestra struck up the music and the great Max Miller sang.

I like the girls who do, I like the girls who don't,
I hate the girl who says she will and then she says she
  won't,
But the girl I like the best and I'm sure you'll say I'm
  right,
Is the girl who never, ever does, but looks as if she
  might!

The last line was spoken rather than sung, full of in-
nuendo and knowing. It brought the house down. I
couldn't even hear him say 'thank you and good night'
amidst the noise of the audience. What a night!

Once the whole cast had taken their final bows and
applause, we filed out into the cold night air. I took
Mum's hand so as not to get lost amongst the crowds
and she buttoned up my coat. Dad was still being
greeted by total strangers who insisted on shaking
his hand. Even the bus ride home was full of people
wishing to congratulate him. 'Well done, Jack, bloody
amazing, Jack.' By the time we got off the bus,
passengers were waving us off like long-lost friends,
with a final 'Good night, Jack' from the bus driver who
wasn't even at the show!

Back at 242, I was quickly put to bed.

'Well, I really don't know. Gone eleven o'clock,
Billy Brown, and you only just in bed!' Mum slipped
Ted in beside me.

'Thanks, Mum. It was a smashing night.'

She bent down and kissed me on the forehead. 'Sleep
tight. Don't let the bedbugs bite.' We both smiled as

she left the room, then Dad popped his head around the door. 'You still awake?' he enquired with mock sternness. He came in and sat on my bed. 'Well, how was that for a night out?'

I sat up and hugged him, my eyes welling with tears. 'Dad, you're my hero.'

He hugged me back and gently put me back under the covers. 'Thanks, Billy, now go to sleep.' His smile washed over me as I slipped effortlessly to sleep, thinking of all the wonderful stories I had to tell on Monday morning.

7

Missions, Markets and Monks

As soon as the first few boatloads of immigrants had arrived, the market traders seized on the opportunity. Greengrocers started stocking green bananas, yams, breadfruit, plantain and much more. Max the Butcher found that our new black citizens preferred to buy their chickens live, especially the white-feathered ones. Lambeth Council even allocated market space so that stalls run by West Indians could flourish. Rolls and rolls of bright material arrived, silk, cottons, taffeta, gold and silver lamé from America. The record shop in Granville Arcade now sold as many imported reggae records as it did tunes from the popular Top 50 chart list that was pinned in the doorway every Saturday. Yes, Brixton was definitely brightening up after the grey austerity of the post-war years.

Even my afternoon Sunday School turned into a gospel mission after six o'clock. Attending Sunday School at three o'clock was a real pain as it interfered with selling firewood. But Mum wouldn't hear of my missing it. 'You're going, young man! If anyone needs to know about good and evil it's you!' So, every Sunday after lunch I would be washed, tidied up, hair brushed and sent off with a threepenny bit in my pocket for the collection plate. The best bit of Sunday School was going in and out of the doorway. Just inside on the left as you went in was an alcove with the greatest picture of Jesus ever painted. It was not the original, of course, but a full-length black and white engraving depicting Jesus in a long white gown with the crown of thorns holding a lighted lantern, knocking on a closed cottage door. It was a fine example of Victorian sentimentality by William Holman Hunt and I loved it. Even the title made my heart soar. *The Light of the World*. Underneath, the reverend had fixed a plaque with the quotation, 'Suffer the little children to come unto me'. And we came. By the dozen.

We boys would always try to sit at the back so we could be out first, but the reverend always spotted us and made us move to the front. The hymns were OK. It was the preaching I didn't like. It was a bit too close to school lessons for me. Children who learnt the text were rewarded with a sticker to be put into a little book, which showed scenes from the Scriptures. Once the book was full you were presented with a small Bible covered in red or blue leatherette. These were supplied by charitable organisations with missions throughout the world. I always liked the magic-lantern shows we had showing mission work in Africa and other far-flung outposts of the Empire.

I had more chance of kissing the film star Diana Dors than winning a Bible. But Beryl Prentis had won two. She asked the reverend to send the second to one of the missions in Africa, for which she received a round of applause and a new book for her text stickers.

I so wanted to win one to impress her. Going about it the only way I knew how, I made it known to my close pals that I wanted to buy texts in secret for a penny each. They flooded in. In no time at all I had more than enough. The hard part was the empty sticker book, kept in the store cupboard behind the lectern. For weeks I had racked my brains trying to work out how to get one. Then, *The Light of the World* shone down on me.

'As from next Sunday we shall be sharing our mission with the new arrivals from the Colonies,' the reverend announced. 'To adjust accordingly, the stock cupboard and Bibles will be moved into the storeroom for more space.' Pausing, he surveyed his congregation over his half-rimmed gold spectacles. 'And I shall require two strong boys to stay behind and help me and Mrs Dawson. Any volunteers?'

My hand shot up as if I'd been electrocuted. 'Me, sir, I'll help.'

He eyed me suspiciously, but as he himself put me in the front row he couldn't ignore me.

'Yes, you and Kevin.'

Sod it. Mister know-it-all Kevin Bradley.

As soon as the hall was clear, the doors to the big store cupboards were unlocked and we were told to stack all the contents on the long mission pews to allow the reverend and Mrs Dawson to move the heavy cupboard. Kevin got to the box of text booklets first and put them so far away from me I couldn't get to them. The thought did cross my mind that he might know of my scheme to win a Bible. Even though I had hand-picked my suppliers, I still had this nagging doubt.

Once the cupboard was moved, it was time to refill it. I kept my eye on the desired box, but Kevin kept it until last. Placing it on the shelf, he closed the doors.

'That's all done, sir,' he said.

'Well done, boys. That's it.'

I made my way to the door with a heavy heart, defeated by Kevin. Mrs Dawson was already outside with him.

'Just a minute, Billy.'

I stopped dead in my tracks. He's told him. The sneaky little shit has told him, I thought. Turning to face the reverend, I waited for the wrath of God to be administered.

'Here, Billy. Get the stores keys from my jacket pocket. I forgot to lock the cupboard doors. Would you be so kind?' His arms were full of old Bibles from the cupboard with the briefcase balanced on top. 'I'll be out at the car.'

The Artful Dodger himself couldn't have removed those keys any quicker. Turning back into the mission, I stopped dead. The late afternoon sun was streaming through the arched stained-glass window above the entrance, flooding *The Light of the World* with amazing colour. Hurrying to the store cupboard, I helped myself to a text booklet, hiding it in my trousers under my jacket. Locking up, I made my way out, walking past Jesus who was still in full colour.

Dad looked at me a bit oddly when I asked if I could have a go with his Parker fountain pen. But Mum said,

'Oh, let him, Jack,' impressed by my keenness to further my writing skills. In my bedroom I carefully wrote over the feint pencil writing. My name, mission class number and home address. It had to be in pen, both the reverend and Mrs Dawson both used Parker pens with blue-black Quink ink, just like Dad. The deed done, I returned the pen.

'That was quick, Billy. What do you think?'

'About what, Dad?'

'The pen, of course. Honestly, I think you go round in a dream sometimes.'

'Oh yes, the pen. It was just perfect, Dad. Maybe I'll ask for one for Christmas.'

Mum joined in, 'Well, we'll just have to see how your school work is, won't we?' Not much chance of me getting a pen then, I thought.

The congregation sat stunned into silence. After the final prayer the reverend had asked if any child had filled a text booklet. I was the only one to put my hand up. Peering over his glasses with a look of sheer disbelief, he said, 'Billy Brown. Are you sure?'

'Yes, sir. Look.' I held the booklet aloft. Although he couldn't remember giving me a booklet, he thought maybe Mrs Dawson had. Making my way to the front, I listened to the mutterings.

'He can't have.'

'Not him. He just can't have.'

'You'll go to hell, Billy Brown.' A voice whispered near me.

'Jimmy. Shut up.' I whispered back.

Up on the dais the reverend scoured the booklet for any missed texts. 'A complete booklet,' he announced. 'Well done, Billy. I would never have . . .' Mrs Dawson cut him off with a polite cough. Looking me straight in the eye she said, 'Will you tell the class your favourite text, Billy.'

I stared unflinchingly back at her as Big Mike had told me to do.

'Of course, ma'am.' I looked out to the sea of faces, all waiting for me to fall at the first hurdle. But I remembered another one of Mum's famous sayings: 'God helps those that help themselves.' Jim nearly fell off his chair.

'*Who* help themselves, Billy. Well done.' The reverend had my Bible open and was busily blowing on the wet ink.

I'll bet that's Quink, I thought.

He showed me the coloured presentation label inside. 'Presented to William Henry Brown aged 9 for learning 24 texts. August 1950'. Motioning the whole of the class to rise, he led the cheers: 'Hip, hip, hurray, hip, hip, hurray, hip, hip, hurray,' followed by sustained clapping.

Emptying out into Sussex Road, my select few gathered round. 'You did it, Billy. You bloody well did it. Tom Sawyer would be proud of you.'

'Who?'

Anthony, our bookworm, continued, 'Tom Sawyer, *Huckleberry Finn*, by Mark Twain. You must have read it.'

'No, can't say I have.'

'But you must have done.'

'No, sorry, Anthony. Why is it so important?'

Smiling, he turned away. 'It's not that important, Billy.'

Walking back, I held my Bible tight in my hand, just in case the reverend came and tried to snatch it back. Most of my pals had gone their separate ways, all except Jimmy who was still laughing: 'God helps those what help themselves! I nearly fell of me chair. How did you do it?'

Before I could answer, a gloved hand slipped into mine.

'Yes, Billy, how did you do it?'

For an instant I thought, Oh God, Mrs Dawson. But then I recognised the voice.

'Go away, Jimmy!' ordered Beryl.

'Right, that's it. I know when I'm not wanted. See you in school, Billy.'

'Bye, Jimmy.'

She still had hold of my hand and wasn't letting go. 'So, tell me.'

'Tell you what, Beryl?'

She stopped and turned to face me. The cat smile was back.

'Tell me how you did it and I'll give you a kiss.'

'What?'

'You heard, Billy Brown. Now tell me.'

'I can't. I'll get all my pals into trouble.'

'I thought so. Tell me.' She wasn't going to let up.

'Anthony said ask someone called Tom Sawyer.'

For a moment she was silent. Then the cat smile softened. 'Billy Brown, you absolute little bugger.' Then she kissed me on the lips. I couldn't believe my luck. Mum was going to be so pleased with me for winning a Bible and Beryl had kissed me twice in one week. Could life get any better than this?

Passing the mission later that day, I bumped into my new black friends, Horace and Toby.

'You coming in, Billy?'

'No, Horace. I've already been in this afternoon. I'm only going down to Ma's sweet shop.'

'Well maybe on de way back. De door is always open.'

It didn't take long to spend the money from the empties and the threepenny bit Mum had given me for the collection plate which I never, ever put in. Four black-jacks, two gobstoppers, twopenny sweet lollies and a packet of sweet cigarettes was me cleaned out. Mum had given me two and six for winning the Bible, which she had promptly put into my money box. I could hear the singing as I left Ma's shop. It grew louder as I approached the mission. It was like nothing I'd ever heard before. In all Dad's records there was nothing like this.

'Won't you come in, young man?' He was the first black man I'd ever seen with pure white hair. I would later come to know him as the Reverend Stone, gospel minister.

'I just wanted to listen a bit,' I ventured.

'Of course you do. Here, just stand inside.'

Standing by the alcove with Jesus, I was mesmerised by the brilliance and enthusiasm of this new religion. 'What is it?' I asked the old man.

'Why, dis is pure gospel, son. Just pure gospel.'

The lectern had been moved to one wall and on the dais a man played a Hammond organ. Beside him a very large lady was singing as if her life depended on it, joined by the whole congregation standing and clapping. The old mission shook to the rafters. It was the most wonderful sensation I'd ever felt, except for being kissed on the lips by Beryl Prentis, of course, but that was different. Horace was halfway down, singing and clapping with everybody. I couldn't help noticing how well everyone was dressed. When the singing stopped, the preacher on the organ began. 'Brothers and sisters,' he said out loud. 'Amen. Amen.' He'd only said three words and they thought he'd finished. But he just carried on, 'My brothers, we come to this land as sinners.' 'Amen, Amen.' There they go again, I'm off, I thought. I looked at my favourite picture and wondered if he approved of his new congregation. It certainly was different. I wouldn't mind their singing in Sunday School.

I nodded to *The Light of the World*. 'Goodbye, Jesus,' I whispered.

The old man leaned closer. 'Never say goodbye to Jesus, son. Goodnight will do.'

'Goodnight, Jesus.'

'Amen,' added the old man.

As the sun had shone on Jesus, making him

multicoloured, it now struck the old man's white hair through the stained glass. I smiled and offered my hand. 'Goodnight, sir.'

He held my hand. 'What's your name, son?'

'Billy Brown, sir.' His face lit up.

'Praise the Lord for Billy Brown.' I thought this was some religious thing until he added, 'Horace told me you got us de machetes!'

''Ere, Billy. You want my job in the market?' Tommy was in the Primrose Café when I had gone for the usual three sandwiches. I had got to know him really well and filled in for him on several occasions at his job with Mr Robinson in the market.

'But I'm working for Big Mike.'

He beckoned me to sit down while Rose cooked the sausages. 'Listen, Billy, the market's where you should be. You seem to know what's what!'

'Well, I dunno.'

'I don't work for Mr Robinson any more. I've got a job with the Monk brothers.'

'Bloody hell,' I exclaimed, covering my mouth in case Rose heard me. The Monk family had more stalls in Brixton market than anyone else and were very influential.

'Listen, I've told Tony Monk about you, and he's willing to give you a try. What d'ya say?'

'What's the pay like?'

'What, what's the pay, Billy? It's the Monks. You'll be set for life!'

'If it's that good why are you leaving?'

'Australia. Dad got a job out there. We sail in three weeks' time, see.' So that was it. No one in their right mind would leave a Saturday job with the Monks unless they really had to.

'What will Big Mike say?'

'Find him a replacement first, then tell him. He'll be OK. He may kill you, but he'll be OK.' His wink told me he wasn't serious.

'Come to Monk's main shop on Monday night when you come for your boxes and find me. I'll introduce you. You'll be OK, Billy.'

Back at the yard, Big Mike was getting impatient. 'You took your time, Billy. Everything alright?'

'Gas ran out,' I lied.

'I'll give Rose a shilling for the meter next time I call in,' he joked.

'This is 'im, Mr Monk.' Tony Monk looked straight at me and out the other side. His piercing blue eyes seemed to be searching for something.

'So, you're working for Big Mike? Are you Bill?'

'Billy, Mr Monk. Me name's Billy.'

The blue eyes bore into me again. 'OK, Billy. Now what's Big Mike gonna say when you come and work for me, eh? He won't thank you, that's for sure!'

'I've got him a new boy.'

'Have you, by God! That was quick work. How d'ya know I'd be giving you the job?'

'I don't, Mr Monk. I haven't told him yet.'

He smiled at me and his face softened. He wasn't that tall but his shoulders were huge and with his close-cropped hair he looked like one of the bouncers from the Palais.

'Stalls every night. Counter-filling here on a Saturday. Ten shillings cash.'

'Ten shillings?' said Tommy. 'I only get eight!'

'Ah, but this lad's brighter than you, Tommy; comes at a price! If he's been at Big Mike's yard for six months and avoided that old bastard Pop, then he'll survive here with the Monks, that's for sure.'

I knew what he meant by 'that old bastard'. In the yard one Saturday I had gone for a piddle behind the big shed as Pop had told me to. While I was relieving myself, Pop came and stood beside me.

As he took out his willie, he said, 'Sod this cold weather, don't half make your dick shrink. I'll have to shake it to get it going. He wasn't shaking it from side to side, but up and down. It was getting enormous. 'D'you want to hold it for me, Billy? Me hands are too cold.'

I knew this was all very wrong and I was piddling on my shoes.

'Go on, Billy, it won't bite.'

I was saved by Mike bellowing from the yard. 'Where the bloody 'ell are you two?'

Pop quickly tidied himself. 'Not a word, you,' and he drew his finger across his throat to reinforce it.

'What the fuck's going on here?' Mike shouted.

I was quickly tucking my willie away.

'Pops?' he said, in a questioning tone. 'OK, Billy. Back to work.' I ran back to the shed and sat on the floor by the stove with Jessie, who snuggled against me.

Behind the shed, Big Mike was going to town on Pop. 'If you've touched that boy, I'll cut it off myself, you old bastard.'

'Honest, Mike,' he pleaded. 'I would never.'

'You would never, would you? What about last year, Pop? All a mistake, was it?'

'The boy was OK. All a mistake, Mike, you know.'

'That's the problem, you old fool. I do know. If that boy is harmed!' There was an almighty crash against the tin shed. The whole thing shook. Dust and cobwebs rained down. 'Now fuck off. Get out of my sight, and think yourself bloody lucky I'm your sodding son-in-law, God help me!'

Pop left the yard immediately. He didn't even stop to get his coat and sandwich box. Mike came into the shed shaking with rage. He understood my questioning look.

'He's still alive. I didn't hit 'im, just the shed. Are you OK, Billy?' I rushed into his arms and burst into tears.

Big Mike was taken aback. 'Hey, steady on. I thought you were tougher than that. You're scaring old Jessie.' She was going round and round in circles with her tail between her legs.

'He frightened me, Mr Mike. He really frightened me.'

'Did he touch you, Billy?'

'No, Mr Mike, but he wanted me to hold his thing.'

'I'll kill the lying old bastard, I'll bloody kill 'im.' Jessie was now distraught, running around the both of us, whimpering. Big Mike crouched down. Still holding me, he quietened Jessie with gentle strokes.

'Mr Mike, your hand!' The knuckles on his right hand were split and bleeding.

'Oh, that's nothing. I'm fine.'

Taking my hankie from my pocket, I wrapped it round his damaged hand and tied it in a knot as Mum had often done for me. 'There you are. Good as new, Mr Mike.'

His huge hand ruffled my hair. 'Jesus, Billy. Life is never simple. That's a fact.'

'I won't tell, Mr Mike,' I suddenly blurted out. 'I won't say anything to anyone.' I suddenly felt ashamed, even though I'd done nothing wrong.

'That's OK, neither will I and neither will that stupid old bastard. Now, if you're feeling OK, you can go home.'

'But Mr Mike, we've only just had lunch.'

Checking his watch he informed me, 'It's three thirty, Billy, what's an hour between friends?' He paid me my half-crown and gave me an extra one.

'What's that for, Mr Mike?'

'For your troubles, Billy. For your troubles.' He suddenly sounded very sad.

I spat on my palm and offered him my hand. 'I'll say nothing, Mr Mike, and I'll shake on it.'

He spat on his hand and took mine. 'God, if only I had a son like you, Billy. Three bloody girls, three bloody girls.' We shook hands and I patted old Jessie goodbye.

'Should I come next Saturday?'

'You bloody well better, or you'll get what the shed got!' he replied, smiling. 'And don't worry, Billy, Pop won't be here for a while.'

I walked home and sat on the playground swings, the last hour's events spinning round my brain. When Mr Meakin, the caretaker, passed I asked him the time. 'It's four twenty.'

Seeing me sitting there all alone he asked, 'You in trouble again?'

'No, Mr Meakin,' I replied. 'Just tired.'

I stayed another minute or two, then went up to 242. Mum took one look at my bedraggled appearance and ordered, 'Right my lad, get those filthy clothes off. It's a nice hot bath for you.' I sat in the bath and scrubbed myself nearly raw with the Wright's Coal Tar soap, tears streaming down my face. Luckily Mum was busy getting the tea and Dad was on his allotment so I was left to cry in peace.

Big Mike didn't argue when I told him I couldn't work for him any more, even after I said that I was going to the market to work for the Monks. I'm sure he thought it was to do with Pop. Pop had been back at the yard for a few weeks and although I was wary of him, I wasn't frightened any more. Suddenly he seemed very old and frail. He hardly spoke to me and sat in the old van to have his sandwich at tea break. I didn't know why but I felt sorry for him.

Joshua, the only black boy in my class and the strongest, was to be my replacement. Big Mike liked him straight away, as soon as Joshua called him 'sir', which I told him to do.

Big Mike and I parted company on a lovely sunny morning. For some reason I was glad it wasn't raining. Shaking hands as usual he said, 'Don't forget me.' I handed Joshua my cut-down gloves. 'If there's ever anything I can do for you, Billy, you only have to ask.'

'Thanks, Mr Mike, I'll remember that.'

'I mean anything, Billy. I owe you.'

'No you don't, Mr Mike, Mum says you never need to owe anything to true friends.'

He smiled as he used to.

'Jesus, Billy, I'll take you and your mum any day.'

He walked back into the shed to show Joshua the magic slip knot, his great boots still going galloup, galloup, galloup. I only looked back once to see old Jessie peering out the gateway, watching me go.

The Monks' main shop consisted of three large arches and it had the only cold store in the market. Working for them was great. The two brothers, Dave and Tony, ran the front, while their mum ran the little office and cash desk. Mr Monk Senior managed the whole fruit and veg business but was usually out and about supplying hotels, restaurants, schools and cafés. Apart from the main business inside the Granville Arcade, they also had several outside stalls selling fruit and veg. They were the number-one market family; if you had a job with them, you'd made it in Brixton Market society! My job was to help clear away and pack up every evening. On Saturdays I would keep the shelves and boxes filled with everything from potatoes to pineapples. And every evening I went off with my pram, which I parked in their store yard. An hour's work, then I'd fill up with firewood and go home.

Saturdays were a mad house. You couldn't move in the market for people. They came from all over south London to shop. By the turn of the last century, Brixton had the biggest undercover market in England and it was the first commercial covered market to have the new electric lighting (hence Electric Avenue). Bon Marché was one of the first true department stores in the country, and Marks and Spencer moved its Penny Bazaar from the railway arches into its first purpose-built store and Woolworths was opened, proclaiming 'Nothing more than sixpence'.

Immigrants had come from all over the world to share in Brixton's good fortune. Areas became Irish, Jewish, Italian and Austrian, with smaller groups of Russian and Chinese in the early part of the twentieth century. Brixton was already the most cosmopolitan area in Britain. There were three theatres and more than six cinemas. Shops and restaurants flourished, serving this amazing melting pot of nationalities. Now, added to this, came the West Indians. The market was already selling soused herrings, salami, black bread, pickles, bagels, dried fish, apple cake, schnitzels and much else besides from Europe. Now there would be everything from the West Indies, including its music and culture.

Even Eddie and Alf, owners of the biggest wet-fish stall in the arcade, had added to their stock. As well as the traditional cod, haddock, mackerel, skate, sole, live eels and fresh crab, they now stocked mullet, red snapper, squid, octopus, tuna steaks and, on rare occasions, shark.

I was fascinated by the way Eddie and Alf dressed. From their reinforced solid-leather hats down to their leather steel-shod clogs, they were like something from a museum. Alf would amuse me by kicking sparks from his clogs on the granite cobbles in the store yard. He would load six or so boxes filled with fish and ice onto his hat, never once tipping them over. Next to their cold store was a marble slab, where I would watch him cut and fillet whole fish ready for the market. 'I'll be charging you to watch soon, Billy,' he'd joke. 'You should be at the Palace, Alf, you're better than the conjurer!' The friendly banter was so different from school, I knew I would fit in well here. At a safe distance a few of the feral cats that lived in and around the market would wait for the scraps cut from the fish. They were only chased away if they got into the open boxes; otherwise they kept the markets free from mice and rats.

Before long I was helping to put out yams, mangoes, sweet potatoes and coconuts alongside the Cox apples, Conference pears and King Edwards. I loved it! By the time I was nine and a half, I was serving on the front.

'Come along, ladies. It's all fresh today.' When one tested the tomatoes I was straight in with, 'Don't squeeze me, til I'm yours, missus.' They loved it and I loved them. I lost count of how many times on a

Saturday I would be called a cheeky little bugger or similar. My close pals would all come to shop at my stall. Holding their paper lists from their mums, they would wait in the long queues that didn't seem to slow down until at least four o'clock. Grabbing their lists, I would fill their bags or an empty box as quick as I could. They all knew the system – be quick!

'Right-ho, that'll be two shillings, always an exact coin to be rung up on the till. As I handed over their purchases, I whispered the correct amount, like five shillings, and back at the flats we would split the difference. I always made sure their mums got the best fruit and veg in the market. One of the Monks' stalls only sold tomatoes and I would cover for lunches. There I stood, with my open brown-paper bag in one hand, shouting to the crowds. 'They're all fresh, ladies, finest Jersey toms, sixpence a pound or ten bob a box, come and get 'em.'

It was all part of the stallholders' spiel. If you simply stood still, you sold nothing. When I asked what to do with the soft overripe tomatoes it had been carefully explained. 'Look, Billy, if they're really spoilt or mouldy, dump 'em in that box for the old girls, but if they're just a bit soft or squashy, put them in the box next to the paper bags. Each time you pick up a new bag, put a crap one in the bottom in the palm of your hand, but in the bag. He demonstrated with the deftness of a conjurer. 'See, now when I put the good ones on top and twist the bag, they won't know until they get home and think it was squashed in their shopping bag.'

'And that's how we get rid of the crap,' I laughed.

'Exactly,' Mr Monk said, 'You're a fast learner.' Continuing the lesson, he went on. 'Always keep the one-pound weight on the scales, drop the bag into the pan and it will sink to the measure straight away. Whip it out, twist it shut, job done.' As he talked he did exactly that. 'Average six tomatoes to the pound. If the customer insists on a reweigh, do it. If it's short, add a tomato, but don't ever say it's short, or sorry. Just do it with yer usual, "There you go, lady". That cheeky smile of yours will do the rest!'

I couldn't believe how simple it was to cheat the customers! I had my regulars, especially from the flats, who all knew that I would only serve them the best produce. A few would give me a list on Sundays when I delivered firewood, which they could collect quickly the following Saturday without queuing. Tony Monk was impressed when he saw the filled boxes with a paper receipt waiting for collection. 'Clever boy, Billy.' He noticed one of the boxes had my name on the receipt. 'What's all this, then?'

'It's my mum's order. I'll pay for it with my wages and take it home in the pram.'

'Honestly, Billy, you and that bloody pram. The whole market knows about Billy Brown's pram. God knows what you'd do with a van.'

He picked up my receipt and tore it up. 'You bring ten or more orders like this, and your shopping's free.'

'Thanks very much, Mr Monk.'

'Mind now. Ten at least, and no taking the piss!'

'How's that, Mr Monk?'

He gave me the piercing-blue-eyes routine. 'No filling her box with expensive pineapples or bags of brazils, got it?'

'Yes, Mr Monk, got it.'

'I'll tell you when there's expensive stuff left over.'

One Saturday I was in full flow with chat. 'There you go, missus, nice hat. 'Here you are, guvner, twenty pound King Edwards, chips for a week!' But on this occasion, I was too cocky. Two black ladies were arguing as to who was next and causing interest from the crowd. I intervened, full of confidence. 'Hold on ladies, don't get your knickers in a twist.'

They stopped arguing instantly. 'Who you calling a nigger, white boy?'

'No, no, ladies, knickers, I said knickers.'

'Nigger. He called me a nigger.'

A group of black people was forming in front of the stall. 'What dat likle shit call you a nigger for?'

'No, I didn't. It's all a misunderstanding.'

Tony Monk arrived from his office. 'What the fuck's going on here?' he demanded. I was sure he'd been alerted not by the commotion, but by the silence of the three tills.

I tried to explain, but was drowned out by the loud black lady. 'Nigger. Dat boy called me a nigger.'

The crowd, of course, was now behind her. 'Yeah, dat's right, man. He said nigger. We all heard him.'

Mr Monk gripped my shoulder and once more gave me the eye inquisition.

'Did you say nigger?'

'No, Mr Monk. I said, "Don't get your knickers in a twist". That's the honest truth. On my mum's life. I swear it!'

The situation had reached stalemate. Mrs Monk leant her head out of the open office window. 'Tony,' she shouted. 'Charlie's on his way.'

Oh, shit. Someone had called the market inspector. Now I was for it. Charlie promptly arrived, resplendent in his uniform of long black coat, black leather gloves, peaked cap with brass badge on which was engraved 'Market Inspector'.

'What's all this lark, Mr Monk? All this commotion? It's holding up the entire market.' He always spoke with a really bad posh accent to reinforce his powerful position.

Mr Monk tried to explain. 'This lady says . . .' That was as far as he got.

'Nigger. He called me a nigger!' She was now sweating profusely, dabbing her face with a hankie.

'Well, Mr Monk, what has the boy to say for himself?'

'I didn't say it, sir, I wouldn't.'

'Of course he wouldn't,' came a voice from the back of the crowd. 'Out of my way.' The sea of black faces parted and a small black man with a trilby hat came through to where I was standing.

'Good day to you, sir,' he addressed the inspector, raising his hat. The pure white curly hair shone like a halo in the sun beaming through the glass roof of the market.

'Well, Reverend?' the inspector began, explaining

the situation. When he'd finished, my white-haired saviour looked straight at me. 'Well now, Billy Brown.' His congregation was stunned into silence. He knew my name.

'He did. He called me a nigger!'

'Delilah, be quiet.' She fell silent, sulking. I suddenly recognised her as the wonderful gospel singer. No wonder she could shout the loudest!

'Well, Billy, what do you say?'

'No, sir. I didn't say nigger.' I then carefully explained again what I'd said.

Stood in the middle, surrounded by the hostile crowd to the front, Mr Monk and the inspector behind me, with the reverend beside me, I felt very alone.

He took my hand and patted the back of it. 'You're sure, Billy?'

'I swear by *The Light of the World*, sir.'

'Delilah, you are a damned fool. You hear what you want to hear. Now go about your business. This boy is innocent.'

'Amen to that, sir.'

He still held my hand. 'Amen to dat, Billy Brown. Mr Monk, dis boy needs a cup of tea!'

The crowd dispersed, with Delilah still trying to convince her now doubtful friends. 'He did, I tell you. He did.'

Charlie quickly pulled off his glove and shook hands. 'Thank you, Reverend Stone. Nasty business all that, very nasty, sir.'

'Nonsense, Charlie, a stupid misunderstanding, dat's all!' The reverend tipped his hat, acknowledging everyone. 'Charlie, Mr Monk, Billy, I bid you a good day. God bless you all.'

'You must lead a very charmed life, that's all I can say. Go and get yourself a cup of tea at Eammon's café. Be back in fifteen minutes.' Tony Monk went back to his office and the inspector went back to the betting shop. 'Nearly very nasty,' he was explaining to a trader as they walked along. 'Good thing I was with the military for a while.'

The trader was patting him on the back with a 'Well done, Charlie, absolutely, good show.' No one wanted to alienate the market inspector.

'Come here, Billy, look at this,' Tony Monk was calling me from the cold store. Inside, six-feet-long stalks of bananas suspended on hooks were being very slowly taken through the store by a motorised overhead rail system. Passing through over a period of days, the bananas warmed up and ripened sufficiently for sale.

At the end of the line Duncan, a big black man, cut the fruit into hands for sale, leaving just the stalk to be dumped.

'There he is, Tony. Look at dis one!' My eyes followed in the direction Duncan was pointing with the knife.

'Bloody hell, Mr Monk. What is it?'

'Spider, Billy.'

'Well, I can see that, but it's a bloody big spider!' The giant hairy mound hadn't moved since falling out of the stalk. 'He's still asleep.'

LONDON COUNTY COUNCIL

EFFRA SCHOOL JUNIOR BOYS'

REPORT FOR YEAR ENDING ___July___ , 19 _50_

Name ___William Brown___   Number in Class _42_

Class ___1 a___   Position in Class ___41___

SUBJECT	ASSESSMENT	REMARKS
ENGLISH Reading	5/20	
Composition	4/20	
Exercises	6/20	
Spelling	0/20	
ARITHMETIC	18/50	
HISTORY	2/10	
GEOGRAPHY	3/10	
SCIENCE	0/10	
ART	10/20	
WRITING	12/20	
HANDWORK	Good	
OTHER SUBJECTS		

RELIGIOUS KNOWLEDGE ___Fair___   Attendance ___Good___

GENERAL REPORT

He makes no effort; hence, this very poor result. He must try and take an interest in his work.

_S.B.er_   Class Master / Class Mistress   _F.A. Nicholson_ Head Master / Head Mistress

My school report, 1950.

Me and Mum, 1949.

Woolies Christmas outing, 1951, with tramlines in the foreground.
Dad, me, Mum and Bob are on the far left.

Me, aged 7½, and full of mischief.

Mum and Dad on Yarmouth Beach, early 1950s. Dad's concession to sunbathing – 'I'll roll my trousers up, but the tie stays on!'

From left: Bob, Mum, Dad and me. Great Yarmouth, 1951.

Me and Barbara
at the entrance to
Ashford House,
circa 1951.

The Guinness
Clock on loan,
1951-1952, after the
Festival of Britain
exhibition. It stood
in the front garden
of our flats for one
month and wasn't
even vandalised.

Dad took this photo of the Brown family on Diss Station/ Norfolk Broads, 1951. From left: Cousin Ruth, Aunty Doreen, Granny Brown, Bob, Mum and me.

From left: Bob, me, Dad and Mum aboard the *Crimson Dawn* at Norfolk Broads, 1952.

Jack Brown (Dad) running bingo at the coronation celebrations at our flats. Next to him is Dolly Hammond – owner of the cabbages!

Dad's amazing display for the coronation which won him £10 prize money and his photo in the paper.

Mum doing what she loved to do – looking after us all at the coronation party, 1953. She's got her best frock on and one of her only pieces of jewellery, a gold flower on a chain that Dad had given her as a wedding anniversary present.

Dad and me, aged 13, pretending to smoke! I never actually did. Note the panelled wallpaper as Dad couldn't get enough of one pattern.

'Well, I'm not going to be here when he wakes up,' I assured him.

He explained, 'They come in the fruit from the ships. Because it's cold they hibernate under the bananas and some survive, like this one.'

Duncan added, 'They're harmless, Billy. You can let them walk on your hands.'

'Not bloody likely!'

'They're harmless bird-eating spiders.' My mind suddenly pictured pigeons being devoured. Anticipating my next question, Duncan continued, 'Very *small* birds, hummingbirds and the like.'

The stowaway twitched and I nearly wet myself.

'Well goodbye, Mr Spider.' Duncan raised a studded boot to crush it.

'Stop!' The boot rested just above the spider.

'What?'

'I want it.'

'What? What do you want with 'im?'

'Never you mind, Duncan.' I quickly found a small cardboard box with a lid. 'Put him in.' Duncan looked at Tony Monk for approval. 'OK. He can have them.'

'Them?' I asked, surprised.

'Yes, Billy. Maybe one or so a month – and I suppose you'll want the scorpions as well?'

'Scorpions?'

'Black scorpions. But they're not harmless, and if fully awake can give you a nasty sting – and they're fast.

'How fast?'

'Billy, use your brain! They've got six legs so they're bloody fast.

'It's a pity McNicolls hasn't got some scorpion in him – West Ham might do a bit better!' His reference to the centre forward wasn't lost on Duncan.

'Ain't dat de trufe, boss. Now, open your box.' While I gingerly held open the box he scooped up the dozy spider with his broad knife, its legs dangling over either side. As soon as it was in the box I shut the lid tight. 'Thanks, Duncan, see you.'

Tony Monk stopped me. 'Don't let Charlie catch you with them. He'll have a fit. You're already in his bad books.'

The timing was perfect, my lunch break. Leaving the Granville Arcade I headed straight for the A1 pet shop. The window was full of kittens, white mice, hamsters and two brown puppies of no particular pedigree. The owner looked up from his *Daily Mirror* as I entered.

'No more kittens!'

'I haven't got any more!'

'What's in the box, then? Some fruit for me?' He chuckled at his own joke.

'If you try to sell me any more kittens, I'll feed you to Crusher!' At the back of the counter in a six-foot-long glass tank was a royal python, sleeping off his last white mouse. Coiled up, he filled the whole bottom of the tank. A card taped to the front of the glass read, 'Crusher. I am a royal python and I am not for sale'. All the kids liked to come in and see him, as he was named after a wrestler in the Diana Dors film *A Kid for Two Farthings*. Further along a wall, a sign read

'Exotics'. In various tanks were cicadas, stick insects and giant dung beetles.

'I've got an exotic for you.' He put down his paper in exasperation.

'Don't tell me. You've got a kitten with six legs!'

'Better than that,' I told him with a smug smile, and promptly opened the box. 'Got any fresh sparrows for him?' I asked.

'Well, well, well! We're moving into Arachnida, are we?'

'What?'

'Spiders, Billy, spiders! Where did you find that?'

'Can't say, but there could be more – and black scorpions, very exotic!'

'Cheeky little beggar!'

'How much will you give me?' I asked, the spider becoming more lively by the minute. It was now spread out and was bigger than my hand.

'Five bob, and three bob for the scorpions.'

'Done – and you can keep the box!'

'When can I expect some more, Billy?'

Spitting on my five shillings as I went through the door, I shouted back.

'When my ship comes in!'

8

Ups and Downs

'Short bar of metal, that's what I need.' I was talking to myself. Looking around, I found the ideal thing, a short piece of old gas pipe. 'Now let's see.'

That was the trouble with working on your own – no one to chat to, only yourself. I had decided that the fewest people who knew what I was up to on the bombsites, the better off I'd be. Taking a couple of turns on the iron pipe, I pulled at the old copper cable. My makeshift handle worked a treat and I had soon freed enough to start rolling it up. This was getting too easy; pull a few feet, roll it up. As I yanked hard on a bit of cable high up in the basement wall it moved something from between the floor joists above my head. Finding an old chair, I climbed up to see what I had disturbed.

There, wedged snugly between two wooden joists, was a black tin box covered in dirt and dust. The metal handle on the end made it easy to pull out. It was a bit bigger than a cardboard shoe box but not as deep. Placing it on the chair, my heart raced as I saw the brass padlock securing the lid. Memories of Jim's story about rich people hiding their treasures in case Hitler invaded flooded my imagination. Staring at the box, I was deciding the best way to get the padlock off when I thought better of it. Taking it to where my pram was concealed, I put it in the well under Dad's piece of plywood. It fitted almost perfectly. Gathering up the rest of my booty and my piece of iron bar, I headed back home. By the time I got to the flats I was almost running. Turning into the gateway, I ran straight into PC Collins and his wife.

'Hold up, Billy Brown. What's your hurry?'

'I'm going to be late home and Mum will be worrying about me.'

'Your mum must worry constantly about what you're up to! What's in the pram?'

'Nothing, Mr Collins, just some old bits of junk, you know me!'

'That's exactly it. I do know you. Let's just take a look, shall we?'

'For God's sake, we're late enough as it is. Leave the boy alone.'

'But Caroline, you don't know this boy like I do. Look at the little bugger. He's been in trouble again.'

'You'll be in trouble if we miss the first film. Now come on.' With that she started to walk away.

'Alright, but I'll be watching out for you next time, Billy Brown.'

'Goodnight, Mrs Collins,' I called out, 'and thank you.' The look on his face was one of total confusion, but capturing me for a bit of old junk against upsetting his wife was an easy decision.

'Next time . . .' he called back, as he hurried after her.

Safe inside my pram shed I took out the box. There had been some white lettering stencilled on it, but due to the dirt and wear I couldn't read it all. I was eager to reveal the treasure within. Putting the box on an upturned log which I used to chop wood, I attacked the padlock with Dad's hacksaw. The steel clasp was very hard and took ages to cut through, but, with a final whack of my rusty axe, it broke. With great anticipation I opened the lid slowly, waiting to be dazzled by gold coins and diamonds. 'Bloody load of rubbish,' I said aloud to myself.

The tin box was filled with crumpled old newspaper, brown with age. I plonked down on an upturned orange box. What a swizz, no bloody treasure, I thought. Remembering how well the box had fitted into my pram, I decided to keep it anyway and began taking out the old paper. Starting at one end, I grabbed a handful and felt something hard. Removing the shreds of paper revealed a china figure of a monkey. I held it up to the light and was amazed by the detail. The monkey was dressed in a frock coat, boots and wig and was playing a violin. A further search of the paper turned up two more; one with a cello, the other with a viola. I stood all three on one of my empty boxes. Ma Kingdom will love 'em, I thought. Now the search was on in earnest. I carefully removed more paper and found a small silver cigarette case embossed with an eagle holding a swastika in a circle; pressing the tab, it flipped open and inside was an inscription in German. The only words I could understand were 'Kapitän' and 'Adolf Hitler'. Wow. Nazi treasure!

The next item beat the three monkeys and the cigarette case by miles. I sat on my box holding the dagger in both hands, still in its green scabbard. Gently pulling it out, I could scarcely believe the perfect condition of the tapering blade and wondered how long it had lain in its hiding place. After making a few slashes in the air, I returned it to its home in the scabbard. I was only halfway down the box, but I already knew I was in possession of three items that Ma Kingdom would be very interested in buying. The remaining half seemed to be filled with only one item. Picking off the paper, I could see what looked like the fold-over black leather top of a handbag, just like the one Mum had for special occasions. Holding the mildew-covered top, I lifted it clear of the tin box and froze. The gun holster was instantly recognisable by its narrowing shape and from its weight I knew it was occupied. It took me a few minutes to pluck up the courage to open it. Every man and boy in the flats would have recognised the gun instantly: there was only one type of pistol that shape. A German Luger. I had held toy guns, but this was very different. I had difficulty holding it in one hand so had to use two. This was beyond my wildest dreams of treasure! Set into the black handle grips was a silver swastika, traces of oil still visible on the long barrel. Holding it in front of me, I looked along the sight.

'Bang, bang, you're dead!' I said. 'Bang, bang, BANG!!' The recoil knocked me off my orange box and for a moment I was deafened. Not thinking, I had pulled the trigger in play. Realising the whole of the flats must have heard the shot, I knew I was in deep trouble. I quickly put the items back in their box and stowed it away in the pram. A few seconds later Mr Austin, the caretaker, arrived.

'I knew it would be you letting off fireworks. Wait till I tell your mum.'

A firework. How brilliant of him, I thought. 'Sorry, Mr Austin. It was only one banger, left over from Guy Fawkes. I haven't got any more, I promise.'

'Stupid little bugger, woke up half the flats. I'll be reporting you to the superintendent. Can't you ever behave yourself?'

'Sorry.'

'Well, don't do it again.' He stomped off, back to sweeping the playground.

Sitting down on my box once more, I decided something had to be done with my treasure and the sooner the better. I tried to imagine what Mum would say and what Dad would do if they caught me with a loaded pistol. It would be just too terrible. As much as I wanted to keep it, I knew I couldn't. Throw it in the emergency reservoir behind the Primrose Café was my first idea, then dump it in the dust chute or bury it in the allotments. Then the solution came to me. Connoisseurs. Tosh's connoisseurs would pay a fortune for a genuine Nazi Luger.

I had to wait for a while for an Irish builder to choose some khaki work trousers and a woollen hat before I could talk to Tosh. As soon as he left the shop I retrieved the tin box from my pram. Turning the sign in his door to 'Closed', I re-entered.

'Oi, what's your game, Billy? I don't shut for another hour.'

'Oh, you'll shut for this, Tosh,' I said, putting the black box on the counter.

'What's in the box then, Billy, Nazi treasure?' His smile was cut short.

'How the hell did you guess, Tosh?'

'Wait a minute.' Quickly he turned the latch locking the door. 'This way.' I followed him through into the back storeroom. A fold-flat table was covered in odd items of army clothing. With one arm he shoved the lot onto the floor, allowing me to put down the box.

'What does it say? I couldn't read it.'

Finding a wet rag, he wiped the lid clean. I'd never heard him so serious before.

'Where did you get the box, Billy?' I recounted the story as to the finding of the box, but no more.

'You couldn't read it 'cos it's abbreviated, see?'

'No, I don't see. What's abbreviated?'

'Shortened, like all military stuff. Look, I'll show you.' He pointed with one of his dirty fingers. 'Brig, that's Brigadier, see.'

'Oh, now I get it. So Gen is General.'

'Exactly, so this box belonged to Brigadier General Sir David Mc . . .'

'MC what?'

'Don't know. Someone has scraped the name off.'

'That's why it was hidden in the floor joists. I bet someone nicked it off him.'

'Possible. We'll never know. What's inside, then?' I

opened the box just enough to take out the three china monkeys and carefully stood them on the table.

'Meissen. Meissen porcelain.'

'You sure?'

'Yes, my ex-wife, she used to read all these books on antiques, see, and these monkeys were her favourite. Got any more? There's a whole orchestra.'

'No, sorry, only the string section. Now, close your eyes and hold out your hand. I promise it will be worth it.'

Something in my voice must have convinced him to humour me. 'Oh alright, you silly bugger. Get on with it then.'

Carefully I placed the silver cigarette case into his open palm. 'You can look now.'

His eyes flew wide open when he saw the insignia.

'One for the connoisseurs, eh, Tosh?' I asked with a smile.

'Too bloody right, boy-o.'

'Open it. There's an inscription. I could only read Kapitän and Adolf Hitler.'

Gently he clicked open the case. 'Oh my God, oh my God.'

'Can you read it? I think it's in German.' He was still staring at the inscription in disbelief.

'Billy, you can't imagine what you've found. Listen. 'Presented to Captain Ralph Spierman of U23 for courageous service to the Third Reich. Adolf Hitler'. Serious collectors will kill to own this.'

'Well, they can start with this then.'

He had to sit down; the shock of the dagger was too

much for him. Without saying a word Tosh withdrew the blade. 'Solignum.'

'What?'

'It's the steel, finest ever made.'

'Why has the case gone green?'

'It hasn't gone green, it *is* green, to represent the sea. This is a German Customs official dagger, only to be used on special occasions. Very rare, very rare indeed.'

'A bit like my Crimea compass, eh?'

'Well that's rare, but this, this is rare, *rare*, Billy.'

'There's more!'

'What? More what? All we need now is a Panzer Tiger Tank to come out of that box and my day will be complete!'

'Shut your eyes and put out both hands.' This time he didn't argue. Squeezing both eyes shut, he extended both grubby hands palms upwards. He wasn't expecting the weight of the pistol and holster, and his hands dropped onto the table.

'Tell me it isn't,' he asked quietly.

'Oh, yes it is, Tosh – and it's loaded.'

'What! You mean you've been carrying round a loaded revolver, Billy?'

'It's a pistol. Have a look.' Opening the flap he peeked inside, instantly recognising the unique handle.

'Sod the tea. I need a drink!' He left the gun on the table and began rummaging on a shelf until he found the half-bottle of Black and White whisky. Throwing out the remnants of an earlier brew from his tin mug, he poured himself a large measure. He sipped it slowly, studying the gun still in its holster.

'I have to be home soon. Mum will worry about me.'

He spluttered on his whisky. 'Worry, why should she? You're abroad with daggers and guns. Who the hell would dare to trouble you! Right, OK, let's have a look. Oh my God, Billy, it's been fired very recently. It may have been used in a murder.'

'It's OK, Tosh. I did it!'

Closing his eyes, he sat in silence finishing his drink while I related how the gun came to be fired. When I got to the part where the recoil knocked me off the box his eyes opened.

'It's a bloody marvel it didn't break your wrist.' Slipping the pistol from its holster, he explained what he was doing. 'Safety on, magazine out.' He pulled back the breech to ensure it was empty.

'Dear God, Billy, you could have shot yourself. Then where would you be?' I wondered if Mrs Thompsit had been in, but thought better of asking him.

'So, what do you think, can you sell 'em?' Pouring another drink, he stroked his stubby chin.

'I don't know about the monkeys.'

'Oh no, Ma Kingdom will have them. I mean the other items!'

'Well, the cigarette case and the dagger should be easy, but the gun, that's a whole different kettle of fish. I'd be breaking the law. It's a prisonable offence to own or sell firearms without a licence, especially those brought back illegally, as I'm sure this one was. I don't know, I just don't think it's right.'

'I'll go halves with you.'

'Halves. Fifty-fifty?'

'Of course; my goods, your buyers!'

'I'll do it, but only 'cos it's you, Billy. I'll need the tin box for authentication.'

'Well, OK. But I want it back.' Although puzzled, he agreed.

'Gonna take a week, maybe two. But pop in when you're passing. I'm sure I can find a buyer. Some of this lot will probably end up in some museum somewhere. You know, Billy, I'm amazed that you trust me to sell your stuff and not cheat you.'

'Big Mike told me you can only be cheated once by someone and I don't think you're the cheating kind.'

'I'm not.' Carefully he put the items back in the tin box. Raising his tin mug he declared, 'To Brigadier General Sir David Mc whatever your name was,' and drained the last of the whisky.

On my way back from Tosh's I called in on Ma Kingdom. At the sound of her shop bell she appeared from the back sitting room.

'Well, if it isn't Billy Brown. I was just saying to Richard, I hadn't seen you for ages. Now, what you got?'

Producing the three porcelain monkeys, I lined them up on the counter. Ma picked one up and immediately turned it over to look at the base before putting it back with its two friends.

'Cheap copies. Five bob the lot.'

'Well, Ma, that's really generous of you.' She'd already put two silver half-crowns on the counter. Taking the money, I pushed one monkey towards her.

'Oi, what all this then?'

'Well, Ma, five bob for the three cheap copies would be OK, but it's five bob each for genuine Meissen figurines. Especially as you've already seen the mark!'

'Who told you, you crafty little bugger!'

'I have my clients, Ma, and one or two connoisseurs who know a real monkey when they see one, same as I do!'

'Well, if you say so. Let's not fall out over a bit of old china!'

'Old Meissen china, Ma.'

'But five bob each, there won't be any profit for old Ma.'

'Oh, I thought you just kept all the stuff I get. You always said you liked pretty things!'

Her tone hardened. 'Ten bob for the three, you're getting far too clever!'

'Twelve and a nice box of choccies for Mum.'

'Ten, and a nice box of choccies for your mum.'

'Done – and I'll always bring you the pretty stuff!'

Smiling to herself, she took the monkeys, replacing them with a box of Cadbury's Milk Tray, Mum's favourite.

'Hello, Tosh. Any luck?' He stopped piling black bootlaces into a cardboard box.

'Ah, it's that Billy Brown, supplier of fine collectibles for connoisseurs of a military persuasion.'

'You what?'

'Never mind. Come out the back and get your money.' We both sat at the fold-flat table, now stacked high with khaki tins full of grease.

'So, come on, Tosh. How did we do?' Removing a two-ounce Golden Virginia tobacco tin, he popped the lid.

'Very nicely I'd say, my young friend.' The tin was filled with coins and bank notes.

'Not all of it. It can't be all of it.'

'Oh yes it is, Billy. All twenty-one pounds of it.' I sat speechless.

'Ha, first time I've known you without anything to say!' Tipping out the cash, he started to divide it.

'Tosh, that's ten pounds, ten shillings each.'

I sat staring at the fortune on the table in front of me, while he read from a slip of paper.

'One presentation cigarette case, four pounds.'

'Four pounds for that!'

'Be quiet. One Nazi Customs official dagger, seven pounds – and last but not least, one officer-issue German Luger pistol with holster – *test-fired*,' he added with a smile, 'ten whopping pounds, Billy! This calls for a drink.' Placing two tin mugs on the table, he produced a fresh half-bottle of Black and White whisky and a bottle of Tizer. We both poured ourselves a large measure, like a couple of pirate captains after a successful day's pirating.

'Did you bring my box back?' I asked.

He lifted the box from under the table and passed it to me.

'There's something in it?'

'Well, you'd better open it and see, hadn't you?'

Inside I found a khaki canvas roll with a strap and buckle fastening. Stencilled on the canvas in black letters were the words 'Tool Kit, Armoured Div.'. Undoing the buckle, I rolled it out across the table. 'Wow, Tosh, how much?'

'I'm cut to the quick, Billy!'

'You're what?'

'I'm wounded. Straight to the heart, that you should think I seek monetary gain from a partner.'

'Oh.'

'It's a small gift, no charge.'

I gazed at the array of tools: pliers, cutters, screwdrivers and spanners. 'No charge?' I repeated, running my fingers over the amazing kit. 'Thanks Tosh, I'll keep it in the pram.'

'That's what I thought. To deal with all those awkward little jobs.'

We both chinked our tin mugs together.

'To Brigadier General Sir David Mc whatever your name was.'

'It's easy, Robin, nothing to it! We do it all the time!'

It was the first time the new boy, Robin, had accompanied us to the bombsites. He'd been welcomed into our group of pals, first because he was good at sport and second, as his dad was in the RAF in Germany. He was quite tall, with straw-coloured hair that seemed to go in all directions. A group of us had decided to go and explore the old Barrington Arms pub. All around it, houses had been flattened by the bombing but the pub had somehow survived almost intact. Windows had been blown out and the doors were gone, but the flat roof and most of the floor were intact. The oak staircase had been removed long ago, so access to the roof was made via the dumb-waiter shaft!

'You'll see, Robin. It's easy.' We all assembled in the basement. Jim went first. Climbing into the empty shaft, he put his back against one wall and his feet against the opposite one. Applying pressure he climbed, crab-like, up the shaft to roof level. Once there, he called back down for the next climber. One by one we all climbed the thirty-foot shaft, leaving only Robin to follow. After much encouragement he began his first-ever ascent. Once he'd got the hang of it he came up quite quickly.

'Well done. See, told you it was easy.'

'Cor, what a view!' We all stood on the flat roof gazing out over the bombsites and Loughborough Road. Jim had a bag of gobstoppers and gave us all one.

'Look at the back of your coat, Jim. Your mum'll kill you.'

'*My* mum? Just look at *yours*, Billy!' We all examined our coats, which were covered in green moss stains from the shaft. After twenty minutes or so, we decided to descend the shaft and go exploring. Once again Jim went first, followed by myself and the other boys. Robin was the last to come down.

'Don't forget. Go slowly. It's harder coming down,' I yelled up the shaft.

From high above came the words, 'I'm OK. I'll be really careful.' We listened to Robin puff and heave as he started his descent.

'He'll be fine,' Jim reassured us, but this was quickly followed by Robin shouting, 'I'm slipping, I'm slipping.'

He screamed as he plummeted down the last fifteen feet. There was a sickening snap as he hit the bottom and fell onto the stone floor.

'Aghh, my leg, my leg,' he screamed. We looked at the bone protruding from the side of his leg, just below the knee.

'Phone box,' I said. 'Where's the nearest one?' No one could speak.

'Bloody phone box, you stupid buggers! He might die.'

This didn't help Robin, who began screaming even louder.

'Over the road,' said Derek. 'The paper shop must have one.'

'Stay with him, Jim. Don't run off. That goes for the rest of you. I'll be back!' I sprinted across the road as fast as I could, narrowly missing a taxi whose driver shouted at me. Panting from my run I began, 'Lift shaft . . . broken leg . . . please hurry!'

'Hold on a minute, lad,' the owner said. 'What lift shaft? What broken leg?' I sucked in air and began again.

'In the old pub. Robin fell down the lift shaft. He's busted his leg.'

'How do you know, lad?'

''Cos it's sticking out the side, mister.'

'Oh, God. Marge, ring nine nine nine and tell 'em to hurry.'

'Now, lad, show me where he is.' Back at the pub, Robin was not looking too good. All the colour had drained from his face and he'd gone very quiet. The man took off his coat and wrapped it around Robin.

'He's going into shock. I saw a lot of this in the army.'

Ringing bells announced the arrival of help. 'Go out and show them the way, lad.'

I went out to the ambulance, to be greeted by a police car, closely followed by a big white Daimler ambulance, which appeared around the corner, bells ringing and lights flashing.

All the other lads had been ordered out to sit on the remnants of the pub garden wall. I followed the two ambulancemen into the basement.

'He's in shock,' advised the man from the paper shop, 'and his leg's broken.' While one of the ambulance crew put an oxygen mask on Robin, the other checked him over.

'What's his name?' he asked.

'Robin. Robin Howard.'

'OK, Robin. We'll have you out of here in a jiffy. Don't you worry son, you'll be just fine.' From a large bag a splint was produced to hold the broken leg still. Once applied, the policeman held the oxygen cylinder while the two ambulance crew gently lifted Robin, who was slipping in and out of consciousness. It seemed to take ages to get him to the ambulance over all the rubble, but all three men had seen service during the Blitz and worked together as a team. The ambulance doors shut on our friend and he was soon speeding his way to King's College Hospital four miles away.

'Now then, you lot,' started the policeman. 'How did it happen?'

There was no point in trying to lie so we told him

the truth. He was shocked when we told him how we climbed to the roof.

'In the dumb waiter?' he replied incredulously. 'Up that shaft? Are you all bloody mad? You could have all been killed!'

'We made him go last,' said Jim.

'Oh, did you now. Well, fine friends you lot are!' More bells signalled the arrival of another police car and within seconds a sergeant appeared around the corner.

'And what do we have here, Constable?' Before he could answer, a familiar voice joined in.

'I'll tell you what, Sergeant. They're the Guinness Trust lads.'

'Did you push him?' he asked.

'What? No, sir. He fell. He was the last one down so he couldn't have been pushed, could he?' The sergeant stood towering over me.

'Smart-arse, are you?'

'No, sir. I called the ambulance!' He seemed to calm down a bit.

'Now, if one of my officers catches any one of you on these bombsites again, you'll be for it! Understand?'

'Yes, sir,' we chorused.

'Now, you're all going for a nice ride home in our police cars!' He led the way and we all filed into the back of the two cars as ordered. It didn't feel at all exciting, returning home in a police car. We all knew just how much trouble we were in. The two black cars swept in through the open gates and came to a halt outside the superintendent's office.

'Out!' barked the burly sergeant. While his three colleagues took three boys each to face our parents, the sergeant drove with the superintendent round to Robin's block to inform his mother. Mum went mad at me when PC Collins told her about Robin's accident.

'You could all have been killed!'

'I'm sorry, Eileen. I often see Billy on the sites and turn a blind eye. But I won't be able to now, not with young Robin in the hospital and all.'

'Thanks, Colin, his dad and I will deal with him, don't you worry!'

PC Collins left me to the wrath of Mum.

'I'm sorry, Mum. We were just playing, that's all.'

'Oh, I'm sure you were, Billy, but Robin is in the hospital and it could so easily have been you!'

'Oh, no, Mum. I've climbed that shaft dozens of times!' As the last words left my mouth I mentally climbed the steps to the gallows.

'What? You *what?* Go and get your money box!' It was pointless to argue. Returning with the wooden box, I handed it over. She took a small screwdriver from her drawer and, swiftly undoing the retaining screw, she emptied the entire contents onto the table.

'My God, Billy. Did you rob a bank?'

'No, Mum. It's all from trading and business. You know, firewood and stuff!'

She eyed me suspiciously. 'Is any of this stolen, Billy?'

'No, Mum. It's from trade.'

Carefully she halved the contents. 'Well, this half

should cover what you've made from the bombsites, so you went there for nothing!'

'Yes, Mum.'

Putting the screws back she said, 'Billy, one day you'll learn: I tell you these things to protect you, not to stop your fun.'

'Yes, Mum.'

'If you had been killed . . .' Her words trailed off and she hugged me so tight I could hardly breathe. When she finally let go her eyes were full of tears.

'Mum, you're crying!' She wiped her eyes with the corner of her apron.

'Billy Brown, go and make us a nice cup of tea.'

My friend Robin was in hospital for six weeks. He had suffered a severely broken leg, fractured elbow and finger. Although badly concussed, he had not fractured his skull. He returned to a hero's welcome and we all signed his plaster cast, even PC Collins.

For some time I had been going to Effra Road Secondary School. I still didn't learn much. My school report read, 'Number in class: 42. Position in class: 42'. The classes were much larger than in Sussex Road, which made life harder for the teachers who, in turn, made life harder for us. The headmaster, Mr Nicholls, ruled with a rod of iron or, more precisely, the cane. All misdemeanours, great or small, resulted in a caning and your name in the book. I had almost a whole book to myself. The only master who seemed tolerant was luckily our class master, Mr Beard, who taught

English. Even though I could never spell correctly, he gave my compositions and stories high marks, once telling the class I had great imagination, to which Jim muttered, 'Yeah, he imagines he's intelligent!' Most of my pals had moved into the same class as me.

Register call in the morning was hilarious. I'm sure the headmaster had done it on purpose to relieve the boredom. It started out normally with Adams, Braithwaite, etc., then carried on with 'Black, Brown, Green, Grey, Orange, White'. It sounded like a paint chart and always made us laugh.

Anthony was still the brightest boy in our class. I don't think I ever saw him without a book in his hands. He was the only boy in our class allowed to take books home from the school library. Because of his looks and studious nature he was a prime target for bullies. Often he would be picked on going home from school when there were no teachers around to protect him.

Walking home past the shops one afternoon, I saw him being harassed by three boys from another class. One of them pulled off his glasses, whilst another knocked the books from his hands.

'Leave him alone,' I demanded.

'Well, well, if it isn't Billy Brown – without his pals. Sod off.'

'Leave him alone, you bunch of bullies.' Two of them turned to face me, one poking me with a finger.

'And what if we don't? You're on your own now – and *he* won't help,' he said, gesturing towards Anthony, who was helpless without his glasses.

'Give him back his glasses.'

'Let him get them himself.' We were now level with the fishmonger's shop, which opened directly onto the pavement. Taking careful aim, the boy threw Anthony's glasses into the tray of live eels. The two bullies looked in the tank and began laughing.

'They'll have his fingers off!'

While they were distracted by the eels, I seized my chance. Grabbing a huge cod fish from the crushed ice tray, I swung it in an arc like a floppy baseball bat. As the first boy turned back towards me, the fish caught him flush in the face, knocking him over into the gutter full of water and fish scales. The second boy managed to get his arms over his face but I still got him in the chest with a resounding thwack. The glasses-thrower had seen enough and was running up the road as fast as his legs would carry him. The one in the gutter was trying to get up but slipping on the wet muck, so I gave him another thwack for good measure.

Hearing a voice at the back of the shop, I returned my marine bat to its bed of ice.

'What's going on here, then?' demanded the fishmonger. 'Oh, it's you, Billy. These boys bothering you?'

'No, I don't think so, Mr Mac, but they were bullying Anthony, my friend.'

By now the aggressor had managed to get upright, covered in filth. 'I'll tell my mum what you did, Billy Brown. Just you wait!' The pair ran off after their comrade, who was streets away by now.

'They put his glasses in the eel tank, Mr Mac.' He fished around and found the specs, wiping them dry on a cloth.

'Don't they bite?' I asked.

'No Billy, not this size. It's only the big Moray eels that are dangerous.'

We both helped Anthony pick up his books.

'Thanks, Mr Mac. I'll be in Friday for Mum's fish as usual.'

'So long, Billy, take care.'

Anthony could see again. 'Who was that nice man, Billy?'

'That's Mr Mac, the fishmonger. I send all my black friends from Somerleyton Road to him for dried fish and jellied eels. They can't get enough of 'em.'

Barbara lived on the other side of the flats to me and was in the same age group. Although separated in classes, boys and girls mixed at playtime.

'I bet I can,' I announced to my group of pals.

'Never. Not a chance! You're a big liar, Billy.'

'I can. I can get Barbara to show us her knickers, but it will cost you.'

'How much?'

'Twopence each.' I had quickly worked out that six of them at twopence was one shilling. 'And if she doesn't, I'll give you twopence each.' This was too good an opportunity for them to resist. If they didn't get to see Barbara's knickers, they would at least get twopence.

'Right, money first.' They all paid up and I pocketed the money. Looking around, I spotted Barbara and called her over. Making the lads wait where they were, I went to speak to her. The lads, of course, thought I was offering her the money I had collected. How wrong they were.

'Shirley Thompsit says you can't do a handstand to save your life!' The captain of the school's junior gymnastics team was furious.

'Oh, does she? She can't even cartwheel properly.'

'That's as maybe, Barbara, but can you?'

'You just watch me, Billy Brown.' And with that, she promptly performed several perfect cartwheels across the playground, returning hardly out of breath.

'See.'

'Yes, but cartwheels ain't handstands!' Her gymnastic prowess at stake, Barbara promptly executed a perfect handstand, holding herself stock-still, allowing her skirt to fall around her shoulders revealing her pink knickers. The boys crowded round and applauded while she held the pose, smiling triumphantly upside down, affording each boy a good eyeful.

'What's going on here?' demanded Mr Nicholls, the headmaster. Barbara righted herself and explained the reason for her display. His hand clamped down on my shoulder in a vice-like grip.

'You disgusting boy, come with me.' I was un-ceremoniously dragged off, to the cheers of my pals.

Before the afternoon session the whole school was assembled in the main hall, where my crime was announced to all.

'This boy,' Mr Nicholls began, 'this vile boy tricked one of our star gymnasts into displaying her under-garments.' No it wasn't, I thought, it was only her knickers. But I didn't say so.

'Hold out your hand, Brown!' Standing sideways on to the entire school, I waited for the lashing pain that felt like your hands were on fire, even hours afterwards. Swish went the first one, the thin rattan cane biting into my palm. Swish. Swish.

'Other hand,' came the command from Mr Nicholls. I had once told Jimmy that I thought Mr Nicholls might have been in Hitler's SS as he had a scar on his cheek and a very distinctive gold signet ring. This, together with real viciousness towards the small boys in his care, only seemed to reinforce my theory. As I turned to face the assembly once more my heart sank. In the front row was Beryl Prentis. For a second our eyes met and she gently shook her head in despair. With all my resolve I readied myself for the rest of my punishment. I couldn't cry, not in front of Beryl. Sod the school, but not in front of Beryl. Swish, swish, swish. I fought back the tears hardly hearing him dismiss the assembled witnesses.

'Now, Brown, let that be a lesson you will not forget. Little prying perverts like you will always be found out.' As he spoke he played with his signet ring, twisting it around and around his finger. Compass and square, with initials and a blue stone. Mr Nicholls was not with the SS, but was simply a Freemason.

'Now, straight back to your class. I shall be watching you very closely in the future, my lad.'

I'm not your lad, Nicholls, and I never will be, I thought. Before returning to my class I went into the boys' toilets and held both hands under the running cold tap. The relief was instant and I waited awhile until the pain subsided. I wanted to stay longer, but was afraid Mr Nicholls would find me. The class fell silent as I entered the room.

'Alright class,' said Mr Beard. 'Just go and sit down, Brown.' Taking my seat at the very back, the tears I had held in check streamed down my face. Mr Beard came over to me, with all the other forty boys turning to look. 'Face front,' he commanded. They obeyed immediately, remembering the caning I had just received. Placing his hands gently upon my shoulder, he spoke softly. 'You'd better come with me, Billy,' and, with that, he ushered me out into the corridor and led me to the sick room and nurse. 'This boy needs some assistance, Mrs Walters. I'll leave him in your capable hands.'

Turning my scarlet palms upwards, she put a hand to her mouth to cover her sharp intake of breath. At that moment the room began to spin and I fell off the chair. I was only out for a few seconds, and when I came round she was dabbing my forehead and wiping away the dried tears with a wet flannel. 'Here, Billy, hold this while I put the kettle on.' The look of horror on my face took her by surprise until she realised that I thought the hot water was for my hands!

'No, no, Billy. It's for a cup of tea. I think we both need one, don't you?'

After a nice cup of tea with two sugars and a custard cream biscuit the colour began to return to my pale cheeks. Mrs Walters applied some soothing ointment to both hands and I started to feel a bit better. Her own son was in my class and they both lived in the Guinness

Trust flats. Her husband was a merchant seaman and was away most of the time.

'Your mum's going to throw a fit when she finds out about this,' she said.

'Does she have to know about Barbara?'

'Not that, Billy, your finger.' I looked at the little finger on my right hand. Where it joined the hand it was now swollen and purple.

'I think it's broken, Billy.' As she spoke the door swung open.

'Where is the little slacker?' demanded Mr Nicholls, heading in my direction. Mrs Walters moved her large body in between us.

'His finger is broken,' she informed him with a loathing in her voice that was not missed by him.

'Nonsense. Let me see.' She took hold of my hand, gently showing him the scarlet palm turning to purple and the rapidly swelling little finger.

'You must have moved, boy. That's it. Tried to get out of the way, must have caught you off-centre, your fault entirely, entirely your fault.' Mrs Walters interrupted him.

'He must go to hospital now,' she insisted.

'Nonsense. He'll be fine in the morning.'

'Then, sir, I'll be putting it in the medical log that you refused this boy proper medical attention, which will, of course, require your signature.' He knew when he was beaten. As the headmaster he didn't select the school nurse; she was provided by the local education authority and answered to them.

Mr Beard drove me in his car to King's College

Hospital, where the finger was X-rayed. The examining doctor was stunned at the sight of my hands and turned on Mr Beard.

'How dare you do this to a child,' he started.

'Please, sir,' I interrupted. 'It wasn't Mr Beard who did this. It was the headmaster, Mr Nicholls, 'cos I got Barbara to show us her knickers.'

Looking at my hands, then at me, he asked, 'Was it worth it, lad?'

I couldn't help smiling at this question, and the memory of Barbara's knickers and the shilling in my pocket.

The finger was only fractured so it was strapped to the next finger to keep it still. My palms were examined then covered in ointment and wrapped in thin bandages. I was given some tablets and sent home. Mr Beard came up with me to 242. Mum was already home from Woolworths and was worried about me. Mr Beard explained the whole thing and apologised on behalf of the school before leaving.

I was in bed asleep by the time Dad got home. I stayed off school for a week while my hands got better. I learned later that Dad visited the school the following day and explained in no uncertain terms what he would do to Mr Nicholls should he ever hurt me like that again. The doctor at King's also sent a report to the education authority.

No other boy was ever caned like that by Mr Nicholls again.

Allowing a few weeks to pass, I felt the time had

come for retribution. I waited until the last lesson one Friday. Asking to be excused for the toilet, I left the classroom. The boys' toilets were outside in a separate block. Quickly I bypassed them to the masters' car park directly behind. There were only ever three cars there, and I easily found the headmaster's two-tone grey Morris Oxford. Taking the large potato I had selected from Mum's vegetable basket that morning, I jammed it into the exhaust pipe, ramming it in flush with a well-aimed kick. Returning to class, I took my seat safe in the knowledge that revenge was mine. All the children left school well before Mr Nicholls and his staff.

At assembly the following Monday Mr Nicholls ranted and raved that his car would not start, and that a mechanic from the local garage had been called. That it had taken nearly an hour before the mechanic had found the cause. He had missed a very important meeting and finally he demanded that the culprit own up. Of course, no one did. As punishment he ordered that playtime be spent inside for a whole week. Maybe my guardian angel was looking down on me because it rained all that week!

The week I returned to school my pals all thought I was a hero, although some of the boys outside my group of pals said I deserved it, as did some of the older girls. I was just pleased to be out and about again. My firewood business had suffered as a result and I'd missed a Saturday at the market, but Jimmy had filled in for me.

As I came out of school on my first day back I walked straight into Beryl Prentis. I was quite surprised to see her as she was always involved in after-school stuff like gymnastics, table tennis, the book club and the art club. I stood, not knowing what to say about the knicker incident.

'How are your hands, Billy, and the broken finger?' she asked. Of course, the whole school knew all about it.

'Oh, they're just fine now. I can take the plaster off my finger in another two weeks.'

We walked along chatting. 'You were ever so brave, Billy. Mr Nicholls is a vicious pig.'

I was surprised by her outburst. 'Beryl Prentis. Such language! It must be the company you keep!'

'So, was it worth it, Billy, just to see Barbara's knickers?' I wasn't sure how to answer but, before I could, she continued, 'If you'd gone behind the store sheds I'm sure she'd have shown you anyway, the trollop!'

'*I* didn't want to see her knickers. It was the other lads.'

'Oh, of course, Billy. You wouldn't, would you?'

'No, Beryl, really, it was for the money!'

'What?'

I went on to explain how I'd got twopence from each boy and then tricked Barbara.

'You little bugger, Billy Brown,' she smiled. 'What a silly cow that Barbara is. You wouldn't have caught me like that!'

'The lads might not want to see your knickers!' She stopped and faced me again.

'Oh, I'm not talking about the lads, Billy!'

We walked home through Somerleyton Passage, both smiling to ourselves.

9

Guinness is Good for You

Everyone was looking forward to the annual summer outing to Sheerness-on-Sea. The whole flats had been buzzing with it for months. Each year the Residents Association in the flats organised a summer day out. In previous years we'd been to Margate, Clacton and Southend. They also organised trips to football matches, West End shows, ice shows and pantos. Dad was one of the first to buy our four tickets at five shillings each. The price included the train down to Sheerness, refreshments on the way, lunch at the Co-op and a gift for all the children. I had got up so early on the appointed Sunday that Mum had to put me back to bed for another two hours. By nine o'clock we were all washed and dressed, having finished a nice boiled egg for breakfast.

Mum had made me wear my smart trousers and jacket with a clean white shirt and new cap. As we approached the front entrance to the flats there were hundreds of families ready for a great day out. We joined up with my auntie Eaddie, uncle John and cousins Ruth, Brian and Roderick who also lived in the Guinness Trust buildings. At nine thirty, six hundred and seventy residents left for the station at

Loughborough Junction. A whole train, called the Guinness Trust Special, was waiting. I felt so proud that we had a whole train just for us. Selecting a carriage, we installed ourselves inside, me bagging the window seat with my cousin Roderick who was two years younger than me. Two men came along with a huge trolley laden with snacks for the journey.

'How many, Jack?' the man asked my dad.

'Four adults and five kids.' Ruth, being seventeen, was not having any of this.

'Five adults, Uncle Jack!'

'Oh, of course, Ruth. Five adults and four kids.' We were all given a white cardboard box and a bottle of drink each. Looking in my box I found a cheese sandwich, a packet of crisps, an apple and a bar of Cadbury's chocolate, the same bar I got from Ma Kingdom's shop.

'Not yet, Billy. Have a boiled sweet.' Mum offered them all round. Auntie Eaddie was the only one who refused, 'on account of me teeth', she replied. 'Broke me plate, the last one did.' What teeth and plates had in common, I couldn't imagine.

The train guard opened the door. 'Tickets please, Billy.' For a moment I was confused. We hadn't got tickets. Then I saw his mischievous smile. 'Oh, Lem, you're pulling my leg.' Lem was a guard on the railway who lived in our flats. He had got himself put on our special for a paid day out.

'Off in about five minutes, dead on ten.'

I watched Uncle John's wristwatch tick away the time. Exactly on the appointed hour Lem's whistle blew and the train pulled slowly out of Loughborough Park Junction on its journey to the coast. Everyone was cheering and waving from the windows. Passing over Acre Lane bridge, people down on the pavements waved back. We played games like I Spy and the First One to Spot, and at about eleven o'clock we had our refreshments. My cheese sandwich was really good, having been made fresh that morning by the Co-op caterers. The crisps followed, all washed down with my bottle of lemonade. Dad chinked my bottle with his to 'cheers' from everyone. It was going to be a great day. The window had been let down by the leather strap to allow fresh air in by mum. Dad, Auntie Eaddie and Uncle John all smoked and the carriage had become thick with it.

Roderick and I took turns leaning out the windows into the rushing wind. It was on my turn that the express train went past from the opposite direction. The sudden whoosh of wind made me draw myself in quickly.

'Billy, where's your cap?' asked Mum. I grabbed at my head and glanced at where I had been sitting, then realised it was on the front of the Golden Arrow Express bound for London.

'Billy Brown, that's the third one you've lost. It's coming out of your money box this time!'

'Oh, but Mum.'

'Oh, but Mum,' Auntie Eaddie mimicked. 'We all have to pay for our sins, Billy.'

I sat with the wind taken out of my sails, or the cap off my head. Then I remembered my bar of Cadbury's chocolate and felt much better. And anyway, I thought, a pramful of bricks would soon cover my costs!

Lem came along the train. 'Ten minutes to Sheerness, ten minutes to Sheerness. Hello, Billy. Where's your cap?' I was about to explain but he was gone, 'Ten minutes to Sheerness' fading down the carriage.

As soon as we saw the signs on the station everyone began cheering. 'Hooray, we're here, we're here.' Once the train had come to a stop on the platform, we flooded off, filling Sheerness High Street. The local traders loved it and were soon busy selling sticks of rock, kiss-me-quick hats, buckets and spades and pints of winkles, cockles and jellied eels.

'Now don't get lost, Billy. Bobby, hold his hand while I get a stick of rock for the two of you.' We waited patiently outside the shop, Bob letting go of me as soon as his older friends arrived.

'Dad, alright if I go off to the fun fair?'

'Sure, Bob. You have a good time. Lunch is at the main Co-op. See you later. Take care.'

'Can I go off for the day, too?' I asked, ever hopeful.

'No,' came the joint answer, 'you stay with us.'

We wandered around the town, and everywhere we went was filled with our friends and neighbours from the Guinness Trust. Everybody seemed in a really happy mood. Outside the Co-op, crowds of people scanned the notices to see which sitting they were at for lunch. Being in the Bs we were with the Benthams: Janet and her mum and dad. As it was twelve thirty we all filed in to the huge dining hall. The tables were arranged in rows the length of the hall; it reminded me of school. Dead on time, two hundred and fifty bowls of brown Windsor soup were served, each accompanied by a bread roll. The sound of two hundred and fifty spoons banging on bowls, together with the incessant chatter, was deafening. It was like the poorhouse scene from *Oliver*. Empty soup bowls were exchanged for two hundred and fifty plates of ham salad with boiled egg and potatoes. Huge glass jars of pickled onions and piccalilli were placed along each row of tables. My first attempt at a pickled onion resulted in it skidding off my fork and across the table, into a lady's lap.

'Sorry, missus. They're as hard as billiard balls.'

Janet laughed, but was told off by her mum. 'We don't laugh at bad manners, Janet!'

'Here you go, Billy.' Mum had placed two on my plate. 'Now just watch what you're doing, they're as hard as billiard balls.' She said the last bit loudly and gave me a wink.

The lady who had been the target for my first onion had retrieved it. 'Thanks, Billy, but I'll only have the one or I'll get terrible wind!' Everyone was laughing. With the ham salads gone it was time for the best bit. The ice cream came in paper rolls to be cut to length, depending on the size of the portion required. All the children had two paper rolls of vanilla ice cream, which we eagerly unwrapped while the adults had treacle tart and custard. I asked Dad if they had the custard delivered by tanker lorry, there was so much of it. He laughed until he had tears in his eyes.

As soon as we were filled up we filed out of one entrance, while the next sitting filed in the other. In the doorway of the exit were boxes and boxes of Kent apples and pears with a notice, 'Help Yourself'. I didn't need asking twice and stuffed my pockets until Mum told me to put some back, but I still had two of each.

'Right then, Billy, time for the beach,' said Mum and off we set. On the way I was bought a tin bucket and spade. Mum got a straw sun hat as she told Mrs Bentham her freckles were starting to multiply. In brilliant sunshine we climbed the steps over the sea wall to the sea – and there it wasn't! The tide was out and the sea was over a mile away.

'Blimey, if Hitler had tried to land here he'd have been knackered by the time he got to dry land,' observed Mr Bentham.

'Alf, mind your language, there's children present!'

'Oh, it's OK, Mrs Bentham, I know what knackered means,' I assured her.

'Oh dear, Jack,' Mum said, 'What are we going to do with him?'

Before any of the grown-ups could decide my fate I was off holding Janet's hand, running down onto the firm sand. Mums spread out their towels and us children were soon changed into our bathing costumes just in case the sea decided to grace us with its presence. We were soon joined by my uncle John, auntie Eaddie and my cousins, fresh from the second sitting, all loaded with apples and pears. Auntie Eaddie had enough in her shopping bag for a pie. The men had armfuls of deckchairs at sixpence each for the day. Alf

Bentham had brought his cricket gear. No sooner had he started to drive in the stumps and mark out the pitch than children and grown-ups turned up from all directions. Janet was upset to be told no girls, so went to dig in the sand.

Instead of the usual eleven per side there were about twenty-five. Mr Bentham took charge, allowing the younger boys to bat first. When it was my turn I held my bat by the top so the umpire, my uncle, could give me middle wicket as I had seen batsmen do in Brockwell Park on a Sunday. Finally I was ready and got clean bowled first ball.

'No, foul! That was too fast!'

'Nonsense, you should have been ready, Billy.'

'Go on. Give him another go,' directed Mr Bentham, 'and bowl a bit slower, Colin.' I nearly choked trying not to laugh. Colin, I thought; PC Collins is Colin Collins. His mum must have had a sense of humour! Wait till I tell the other lads. I watched as he walked back from the crease, thinking of the pleasure he must have just had nearly taking my head off with the fast ball. Charging down to the crease he let fly with the ball, but not as fast as last time. I closed my eyes and swung the bat with all my strength, to be rewarded with a resounding thwack, opening them in time to see the ball disappearing into the distance.

'Run, Billy, run,' shouted Dad.

At the other end was Jim. As we passed for the first time I said, 'His name's Colin.'

As we passed again Jim asked, 'Who's Colin?' I had

to wait for the return run before I could answer and was getting short of breath.

'PC Collins is Colin.' His reply trailed off into the distance.

'W-h-a-t?' The fourth run produced, 'You're lying, you bugger!'

I had time to reply, 'No, it's true,' as we had both slowed considerably.

Before I could continue this running discussion, Jim yelled, 'Stay,' as Colin Collins returned, puffing, with the ball. When Alf said, 'You're out of condition, Colin,' Jim held his thumb up to me from the other end of the wicket, smiling.

The next ball I was clean bowled. I went off to field near Mum so I could have a drink of Tizer.

'Billy, you're crap at cricket,' observed Auntie Eaddie. 'You got my rabbit yet?' Still watching the game I replied, 'Won't be until next Saturday. Big Mike's in Ireland this week.' I didn't like lying to my aunt. I *had* got a rabbit from Big Mike, but it was such a big fat one I had given it to Mum instead. I looked to see if she was cross with me for lying, but she just smiled and gave me one of her lovely winks.

'Catch it, Billy!' came the shouts. PC Collins had hit the ball skyward in my direction. Running backwards, I kept my eye on the descending ball. As I cupped my hands to catch it I fell backwards into the excavation Janet and the other girls had been digging. I lay there clutching the ball, semi-stunned. As my eyes focused an angel appeared; Beryl stood there, gazing down into the hole. Her back was to the sun and her blonde hair cascaded down around her face like a halo. I had never seen her in a swimming costume before.

'Close your mouth, Billy, you might swallow the ball,' said Janet.

Beryl jumped into the hole and knelt down beside me, her bare leg brushing against my arm. 'Are you alright, Billy? Is anything broken?'

'He's fine. Get up,' ordered Janet. I was fine, but I wasn't in any hurry to get back to the game. Then Dad arrived.

'Honestly, Billy, you scared the hell out of me when you disappeared.'

'I caught it, Dad,' I exclaimed. 'Colin Collins is out!'

Then Alf arrived. 'Bloody hell. He caught it!' he shouted and, turning to Collins, announced: 'You're out.'

From far off a loud voice I knew all too well said, 'Bugger 'im'. Dad helped me out and sat me on the towel.

'Stay there and recover, Billy. Bloody brilliant catch, bloody brilliant!'

Mum gave me some Tizer. 'You'll break your neck one day, Billy Brown, and then where will you be?' It's Mrs Thompsit again, I thought.

'We'll look after Billy, Mrs Brown,' said Beryl. Mum noticed my instant smile.

'OK, girls. Here, have some cake.' We all took one of Mum's famous fairy cakes and sat on the edge of the excavation. I thought it wise to sit between Janet and Beryl. Besides, I was the hero, so I could choose.

*

226

The game finally ended, Alf declared a draw, much to everyone's satisfaction, and several people came over to see how I was.

'Funniest thing ever,' said Jim. 'Better than that Houdini bloke! Best disappearing act I've ever seen.' Jim sat next to Janet on the crater's rim.

'This is almost as big a hole as our bomb would have made, eh, Billy?' As soon as he spoke I knew we were in for it.

As one Janet and Beryl said, 'Your bomb?'

'Shush! Be quiet or my mum'll hear you.'

Beryl was first to speak in a hushed voice. 'I knew you two were up to no good.'

'No good?' I retorted. 'Me and Jim saved everybody!' I made a grand gesture towards all the Guinness Trust people on the beach.

'You'll have to tell us now, Billy, won't he, Janet?'

'You promise you won't tell a soul. Cross your heart and hope to die.' In hushed voices they both repeated the sacred oath without raising their right hands so as not to give themselves away. Jim and I related the story of the unexploded bomb in The Lodge. When I got to the point about chalking a message on the grand piano Beryl nearly exploded.

'You did what? You wrote on a beautiful grand piano, Billy Brown? You're a philistine, a barbarian.'

'It's alright. It was knackered anyway,' Jim joined in. 'What's a philistine?'

'Huh! Boys!' exclaimed Janet.

Ignoring her, I continued with the story.

'And you told PC Collins?' they both asked, disbelievingly.

'Well, not exactly told, more like pointed to,' added Jim.

'So all that hero stuff in the paper . . . ?'

'Bullshit, Beryl, but he did go and look. You should have seen his face when he came back. I thought *he* was going to explode, let alone the bomb!'

Beryl took my hand in both of hers. 'So, *you're* the real hero, Billy.'

'And me!'

'Oh, of course, Jimmy, and you, but Billy left the message that saved us all.'

Jim tried to hold Janet's hand, but she wasn't having any of that, thank you very much.

Mum came over with a fresh bottle of Tizer and more fairy cakes. We all took one and passed round the Tizer bottle, Janet and Jim going first. When it came to me I offered it to Beryl who tipped it back and took a swig. Before passing it to me she went to wipe the top with her hand but stopped short, passing me the bottle with a smile. I understood immediately and took my turn enjoying the second-hand kiss she had offered me!

The queue for fish and chips at teatime was so long we had to wait over half an hour and, by the time we got to the counter, our mouths were drooling with the smells of fish and chips cooking. The owner must have made a small fortune that day.

'Right, that's five cod and chips, four haddock and chips, one pie, one sausage and chips, ten pickled onions and ten whallies [gherkins].' The men all paid their share and we walked back to the promenade. The whole mile or so of the sea wall was covered with holidaymakers eating their tea. Fish and chips, pies, jellied eels, chip butties, sandwiches, anything portable was being eaten in the late afternoon sun. Many bottles of beer, lemonade and Tizer were drunk. Wish I could have all the empties at tuppence a go, I thought. I'd have made a fortune! Mum rolled the paper down on my stick of pink peppermint rock, and as I looked at the word 'Sheerness' written on both ends, I wondered if it really did go right the way through!

As we all made our way back for the seven thirty train everyone agreed what a splendid summer outing it'd been. My brother, Bob, arm in arm with two girls, found us at the station. All three were wearing silly hats and one girl had a large teddy bear under her arm that she'd got at the fair.

'Bobby won it for me,' she claimed proudly, clinging to his arm.

'And Billy made the greatest catch in cricketing history,' retorted my uncle, 'and the best disappearing act ever seen at the same time.' We all laughed out loud. We laughed even more when we saw the station sign. Someone had crossed out the word 'Sea' with lipstick and written beside it, 'Mud'. From then on it would always be called 'Sheerness-on-Mud'!

The train pulled into Loughborough Junction dead on nine o'clock. Disembarking, six hundred and seventy weary, but happy, residents made their way to the exit where there were two large boxes, one for the boys, one for the girls. I went with my cousin Roderick to the boys' box and was given a model kit for a balsa-wood aeroplane with an elastic-band motor to make it fly. We walked the half-mile up Loughborough Park Road in full song. We were like a conquering army returning home after their greatest victory. Lights came on and people came to their gates to wish us goodnight.

Only a few short years before, this whole street would have been blacked out and no one would have had anything to sing about. Our little group sang as loud as anybody. It had been a truly memorable day. As we approached the flats, every light had been put on by those who had not been able to join us. The entire flats was like a huge beacon welcoming us home.

Then it happened. My poor cousin Roderick, not looking where he was going, slipped and fell into a huge pile of freshly deposited, steaming wet horse dung, covering him from top to toe. The singing stopped, to be replaced by hails of laughter all round. He stood in the light from the flats and began to cry with the humiliation of it all. My aunt and mum stepped forward together, taking a hand each to avoid the muck on him and trying not to laugh. As they walked in through the gateway, I stood staring at the pile of horse muck as Jim came along with the girls.

'What are you doing, Billy?' he asked.

'Whole bucketful there, Jim. Worth a shilling. I'll have that, first thing in the morning.' From behind me I could hear Beryl's voice.

'Billy Brown. You're disgusting!'

*

'You going to the clubroom tonight?' Derek asked. He was referring to the large meeting hall which ran above the superintendent's flat, workshops and boiler rooms. It was the equivalent of a village hall and held all manner of functions from wedding receptions, dance and gymnastics classes to bridge, gardening and model-making clubs, along with the Saturday-night film and variety shows. The hall had its own well-appointed kitchen and toilets. The dance floor held two hundred dancers with ease on its sprung maple floor, with a raised stage at one end accommodating the film screen, bands and other acts. It was in the centre of our flats and was the hub of our social life.

'You bet I am. Mum says they've got a new film.'

'It's about time. If I see *Steam Boat Willy* again I'll scream.'

'Yeah, me too. See you at seven thirty.'

By seven fifteen a crowd of children and a few parents had assembled by the doors. Me and my pals were always eager to get in the front row. At seven thirty on the dot Mr Meakin, the caretaker, would open the doors from the inside and stand back. We all rushed up the curved stairs through the double doors, past the bar and straight in. I quickly took off my jacket and put it on the seat next to me.

'You can't save seats, Billy Brown.'

'Sod off, Barbara. It's not for you.'

'Oh, we all know who *you're* sweet on. It's the talk of all the girls. What she sees in you I don't know. You're terrible. My mum says you'll come to no good.'

'Your mum's an old misery guts,' I retorted, much to the admiration of my pals.

'Yeah, that's it, Billy, you tell her! Show us your knickers, Barbara!'

'Huh! You boys are revolting. I'm going to tell my mum of you lot.'

'Tell her, smell her, lock her in the cellar.' Barbara retreated back to her group of friends at the end of the row.

The hall was filling up. All the dads were at the back getting a beer for themselves, tea for their wives and lemonade or Tizer for the children. As usual Mum was on teas, wielding a huge brown enamel teapot. She would only tip it once and run it over a dozen cups, filling them all without spilling a drop. Slabs of bread pudding were sliced into smaller pieces for tuppence a lump. They couldn't sell it quick enough!

The clock on the wall above the bar told me it was seven fifty-five and nearly show time. I stood on my chair, looking around.

'I bet she doesn't come – and even if she does, she won't want to sit with us!'

'Shut up, Jim. You're only jealous.'

'I'm with Jim, Billy. She's too posh for the likes of you.' I was disappointed that my pals had no faith in my ability with the girls, especially this one.

The curtain opened and the superintendent, Mr Robson, greeted us all. 'Ladies, gentlemen, boys and girls.' To acknowledge being recognised we all cheered loudly. 'Now, now, you little monsters in the front.'

Before continuing he waited to allow a latecomer to

find a seat. We all turned to see who would dare interrupt Mr Robson. My heart stopped and I held my breath. Coming down the centre aisle was Beryl Prentis, her yellow dress swishing as she walked. The tiny heels of her white shoes made a staccato noise on the sprung maple floor. Her hair was tied back with a new yellow ribbon and she had a white handbag. The spotlight illuminating Mr Robson just caught her blonde hair. To me she looked like an angel. She marched all the way to the front row and stopped at me. I could hear all the other girls muttering. 'Huh! That Beryl. Who does she think she is?' And, 'She's got her own handbag! Thinks she's Jean Harlow, she does!'

'Is that seat taken, Billy?' I snatched my jacket off the reserved chair.

'No, no. It's for you, Beryl.'

She sat down carefully, crossing her legs, pointing her toe down as she had been taught in Miss Betty's Deportment Class. My pals were stunned. 'See that, she came! I'd never have believed it. The lucky bugger!' I heard them mutter.

'When you have quite finished in the front row,' continued Mr Robson, eager to get on. 'A few notices before we start. Mrs Jones of 136 had a little girl on Tuesday; seven pounds and four ounces, mother and baby doing well.' A rapturous round of applause broke out amongst the assembled tenants. A lady two rows back commented, 'That's her third girl. I bet she tries again.' Mr Robson continued. 'A box of fruit and some flowers were sent by the Committee to old Mrs

Howard, who has been quite poorly.' (One block of our flats was only for widows, many from the First World War and two from the Boer War.) The announcement was followed by the customary round of applause. Several more items followed concerning rubbish collections, tenants' cats on allotments, the next week's summer outing and repairs to the swings. Finally he announced a special vote of thanks to Jack Brown of flat 242 for constructing a metal wheelchair ramp for the OAPs block. I clapped as hard as anyone.

'Your dad's ever so clever, Billy. My dad doesn't do anything like that.'

'Never mind, Beryl. I guess it's on account of his back troubles.'

'Oh, yes. His back troubles.' I looked at her as she looked up to heaven and smiled.

The announcements over, Mr Robson declared, 'On with the show,' to another round of applause. The lights dimmed as the white film-show screen rolled down. The flickering first film started and we all counted down the numbers: 5–4–3–2–1 . . .

It was *Steam Boat Willy*.

'Oh no! Boo! Boo!' The front row was in uproar. Mr Robson's voice came over the tannoy system.

'Now, now. Quieten down, you lot.'

The vintage cartoon was followed by Laurel and Hardy, Buster Keaton and Harold Lloyd, which had all been shown for the last six months. We were all getting restless.

'Boo. It's a swizz. Where's the new stuff, Billy? You're such a liar!'

'My mum said . . .'

'Oh, sure. Your mum knows it all.'

'Shut your gob, Brian!'

'Why don't ya shut it for me!'

Beryl nudged me. 'Don't take any notice, Billy. Here, have some toffee. My mum made it.'

Halfway through Harold Lloyd, the film broke. This is what we had all been waiting for. As one, we stamped, clapped and cheered, immediately followed by a rousing chorus of: 'Why are we waiting, whyy-are-we-waiting!' The house lights came up while the film was fixed. As soon as it was done the hall darkened and Harold Lloyd was allowed to continue, defeating the baddie and saving the heroine.

We all fidgeted and made noise while the next film was loaded, but when the screen finally lit up we couldn't believe our eyes. It was Buster Crab in *Flash Gordon*. It took a while for the clapping to subside. We sat enthralled, cheering for Flash Gordon and booing the wicked emperor Ming. At the end of the first episode our hero was left in the grip of the death ray. The final few frames announced, 'Tune in next week'. The lights went up.

'See, Brian. I told you my mum knew.'

The tannoy system boomed into life. 'There will now be a fifteen-minute intermission.'

'Do you want an ice cream, Beryl?' I asked.

'Oh, yes please, Billy. Here, I've got some money.'

I held out my raised hand to stop her. 'Oh no, Beryl. I'll pay.'

Jim gave me a look as if I'd gone mad. 'Bugger me, it must be love.'

'Shut up, Jimmy,' reproached Beryl.

I went off to the toilet first. As I stood in the stall, Jimmy came into the next one. 'Are you mad, Billy? She was going to pay.'

'Jim, you should never let a lady pay. That's what my dad says.'

Jim gave it some thought, while seeing how high he could pee up the urinal.

'That's no lady, that's Beryl.'

'Exactly, Jim . . . Oh, and dry your shoe.'

Jim looked down. 'Oh bugger,' he said, and wiped it on the back of his socks.

Mum served me two ice creams in cones. I offered to pay, but she just gave me her 'don't be stupid' look which I knew so well! Turning round, I bumped into Janet.

'Two, Billy! You are a pig!'

'One's for Beryl,' I said.

'Oh, one's for Beryl!' she mimicked. 'Who does she think she is, coming in late and going straight to the front seats?'

'I saved one for her.'

'Oh, did you now! And I wonder why?'

As I got back to my seat the lights dimmed signalling the start of the second half. This always comprised live acts from inside and outside the flats, giving new talent a chance to appear before a live audience. Mr Penn, a bus driver, was on first. He rode a unicycle and juggled at the same time. We had all seen him before as he lived in the flats. I liked to watch him coming and going to work. He rode on a unicycle to Brixton Bus Garage for practice. But even more unusual, he held the handlebars, front forks and wheel, of a normal bike so that people wouldn't be confused. His act was followed by a terrible pub singer who got booed off and a conjurer who forgot his tricks. We lads thought it was hilarious.

The curtains closed and we waited for the next act. Word had already gone round that the sisters were in the show. Their music started with a few clicks and scratches as the stage man lined up their music on the gramophone, and Mr Robson announced . . . 'Ladies and gentlemen, boys and girls, the fabulous Brook Sisters!'

The curtains parted and there they were, the sixteen-year-old twins Jean and Joan Brook. They'd been at stage school since the age of nine and had already been in West End shows. We boys thought how lucky we were that they lived in the Guinness Trust flats. They wore very daring costumes with tight sparkly bra tops and pants, a sequinned headdress and white roller boots for their skates. Now all the girls knew why we had grabbed the front seats! Their type of act was all the rage in America, where roller-skating duos were on every TV show. Skating on a large raised circular platform, they amazed us. One held and spun the other upside down, causing her top to come down slightly, making her breasts look even bigger. We clapped and cheered our heads off. Round and round they went.

During one intricate display Jim was chanting, 'Now you see it, now you don't. Now you see it, now you don't.'

'Jimmy, you're disgusting. Isn't he, Billy?'

'Oh yes, Beryl. Very.' Although *my* mind was now going, 'Now you see it, now you don't'! The strenuous routine was taking its toll on Joan's top. Jim was the first to spot it, as she hung upside down.

'Her tit's out!' he whispered.

'Don't be so filthy,' admonished Beryl, but it was true. The news spread down the front row like wild fire. Soon the whole audience knew. Oblivious, the twins span on, round and round, upside down, finally coming to a full stop, both on one knee with arms outstretched ready for their adoring fans to show their appreciation. They looked slightly confused at the silence, until Jean noticed her sister's chest heaving out of its bra. Joan quickly understood her look and adjusted her top, smiling all the while to the crowd, a true professional. The applause that followed was deafening, especially from the dads by the bar.

'Tart! She did that on purpose,' said Beryl.

Filing out of the clubroom, we stood in the cold night air, not wanting the evening to end just yet. Amongst my pals there were only two topics of conversation: Joan's revealing act and Beryl's late entrance to sit with me. The girls could only talk about Beryl. 'Who does she think she is?', 'My mum says she's a proper little madam!', 'She waited for that spotlight, the cow!'

I stood with Beryl and Jim, who offered us a

gobstopper. Before I could take one she put her hand over the bag. 'No thank you, Jimmy – and Billy doesn't want one either.'

'I don't?' She turned to face me and made a cupid's bow with her lips. 'No, you don't, do you?' she asked me. Jim didn't miss my Cheshire cat's grin.

'Ah, I see, no, you two definitely don't.'

Our conversation was interrupted by the twins leaving the clubroom. Their skates were in a bag and a long coat covered their outfits.

'You got our stuff yet, Billy?' Joan enquired.

'Don't forget, forty denier, black tops,' added Jean.

'I know, I know. I wrote it down. They're on their way.' Joan parted her coat to her thigh. 'What do you think, Billy? Ready for silk stockings?'

'I suppose so, Joan, if you say so.'

'Oh, leave him alone, Joan. Come on. I'm getting cold,' said Jean. Joan wrapped up again. 'Bye, bye, Billy, see you soon.' And with that they walked off arm in arm to their block.

'Bloody hell, Billy,' exclaimed Jim. 'She's got great pins!'

'What's going on, Billy Brown?' demanded Beryl. 'Why did that tart show you her leg?'

'Stockings, Beryl. I'm getting her some nylons.'

'You're what?'

'From a man I know. They come from America on the ships. Real nylon stockings.'

'Huh! Cheap tart! My mum always wears silk ones.' The thought of the ample Mrs Prentis in silk stockings was not something I wanted to imagine.

'It's business, Beryl. Just business, that's all.'

'It had better be.'

We said goodnight to Jim, who couldn't reply, his mouth being full of gobstopper, but he did give me a knowing wink.

At the entrance to her block Beryl went up one step again and stopped.

'I'm really sorry about Joan,' I said.

'Shut up, Billy.' Once again, the cupid's bow lips beckoned.

10

Mischief, Mayhem and a Night to Remember

'You coming, Derek?' I asked.

'We won't be back too late, will we, 'cause Mum's taking me out later.' I reassured him and we headed off to Brockwell Park. It was named after Lord Brockwell who built a mansion on its highest point, then laid out the parkland around it. After the First World War it had been given to the people of Lambeth because the family couldn't afford its upkeep. The early Georgian grand house was now offices and a teashop.

We headed for the shrub border backing onto the row of Georgian houses fronting Tulse Hill. The large family homes had two-hundred-foot-long back gardens running down to the wall surrounding the park. We aimed for my favourite, which had its own orchard.

A convenient tree gave us easy access to the top of the wall. Ensuring no one was about, we hopped down onto the compost heap and made our way to the enormous pear tree, laden with fruit ripe for the picking. An old tapering fruit-picker's ladder was laid on the ground, just right for us to pitch up the tree. It wasn't too long before the two of us were in the highest branches, filling our tucked-in jumpers with ripe pears. Within twenty minutes I couldn't hold any more.

'That's it, Derek. I'm full. You coming down?'

'Just a few more. There's a whopper up here that I must get.'

'OK. I'll see you back at the park.' Descending the ladder, I was on my way to the compost heap when there was a shout.

'Hey, you! What do you think you're doing?' I didn't look around but ran up the heap and climbed over the wall.

'I'm calling the police!' shouted the voice after me. Then I remembered Derek. The man must have caught him. Now we were both in serious trouble. I moved down the back of the border to another tree affording good cover. I could now see the man in more detail. By his overalls and boots he was clearly the gardener. I was surprised that he wasn't holding Derek. Looking up at the top of the pear tree, I was stunned when I saw him partially hidden in the foliage.

'Bloody kids,' shouted the gardener, and duly started work. By my reckoning it was about two o'clock in the afternoon. My mind was buzzing trying to think of all our options for escape. Derek could give himself up. I thought about this for a moment but dismissed the idea due to the trouble we'd both be in. Maybe the gardener would go in for tea, allowing Derek to escape, or maybe he would stay working until it was dark. Either way, all I could do was wait and see what happened so I settled down in a large bough and watched intently.

Several people passed by on the path next to the border I was concealed in amongst the shrubs, but I didn't move. I hadn't been there five minutes when fate intervened. A lady came from the back door of the house and called, 'John, the coalman's here. Will you open up the coal hole for him?' All the circular metal coal holes were at the front of houses, allowing coal to be tipped straight into the cellars. I knew this would be Derek's only chance of escape, and he'd best be quick.

As soon as they'd gone back into the house I called out to him. 'Derek. All clear. Hurry up!' He didn't need much encouragement and descended the tree like a squirrel. Sprinting down the garden, he was over the wall in one go.

'I thought he'd got me,' he said, gasping for breath. 'Let's get out of here in case he does call the police.' We stayed hidden in the dense shrubbery, making our way towards the cascade ponds. Surrounding the back of one pond was a dense thicket of bamboo. Hopping over the low iron-hoop fence and totally ignoring the KEEP OFF THE GRASS sign, I led Derek into the secret hidey-hole in the bamboo. There was a small clearing in the middle, just enough for the two of us. Surrounded by a fifteen-foot-high wall of bamboo, we could just see out to the path, down to the pond and the rear of the old potting shed now mostly covered with bamboo and ivy.

'It's no good. I've got to have a breather,' declared Derek, sitting down and taking out the prize pear from inside his jumper.

'Wow. That's a beauty,' I told him and sat down with him to enjoy one of my own scrumped pears, watching as grown-ups with children passed by, un-aware of our presence.

'Look,' I whispered, pointing towards the path. A lady and man seemed to be staring in our direction. For a moment or two they looked up and down the path, then, seeing no one, hopped over the fence and came directly towards us. The two of us crouched down as low as we could get, waiting to be discovered, but at the last moment the man led the lady straight past us and into the old potting shed. Sitting in silence, we both heard the door creak open, then close.

'That's queer, Derek. What do you think they've gone in there for?' I beckoned him to follow me, and together we crept to the side of the shed and positioned ourselves just below the window. Listening intently, we could only make out some strange, faint squeaky noises. With a thumbs-up sign to Derek, I began to stand up very slowly, until my eyes drew level with the windowsill.

It was still quite dark in the shed, what with all the vegetation covering the other window, but the light coming through my window was just enough to make out what was going on. I gently motioned to Derek to join me, hearing his sharp intake of breath as he got his first look in. Stood with his trousers around his ankles, the man had his back to us and the lady was bent over the old potting bench, the cause of all the squeaking. We couldn't see much but we both knew what they were up to. Turning to Derek, I made a rude sign with my thumb and fingers. It was the first time either of us had seen two people having sex. We both watched for a minute or two more, then decided it was time to go before we got caught. Creeping past the front of the shed, I noticed it had a new hasp and staple catch and glancing round I found what I was looking for. The new padlock was in the grass by the door. Quietly picking it up, I closed the hasp over the staple and hooked the padlock through it, locking them both in. Derek had his hand over his mouth to stop himself from laughing. We crept away to a bench higher up from the potting shed, overlooking its access path. Sitting down, we both had another pear and waited. More people passed, oblivious to what was happening just a few feet away from them.

At first the banging was quite restrained. As it became louder people began to stop and look in the direction of the noise. By the time shouting was coming from the shed, quite a crowd had gathered. One of the park keepers had been summoned and he pushed his way through.

'Now then, what's all the commotion about,' he wanted to know. The shouting soon answered his question.

'Stand back, please. I'll deal with this.' By this point Derek and I were in fits of laughter in our grandstand seats. Everyone could hear the commotion from behind the bamboo screen.

'What the hell's been going on in here?' the keeper wanted to know.

'Some bugger locked us in,' came the reply.

'But why come in here in the first place? What on earth could you find to do in this old shed?' Then the realisation dawned on him, his suspicions were soon confirmed when he glanced down. There, under the potting bench, were the discarded knickers.

'Right, so that's ya game, is it?' He tried to restrain them, but the two lovers were off. It was like one of the Buster Keaton chases from the Friday-night film shows. The couple leapt the low fence together, heading for the gate onto Tulse Hill. They were hotly pursued by the keeper, who was trying to rouse support from onlookers.

'Caught in the act,' he shouted to anyone who would listen, 'and left her drawers in the shed, she did!' he told a mother with three young children. She covered the oldest girl's ears with her hands and hurried all three away.

'Will this do, Billy?' said Derek, holding up a wooden back door blown off during the Blitz.

'Perfect. Load it on the pram with the other wood.' It took both of us to push it back up Sussex Road to the flats. All of our pals had been at it for weeks. Every spare pram shed or hidey-hole was filled with old boxes, tea chests, doors, chairs and lumps of timber. At the back of the flats between two walls were six sheets of old corrugated iron, also trundled up from the bombsites. Operation Guy Fawkes was well under way. It had been like this for as long as I could remember, each generation of children taking over from the last. It was planned with almost military precision, even the caretakers turning a blind eye to the goings-on.

'This should make it burn.' Jim was rolling out a forty-gallon drum of old sump oil he'd found in a derelict garage.

'Are you completely stupid, Jim? If that goes on the bonfire it'll explode like an incendiary bomb, only a hundred times worse.'

'Well, maybe not then, but it wouldn't 'alf have warmed the guy's arse!' Still laughing at his joke, we carried on filling prams and karts.

A couple of the lads came along from the Old Barrington Road flats.

'Oi, this is our stuff! Piss off, you lot!' Jim gave a shrill whistle and our other six pals appeared out of various ruins.

'I think *you* should piss off!' advised Jim.

'Look mate, there's enough for us all. There's bloody hundreds of bombed houses.'

'You're Billy Brown, ain't you?'

'I might be. Who's asking?'

'I'm Johnnie, Suzie's brother. You know Suzie, my eldest sister, in the shoe shop.'

'Oh, that Suzie.'

'Shall I hit him?' Jim had found a piece of metal pipe.

'No, Jim, he's a friend of a friend.'

'Oh, that's OK then, but just say the word and I'll do the pair of 'em!' He went back to loading wood.

'Who the hell was that?' asked my new friend.

'Oh, it's only Jim. Must be a full moon again.' We all laughed at Jim's expense.

'Suzie was saying how she wants to see you for some more stuff.'

'OK. I'll call in on Saturday sometime, tell her. But if she's after pure silk again, it's a no-no! Afraid it's only nylon at the moment.'

'I'll tell her. It's all she wants to do, go to the Palais with all her mates for a good time.'

'I know the sort of good time your sister wants if she needs silk stockings,' said Jim. Johnnie wanted to say something in his sister's defence but thought better of it, just in case it *was* a full moon.

'I'll see you around, Billy. If any more of our lads show up just tell 'em Mick and Johnnie say you're OK!'

To raise money for fireworks, several of us had been out collecting a penny for the guy. My guy was life-size, being made of a pair of Dad's old trousers stuffed with straw from the stables, an old sack with one of his jackets on and a pair of old black wellington boots. Mum made me a great head with a felt beard, moustache and eyebrows, topped off with an old hat of Dad's.

Once loaded into my pram he was easy to transport to Brixton. We set up outside Woolworths on Brixton High Road, the very best place, right next to all the bus stops. I got Derek to come with me for a share of the cash. We each had an empty baked-bean tin that had been washed out, with a new paper wrapper declaring 'Penny for the Guy'. Mum had told us to put a few pennies in first so we could rattle the tin to encourage people. It worked a treat. Her other piece of advice was always to say thank you, sir or madam. 'Manners cost nothing but earn a lot,' she said. We went back on several occasions in the week before Guy Fawkes night and filled the tins many times over. Lots of people said he was the best guy they had ever seen, thanks to the brilliant face Mum had put on him.

Several ladies out shopping from the flats gave us money. Mr and Mrs Prentis stopped when she recognised me.

'Honestly, Cyril, if Billy isn't a millionaire one day, I'll be very surprised. Go on, give them sixpence each.' Mr Prentis took out a small leather purse from his pocket and dropped a coin in each tin.

'So, you're the infamous wood-seller Beryl can't stop talking about.' I was thrilled that Beryl talked about me.

'Yes sir – and horse muck!'

He was quite a slight man with a small, neat moustache. 'No sale there, Billy. I don't have an allotment.'

'I know, Mr Prentis, on account of your back.'

His surprised look made me think I'd said too much. 'Exactly, Billy. We're not all as fit as your dad.' I smiled at the reference to my dad.

Mrs Prentis hurried him on. Before he left he tapped the nearly full money tin.

'Put half in the post office, Billy, there are always rainy days!'

Derek had overheard his advice. 'Sod the post office, I'm spending mine on fireworks. I want the Paynes giant box.'

'What a nice man. No wonder Beryl's so nice,' I said, not hearing a word he said.

'Bloody hell, Billy. Is she all you ever think about?'

On the last day before Guy Fawkes night, Derek and I sat in my front room and counted out the money. Mum gave us both a cup of tea and a slice of her home-made bread pudding. We sat facing each other with the guy on a chair between us. Soon the middle of the table was stacked with assorted coins in piles of one and two shillings. Mum was amazed at the money we had raised.

'You two look like pirates divvying up the treasure,' she said, which we took as a huge compliment. Although mostly pennies, there were plenty of three-penny bits, a few sixpences and even one half-crown that a drunken man had put in. After much deliberation and shuffling of coins we both agreed a total of three pounds, three shillings and threepence.

'That's lucky, Billy. Three threes. That's very lucky.'

'It'll split three ways nicely.'

'What? Why three ways, Mum?'

'For the guy. After all, I helped to make it. I did the face, Dad supplied the clothes and boots. It's only fair.' She waited a while longer, enjoying the look of horror on our two faces before adding, 'Only kidding, boys!'

'Oh, Mum. You *are* awful. We thought you were serious!'

'But you're putting your half into your post-office book, Billy Brown, and I'm serious about that. You can spend five shillings on fireworks that'll be gone in seconds, but that's it.' My idea of filling the pram with thirty bob's worth of fireworks had gone up in smoke!

'Have you been talking to Mr Prentis?' I asked.

'Not lately, Billy. He's not a well man. Why do you ask?'

'Oh, nothing, Mum.' They must both have shares in the post office, I thought. Derek went off with his half of the money and Mum divided up my share, pushing the coins to one side as she did so.

'Now, let's see. One school cap, three shillings and sixpence.'

'Oh but, Mum.'

'One lost satchel, four shillings.'

'Mum,' I protested.

'Two ruined hankies, sixpence.'

'I brought them home,' I protested.

'Yes, covered in green paint.' It was true. We had been in Brockwell Park and had gone on the slide, not seeing the WET PAINT sign. I had wiped it off my new shoes with her hankies.

'That's the lot, isn't it, Mum?' I asked, getting worried now.

'One last thing, young man.' There it was, the 'young man' again. Now I knew I was in trouble.

'Threepence for half a tin of black boot polish. Didn't think I'd notice, did you? What on earth did you want that for, Billy?'

'I gave it to the mission for Africa,' I said. 'Reverend and Mrs Dawson have been collecting old shoes for the children in their African missions so they needed some shoe polish for them.'

She eyed me up suspiciously. 'Is that the truth?'

'Honest, Mum. You can ask Mrs Dawson!'

She slipped me back the threepenny bit she had taken, still not quite believing me. The story about the African children was true, but I'd made up the bit about the shoe polish. A few weeks earlier whilst delivering firewood, my pram was pushed over with all the boxes of wood in it. When I came down from the last flat I found it all over the path. Looking up the road I spotted the culprits, the twins, riding away on their tricycles. They were seven years old, each with bright red hair and always up to no good. As soon as they saw me they started to make faces and call out 'Billy's lost his firewood'. I didn't bother chasing them as I had orders to deliver, and I knew my chance would come. The twins always left their tricycles in the entrance to their block, which is where I found them at lunchtime. Taking the black boot polish from my pocket, I smeared it all over their saddles and handlebars. I didn't have to wait too long to find out if it had been a success. That evening it was all over the playground how they had been covered in black shoe polish. There were plenty of suspects as the twins had upset lots of other children with their antics.

'We know it was you, Billy Brown,' they accused me.

'Not me, boys, must have been one of your other victims.'

All my pals were glad that the twins had finally been caught out at their own game.

Dividing the rest of my hard-earned cash, Mum said,

'Right, this lot is going in your post-office book. You can have five bob to spend on fireworks, but the rest goes in your money box for a rainy day.' She *must* have been talking to Mr Prentis, I thought to myself.

Feeding the coins through the slot of my old Mother Hubbard money box, I thought to myself what a swizz. My guy earns us three pounds, three shillings and three-pence and all I get to spend is five bob. I always smiled at the money box, made by my dad from a *Hobbies Plan*. The whole thing was fretwork cut from plywood on his *Hobbies treadle fretsaw*. A cut-out Mother Hubbard held her hand out to the little door, which opened to reveal the money slot. Below, a cut-out dog, begging, waited for a bone. If I could get my hands on the cash inside, I thought to myself, he could have the whole bloody butcher's shop.

November the fifth finally arrived and we all waited for seven thirty. As the superintendent's clock clicked on to the appointed time, the prearranged plan swung into action. Older boys dragged out the corrugated-iron sheeting and covered the tarmac road outside the flats' gates. Us smaller boys piled boxes, chairs and old tables on top with all the lumps of timber on top of them. Sacks of old straw were shoved under the base of the bonfire and set alight. The stack roared into life, sending sparks and smoke skywards at a rate of knots. It was soon blazing well. The whole operation took less than fifteen minutes, the same as last year and, I hoped, the same as years to come. The whole flats turned out, even PC Collins, who stationed himself at the junction with Sussex Road to divert the traffic!

The only lawns not ploughed up for the 'Dig for Victory' campaign were along the front facing the road. They were now covered with families letting off fireworks. Mums had brought out flasks of tea and biscuits, dads had provided fold-up chairs and we children were having one of the best nights of the year.

The flames of our bonfire were over twenty feet high now and reflecting in the windows of the flats. The red glow from the flames was making it look like something the devil would have been proud of! Beryl and the girls were being chased by Jim. They screamed hysterically, still holding their sparklers as he fired his Roman candle after them. The air was heavy with the smell of smoke and saltpetre. Derek was letting off his giant box of fireworks, filling the sky with cascading lights. Bangers and jumping crackers were exploding everywhere. My scarf kept getting in the way so I gave it to Mum.

'Don't get cold, Billy,' she warned, moving her chair back from the bonfire which was threatening to singe her eyebrows. At any sign of the fire dying down, more old doors and wood were thrown on, causing sparks to fly into the night sky.

At eight thirty we all brought our guys to the fire. It was a tradition that they all went on at once. Dad rescued his old wellingtons and hat from mine just in time. With a 'One – two – three,' some twenty-odd guys were hurled onto the fire and a huge cheer went up as one looking like Hitler was consumed by the flames. I decided it was time and wheeled out my firework on the back of my go-kart.

'What the 'ell is it, Billy?' asked Jim.

'It's my one and only firework.'

'What, you mean you only bought one, you tight bugger!'

'Yes, but it cost ten bob,' I announced proudly. Word spread like wild fire. 'Ten bob, I tell you, for one firework', 'No, can't be just one', 'That's what Jim said', 'Young Billy, Jack's boy', 'One firework, ten bob'.

'What have you done now, Billy?'

'Hello, Beryl. You're just in time.' I pulled my kart between the two pillars of the open gates. The firework was a huge square shape, almost filling my wooden apple-box seat. It was covered in red, gold and silver paper with a Chinese dragon winding right the way round the box.

'Well I never!'

'Did you ever see one that big?'

'It'll blow the gates off!'

'I wonder where he got that from?'

Pulling up the blue touch-paper, I beckoned Beryl forward. She shook her head, refusing to move.

'Please, Beryl, come and light it. I bought it for you.'

'Oh bloody 'ell,' sighed Jim, 'it must be love.'

'Shut up, Jim,' retorted Beryl. 'It's very sweet.'

'Go on, love. Light it up. Let's see it.' The crowd were now getting impatient.

'Come on, Beryl. The dragon won't bite!' There were hardly any other fireworks being let off now, although the occasional rockets streaked across the night sky. Beryl, along with most of the flats' tenants, had gathered to see my firework. She came forward, to the applause of the crowd. I could see Mum and Dad a few rows back. Mum shook her fist at me, but she was smiling. Beryl stood beside me, dressed for the occasion as usual in a pillar-box-red coat and hat, with black shoes and matching woollen gloves.

Taking the matches from me, she crouched down and lit The Imperial Dragon. Everyone stood back as the blue paper smouldered, then died. 'It's a dud. He's been had. Ten bob, I wouldn't give tenpence!'

I stood, praying for a miracle, that I wouldn't be humiliated in front of Beryl and the entire flats. Then the dragon spoke. The first bang and blinding white flash blew the cardboard lid off clean. No one saw it go as they rushed back from the exploding kart. Suddenly, the sky thirty feet above us was filled with hundreds of exploding white stars, but the dragon in the box was only warming up for the big event. White stars were followed by red, blue, green and gold, shimmering clouds of coloured smoke hiding more stars and sparkling explosions. On and on it went, one minute showering cascading fountains of white rain into the air twenty feet high, and the next booming bombs resonating through the night air, followed seconds later by a giant starburst across the sky. Now my dragon was in full cry: bang – bang – bang! I was beginning to think it would never stop. I was so absorbed by it all I hadn't noticed Beryl clutching my arm tightly and hiding her face against my chest. 'It's OK, Beryl. I'll look after you.' We gazed out together at the pyrotechnic masterpiece. I looked at the clock in the light from the bonfire behind us. My dragon had been spouting his display for nearly twenty minutes. Everybody now realised this was no ordinary firework and that it was building to an incredible crescendo. As if to answer their questions, the dragon went to sleep but with one eye open. The explosions stopped and just a flickering flame was left in the centre of the blackened box. People started to applaud and cheer.

'Well done, Billy.'

'Bloody marvellous.'

'Never seen anything like it.'

Then my dragon woke with a vengeance. Nothing that had gone before was like it. Starting slowly, it built and built, silver, red, blue, green and gold lit the sky. More clouds with coloured smoke, small whistling bombs exploding like silver snowballs, falling and turning fiery red. Finally the box went off so loudly it reverberated around all the five-storey flats. In the sky the last bomb exploded with a tremendous bang. For a second or two the crowd was stunned into silence. The white star that burst above them was truly awesome. It lit the sky for miles around, silver stars rained down and exploded in thousands of little bangs and the dragon was gone! I looked at Beryl. She was crying.

'Beryl, are you hurt?' I asked, concerned. She turned to face me.

'No, Billy. It's just that that was the most beautiful thing I've ever seen in my whole life. Thank you.' Then she kissed me on the cheek. The crowd was ecstatic.

'Where did you get that from?' Derek asked. 'It made my giant box of Paynes look crap!'

I wasn't really listening, Beryl still clinging to me tightly. My dad came up to me. 'Bloody amazing, Billy, bloody amazing. Your mum was in tears. What's up, Beryl?'

'Nothing, Mr Brown. Absolutely bloody nothing.' We both laughed at her use of bad language.

'That was some show, Billy – and don't worry. I'll fix your kart,' Dad added. We all looked in the direction of the smouldering kart. The last great burst had blown the apple box to bits and one wheel had come off, but I didn't care. All the cheers and congratulations had paled into insignificance. All I could hear were the words from the pretty blonde girl in the red coat hugging my arm.

'I love you, Billy!'

After that, all there was to do was watch the bonfire die down to a huge pile of glowing embers. Some of the children had long garden bamboos with sausages on and were cooking them in the remaining heat. I stood with Beryl still hugging my arm.

'Alright, you two love birds. You're gonna make me throw up in a minute!'

Even Jim's comments couldn't make me let her go.

'Where the bloody hell did you get that from, Billy?'

'Chinatown.'

'Soho? You've never been to Soho.' Just the notion of this dangerous and exotic part of London was scary.

'No, of course I haven't, but Mr Woo has.'

'Who?'

'Mr Woo. The man who owns the Chinese restaurant in Acre Lane.'

'How do you know a Chinese man, Billy?'

'Rabbits. I get him rabbits from Big Mike. The Chinese invented fireworks for the emperor's birthday. I read it in a book so I asked him to get me a big one next time he went shopping in Chinatown, see? That was the biggest one they had left over from Chinese New Year.'

We were all distracted by the clanging bell of Brixton's bright red fire engine coming up the road. Standing back, we watched as the firemen in their black uniforms quickly extinguished the fire with the hose reel of their tender. The chief came over to our little group.

'Now don't light it again tonight, OK? Especially you, Billy Brown.' We all stared, open-mouthed, that the chief fireman knew me. Then I recognised him.

'Hello, Mr Hendrick. Busy night?'

'Cheeky bugger! No more bonfires!' and with that, he mounted his fire engine and was gone.

'Who on earth was that?'

'He lives next door to my aunt Eaddie. I didn't even know he was a fireman until tonight.'

With the fire now reduced to a pile of soggy ash we began to walk back to our flats, leaving it for the council cleaner in the morning. After saying goodnight to Jim, Beryl and I walked back to the entrance to her block. Once again, she climbed the first step to be level with me. This time I didn't wait to be asked and kissed her flush on the lips. When we parted she held me close and whispered, 'I do love you, Billy.'

'I love you too, Beryl.' I had never said this to a girl before, but I knew I meant it.

11

Supply and Demand

'I want a word with you.'

Big Mike had called me over as I passed late one afternoon on my way to the market. I hadn't worked for him for nearly eighteen months, but had always kept in touch as he seemed to have a constant supply of dead rabbits.

'Hello, Mr Mike. What can I do for you?'

Beckoning me into the first shed, he said in a whisper, 'Durex.'

'Pardon, Mr Mike?'

'You know, Billy, Durex; rubbers, johnnies, whatever you wanna call 'em.'

'Oh, I get it. You want something for the weekend, sir!' I said, mimicking every barber in Brixton.

'That's it, a gross.'

'What? That's a lot of weekends, Mr Mike. You'll exhaust yourself!'

'No, not for me, you cheeky bugger! Now, can you do it or not?'

'Well, I really don't know. I'll have to ask around. Can't you just go to the chemist, Mr Mike?'

'Too expensive, Billy. Two and six for three. I want one hundred and forty-four – a month,' he added.

Even at my tender age I knew that that was an awful lot of shagging.

'I'll make enquiries, Mr Mike, soon as I can.'

'Good lad, Billy. Do ya want a rabbit to help you with your enquiries?' Slipping the rabbit into the bottom of my pram I headed off, waving him goodbye, making a mental note to look out for Mickey Finn. People always laughed at his name as it was a nickname for a drugged drink, but there was nothing dopey about Mickey. Some of the boys called him Ferrety Finn on account of his sharp, thin nose. I didn't care about that. All I knew was that Mickey Finn's nose could sniff out anything you wanted.

'*How* many?' asked Mickey when I caught up with him later that day.

'A gross.'

'You'll go blind, Billy.'

'No, no, Mr Finn. They're not for me. I haven't . . .' I stopped short, not wanting to make such an admission, even at my young age.

'Of course you haven't, Billy. You wouldn't be so tall otherwise. Stunts your growth, you know. Look what it's done to me! Now, who's it for?'

'Sorry, Mr Finn, first rule of business. Never let your right hand know what your left hand's doing.'

'I know what your right hand's being doing, if the Durex are anything to go by, Billy!'

'Look, if you can't do it I'll have to try Harvey.'

At the mention of Mickey's rival supplier, his attitude changed. 'Hey, hold on, you stroppy little sod! I didn't say I couldn't. What about the cash?'

'Payment on delivery, but I'll have to know in advance.'

'So you can get it from whoever the sex maniac is, eh?' I so wanted to tell him it was Big Mike Gallagher just to shut him up, but thought better of it.

'Wait there. Give us tuppence.' He took my coins and went to the phone box on the wall of the arcade, returning a few minutes later.

'Gonna cost you a fiver, Billy, one gross, packets of three, that's four hundred and thirty-two johnnies, one a night for a year and then some. Who are you supplying, the Guards' regiment?'

'Five pounds cash. When?'

'Here tomorrow, same time. Don't be late. I don't want Phyllis to catch me with a gross of johnnies. She'll think I'm one of those sex fiends!' The whole market knew Mickey's girlfriend Phyllis was what they called hot stuff and easy, but no one would tell Mickey that!

Mike didn't even argue when I told him the price of five pounds ten shillings. He just gave me the money and said he'd keep the yard open until I got back. Mickey Finn was waiting with a paper carrier bag and a folded copy of the *Evening Standard*.

'Got the money, Billy?' Carefully I took the five one-pound notes out of my shoe.

'You're a smart lad, Billy boy, but not that smart. You should have done that round the corner. Now I know where you keep yer cash!' Saying so, he tapped his finger against the side of his thin nose, knowingly.

'Here's yer goods, and goodnight.'

263

'Hold on, Mr Finn. I want to know if it's all there.'

'Billy Brown, you cheeky sod! I'll excuse that on the grounds of your young years. When Mickey Finn makes a deal he stands by it, see, or word soon gets around and Mickey Finn would be out of business. You get me, Billy?'

'Yes, Mr Finn, but I don't know what a gross of Durex looks like!' Taking the bag from me, he opened it up.

'Like that, Billy.' The purple and pink box printed with *Durex, packets of 3 x 1 gross* stared back at me.

'What's the wrapper around it, Mr Finn?'

'Oh, thanks for reminding me, Billy.' As he pulled off the green paper I just had time to read 'US Army Supplies Department'.

'We all set? Deal done?'

'Deal done, Mr Finn.' I spat on my palm and offered it to him. He had to change the *Evening Standard* paper he always carried to his left hand. In doing so, he caught my knuckle with it.

'Ouch! That's a bloody hard paper!' Smiling, he opened out the folded paper. Inside was a heavy steel tyre lever the length of the paper.

'You never know, Billy. You just never know. But just like the boy scouts, always be prepared.'

He went off whistling, covering his paper. The lights were on when I got back to the yard where Mike was waiting for me. Once inside the shed I produced his box.

'Just what the doctor ordered, Billy. You're a bloody magician!'

'Thanks, Mr Mike. I'm off home.' As I made to go he stopped me.

'D'ya want some biscuits, Billy?' Without waiting for an answer he produced two big tins of Party Time assorted biscuits. With a razor blade he carefully cut the sealing tape at the join between the lid and the tin. I wondered why he was being so careful with just the wrapping. Lifting the lid, he slowly removed the first full layer of biscuits in its cardboard tray.

'Here, give us your bag, Billy.' Handing him the paper carrier bag, he tipped the rest of the biscuits into it, followed by the second tin, treated in the same careful manner. My bag was now almost full of nice biscuits.

'Now for the good bit.' He looked at me and winked. Tearing open the box of Durex, he lined the bottom of each tin with them, half filling the tin, then replaced the top layer of biscuits level with the top of the tin. Once he was satisfied the lid went back on. Very carefully he resealed the two tins with new Sellotape, smoothing it down with his thumb.

'There you go, Billy, fool the Pope himself!' At his own mention of the Pope he crossed himself.

'They're not for the Pope, are they?' I exclaimed.

'Bless you, no, Billy. He'd have me excommunicated if he found out. Listen, I'll explain.' I sat on a box and ate a biscuit while he told me all.

'In Southern Ireland you can't buy Durex. The Catholic Church is so strong it's prevented the sale of 'em.'

'Why, Mr Mike? Don't they want people to have a shag?'

'Oh yes, Billy, but only to make good Catholic babies, see? So, when I go to Ireland I take these with me and make a nice little profit, at the same time helping people who've got enough kids already not to have any more.'

'Ah, that's why you wanted a gross!'

'Exactly – and if your man can do it, one box a month.' Picturing the US Army Supplies Department wrapper, I reassured him.

'No problem, Mr Mike. One gross each month.' As I walked home pushing the pram loaded with boxes, a rabbit and a bag of biscuits, I pictured nice Irish couples welcoming Big Mike with open arms while Parish priests wondered why the baby count was down this year!

In my flats, each block was served by two dust chutes and at the bottom of each was a brick store containing a dust cart. Anything of value was put on top of the store ready for the dustmen to collect and recycle, from aluminium pans, newspapers, glass and old tools. By first thing every Friday morning, the store was full to bursting.

So, each Thursday afternoon I used to visit all twenty-two dust chutes before the dustmen came. It was a cat-and-mouse game of Dodge the Porter, but I knew their routines by heart. Once the pram was loaded, it was back to my shed and then off for the next load, often doing three of four pram-loads before

I was finished. Any metal or tools went to Big Mike for scrap money. I left the jam jars, but took any decorative glass such as vases or bowls, which I sold to Ma Kingdom. On occasions, other treasures appeared. A hand-operated Singer sewing machine sold for five bob down the second-hand shop, as did a Decca wireless. Even the old gas masks fetched two bob each from Tosh. But the newspapers were best of all.

Nearly every household in the block of four hundred flats had at least one daily newspaper and on Sunday two or three. Tied in bundles of fifty, I got two shillings and sixpence a bundle from Reggie the rag-and-bone man. He called twice a week, on Saturday and Wednesday mornings. He was not allowed to drive his green three-ton Luton Bedford van into the flats so he parked just outside on the road. Once parked, he set up for business. He bought old clothes, shoes, bed linen, cardboard and newspapers. A large set of spring scales hung from the roof of the van to weigh the items and current salvage prices were chalked on a board screwed to the inside of the back door.

Those who wanted a better deal could trade their items for goods. On the back of the van were wooden boxes filled with assorted merchandise including washing powder, bars of soap, clotheslines, tea towels, hot water bottles, comics, balloons and oranges. The business was simple; Reggie weighed your items or simply assessed them, then called out what you could have. 'Right now, luv, washing powder and two soaps or clothesline and tea towel.' It just depended on what he'd got.

He was always pleased to see me. I usually caught him on Wednesday morning before school as he made a special effort to arrive early.

'How many, Billy?' he asked, as I unloaded the bundles of newspapers from my pram into the back of his van.

'Six bundles, Reggie, and a sack of rags.' After checking the contents of the sack he hooked it onto the spring scales.

'Twelve pound of rags at four pence a pound, that's forty-eight pence. Call it four bob, Billy, so that's a total of . . . ?' He gave me one of his quizzical looks.

'Nineteen bob, Reggie, thank you, but I'll trade some.'

'Ah, good lad. Now, where did I put them?' After shifting a few sacks and boxes he found the big cardboard box he was looking for. Placing it on the back of the van, he opened the lid. It was almost full to the top with comics.

'Good, ten bob's worth in there, Billy,' he said. I closed the lid.

'Seven and six, that's all I'll give you.'

'Seven and six; it's a deal.' We shook hands and I loaded the box into the pram. I knew Reggie had to sell the comics to someone like me as they were no good for waste paper. The processing plant couldn't use any paper with coloured inks in it. I sold them on for one or two pence each to all the children in the flats. I knew I would clear the whole box on Sunday afternoon after Sunday School. As he counted out the remaining eleven and six, he stopped.

'Hold on just a minute, Billy.' Once again there was a great deal of shifting and moving of boxes in the back of his van.

'Ah, got you, my beauties!' he exclaimed. Stacking two more large boxes at the back of the van, he beckoned me inside.

'Not for everyone's eyes, Billy,' he told me. My curiosity aroused, I couldn't wait to see what was so special about more comics.

Opening the first box, he took out a magazine and handed it to me as if it was some priceless museum exhibit. I took it and glanced at the cover. A full-colour illustration of a girl in stockings smiled back at me with a wink in her eye. It was a men's magazine, entitled *Wink*.

'Have a look, Billy,' he encouraged. I didn't need much encouragement and duly flicked through the pages of pretty young women clad in only their underwear; Kim of Hollywood, Layla from Hawaii, Mona of New York. They all smiled out from the pages. Reggie picked up another entitled *Peep Show*. The cover was a cut-out keyhole revealing a pretty girl adjusting her stockings in full colour. I don't care if the paper mills don't want them. I do, I thought.

'How many and how much?' I asked.

'There's over fifty in each box, Billy. Come from the Yanks, they did. You can have them for a quid a box.'

'I'll give you what you owe me for the two, plus one pound – and I'll buy any more like them.' He didn't need long to think.

'Done. I've got at least two more boxes of them at

the yard. I'll bring 'em next week. Always a pleasure, Billy. See you next Wednesday.' I pushed the laden pram back to my shed, then headed off to school with two of the American magazines in my satchel.

Once lunch was over I headed for the playground. I soon had my select group of pals around me. They'd never seen anything as daring as these magazines before.

'How much do you want for them, Billy?' Jim wanted to know.

'A shilling each – and I may have more.'

'I haven't got a shilling. How about nine pence?' offered Jim.

'Sorry, Jim. No can do. This is hard-to-get American stuff. You won't find these in your local paper shop.' No one seemed to have the required amount of money, so after letting the lads have a good look inside I put the magazines away. Walking home, Jim and I were joined by Anthony, the bookworm.

'Do you still have those American magazines?' he enquired. Jim and I both stared at each other in disbelief.

'Yes, Anthony – and they're still a bob each,' I told him. To our utter amazement he promptly produced a two-shilling piece.

'I'll have both of them, please.' I took his money and handed over the merchandise, which he placed in his briefcase without even looking at them. 'I trust you'll be discreet?' he asked us.

'We'll be what?' Jim asked.

'Don't tell anybody, *please*,' he explained.

'Oh no, of course we won't, will we, Jim? Our lips are sealed.' Anthony ran off ahead of us.

'Well, I'm blowed,' Jim said. 'It's always the quiet ones!'

By Sunday, word had got around and there was quite a group gathered around the entrance to the clubroom. I dealt with the youngest first and sold lots of comics, swapping ten for a really good regimental cap badge from the Gordon Highlanders. The older lads wanted to see the new magazines so I passed out a copy of *High Heel*, 1937 vintage. They were all seriously impressed and I soon sold the ten I'd brought with me.

The lads all disappeared except Jim, and a few young ones sat on the stone bench reading their comics.

'What's up, Jim?' I asked.

'No money, Billy, that's what's up. Or I'd have bought one of those American mags.'

'How would you like to make at least a quid every Sunday?' I asked him. He looked confused.

'I don't know how.'

'I'll sell you half the firewood businesss, Jim, that's how. I've got too much on the go, so how about it?' He still didn't seem too happy.

'I haven't got any money to pay you for it.'

I explained that I'd sell him the half of the flats on his side for five pounds, plus the complete list of customers and orders.

'What about the wood?' he asked.

'You find a pram and I'll show you how to collect it. You can pay me ten bob a week until it's paid. How's that?' He thought for a moment.

'What if I don't make ten bob?'

'Oh, don't worry, Jim. You will. There's over fifty customers on your side so you'll do OK.'

'He'll do OK at what, Billy Brown?' Beryl and Sally were arm in arm, wearing their best Sunday School clothes. 'Every time I see you and Jimmy together, I know you're up to something.'

'No we're not!' exclaimed Jim. 'I'm just going into the firewood business, that's all. I'm taking over half of Billy's customers.' I smiled and Beryl eyed me with suspicion.

'If you're giving up half of your firewood round, Billy, then you're up to something else!'

'He's only selling mags, Beryl, that's all.' Jim knew the instant he opened his mouth that he shouldn't have.

'Magazines? What kind of magazines, Billy?' asked Sally. 'Show us one.'

'Sold out. All gone,' I informed them, but Beryl was not giving up that easily.

'Urgh! You're both disgusting. We should tell your mum, Billy Brown.'

Sally caught on instantly. 'Good idea, Beryl. We'll see her at the next club night when she's on teas and cakes. We'll tell her then.'

'Oh, come on girls, have a heart. I've got to make a living. I've not sold them all yet.' Now it was my turn to feel completely stupid!

The two girls turned away in a huddle, whispering to each other. I looked at Jim, who shrugged his shoulders. Finally the girls turned around.

'We want to see one!' demanded Beryl. 'Or we'll tell.'

'But you can't,' I protested. 'They're for American soldiers. You know, men's stuff.' But Beryl knew she had me trapped.

'Fine, we'll just tell your mum on Friday.' And with her passing remark she took Sally's arm and started to walk off.

'OK, OK. You win, but you've got to promise not to tell a soul. Word of honour.' They both agreed and made the cross-your-heart sign.

I led the way to my pram shed and stopped at the door.

'Promise again, no telling.'

'Just get on with it, Billy,' ordered Beryl. 'After all, if we tell on you now, we'll all get into trouble.' I saw her logic and unlocked the shed, wheeling out my trusty pram before ushering them inside.

'There's only two boxes to sit on,' I told the girls, trying to put them off.

'I'll sit on Jim's lap,' said Sally, much to Jim's amazement.

'Then I'll sit on yours, Billy,' said Beryl. There was still enough light in the shed to see by as it was one of the few that had small grilles high up, allowing ventilation and sunlight in. Sat side by side with our backs against the wall, Jim and I allowed the girls to sit on our laps.

'That big box there,' I indicated to Beryl, unable to reach it myself. Opening the lid, she took out a magazine. *Reel Humour*, fifteen cents. On the front was a colour illustration of a bubbly blonde wearing a red bikini seated in a rowing boat, showing her long, shapely legs.

'Billy Brown!' exclaimed Beryl, opening the magazine. Inside were black and white photos of various Hollywood stars and hopefuls in very scanty costumes or underwear: Joan Blondell, Ann Sheridan, Bette Davis, Alice Faye and Ginger Rodgers to name but a few. The lesser-known starlets were posing in stockings and suspenders. Sally was the first to speak.

'They're shameful. You can see their knickers!'

'I told you, they're for men, Sally.'

Beryl reached for another magazine.

'You sure, Beryl? Some of these are a bit daring, you know!' Ignoring me completely, she retrieved a copy of *High Heel*, 1937. The cover showed a pretty blonde bending over to straighten her seams. Holding it up into the sunlight, she studied the pin-up intently.

'Her legs are a bit fat!' she commented. Beryl and Sally turned the pages together. At each turn they whispered the name of the story accompanying the photos.

'*Miami Mammy, Three for Company, Love on the Rocks, Sheer Nonsense.*' Beryl stopped at a double-page spread of a pretty girl sitting on a piano with her skirt hitched up, entitled *Baby Grand*.

'That's terrible,' she commented.

'Why? She's not showing her knickers?' said Jim.

'I can see that, Jimmy, but her high heels could scratch that piano!'

'Right, that's it. Time to go!' I tried to stand, but Beryl stayed put.

'I want one,' she suddenly announced. All three of us were shocked at her demand.

'What for?' asked Sally.

'I want to read the stories. I want to know what all the boys see in them.'

'But, Beryl, they're not for nice girls. They're for older men, soldiers, you know.'

'Give me one or I'll tell,' she declared.

'You promised, on your honour,' Jim reminded her.

'Then give me one and I won't! I'll give it back when I've read it.' It was hopeless to argue with her.

'Help yourself, but just one.' With Sally's help she selected the magazine and slipped it under her jacket.

'If your mum catches you, I know nothing about it, Beryl,' I told her. 'You can tell her it was on top of one of the dust chutes with some newspapers.'

They waited while I put the pram back and locked up the shed. Sally now had hold of Jim's arm.

'Jimmy's going to walk me home, aren't you, Jimmy?' she told him.

'I am? Yes, I am, if you want me to.' Once more, Jim looked at me and shrugged his shoulders with that I-don't-know-what's-going-on expression.

'And Billy's taking me,' announced Beryl, at which point we parted company and I walked Beryl home to her block.

'Is there nothing you won't sell, Billy?' she suddenly asked me.

'Children, horse meat and me granny,' I told her.

'Be serious or no kiss.' I looked into her pretty face.

'I don't know, Beryl. It seems that you can sell

anything, you just have to have the right goods.' She tapped the men's magazine concealed under her coat.

'Are these the right goods, Billy?' she asked.

'You know they are, Beryl. The lads couldn't buy 'em quick enough.'

'Well, once I've read it, I'll know what all the fuss is about.' Turning, she made as if to walk up her stairs, then stopped.

'Well?' she said, turning back towards me. 'Do you want to kiss me or not?'

'You know I do, Beryl,' I said, and, going up one step, we were level again and she closed her eyes and pursed her cupid's-bow lips. When I didn't kiss her she opened her eyes in surprise.

'Do you want to kiss *me*?' I asked. Without giving an answer she kissed me flush on the mouth.

'There. How's that?' she asked. And quick as anything, I replied, 'Not out!' and kissed her again.

Rationing was a real boon for me. Clothes, bread, jam and petrol were derationed by 1950, but tea, sweets, eggs, cream, sugar, butter, cheese, marge, cooking oil and meat still required ration coupons. So, with this in mind, I went to see Horace and Toby, the local poultry farmers.

'Billy man, have a cup of tea.'

'Thanks, Horace. Two sugars please.'

'You'll get one like de rest of us and dat's dat!' He poured the tea while we gazed out at the chickens pecking away in the now cleared back garden.

'How are they, Horace?' I asked. 'Started laying yet?' In answer he showed me a tray of assorted eggs.

'So, what are you doing with them all, then?' He eyed me suspiciously.

'Why you want to know?'

'Well, if you've any left over, I'll sell 'em for you.'

'Ha, I can sell them myself. Everybody in the road wants some.'

'Well, I'll swap you for them then.'

'Swap? What's dis swap t'ing?'

'You know, Horace. You give me your spare eggs and I give you stuff in exchange.'

'What stuff?'

'Whatever I can get. You know, tea, butter, nylons.'

'Did you say nylons, Billy?'

'Sure, Horace. Sometimes pure silk stockings. I might be able to get anything, provided the eggs keep coming!' I suspected the eggs would because, since the first chick deliveries, they'd had three more and Toby's garden had been cleared for some of them.

'How many for a pair of nylons, den?'

'One dozen.'

'And for silk?' I quickly worked out that silk stockings were three times the price of nylon ones.

'Three dozen.'

'What! Dat's daylight robbery.'

'Silk is scarce, Horace. All been used for parachutes. I could try and get you some silkworms from the pet shop and you can make your own. Come on, Horace. Your eggs are free; I have to pay cash for silk stockings!'

'Alright, alright. You'll have me crying me eyes out for you in a minute. Scotch?'

'No, I'm English.'

'No, you fool. Can you get Scotch, you know, whisky?'

'Bloody hell, Horace. What kind of a party are you thinking of having, what with silk stockings and whisky?'

'Dat's de only kind of party, man,' he continued, slapping his thigh and laughing. 'De only kind. You'll learn.'

'I think I'm learning too much from you already. Look, I'll see a man I know about the whisky, but I can't promise anything. That's big stuff. What stockings do you want?' I didn't tell him that I had some already. Every older girl in the flats had got to know about them so I kept some in reserve for my regulars! Mickey Finn seemed to have a limitless supply.

'Two pairs of nylons and if she turns out to be worth it, maybe silk, just maybe.'

'How big is she?'

'How big? You cheeky bugger. What do you want to know dat for?'

'Knickers, Horace. I've got two pairs of black silk ladies' knickers but they're big, too big for any of the girls in my flats. Cost you a dozen and a half per pair. They'll make your party go with a bang!'

'How wide, Billy? Show me.' Holding out my hands, I estimated the width.

'Sold. Bring dem with the stockings.' Judging by the

size of the knickers he was going to buy, Horace went up in my estimation.

'Tomorrow after school. Can I take these on account?'

'Yes, man. Dat's fine, but don't forget the Scotch, if it's possible,' he added.

As I was on my way to the market for wood I put the eggs in the bottom recess of the pram and covered them with Dad's piece of plywood. Mickey Finn wasn't hard to find if you knew where to look.

'Hello, Mickey. How's tricks?' He eyed me up and down over his cup of tea, the *Evening Standard* unopened next to him on the table.

'Oh, it's you, Billy. I was expecting someone else.' Mickey was always expecting someone. 'What you after now? I haven't got any of them TVs, if that's what you want.'

'No, Mickey. They're a waste of time. Records are much better! No, I just wondered if you could get me a bottle of Scotch. You know, whisky.'

'You're a bit young for that, ain't you?'

'Oh no, it's not for me, it's for a grown-up.'

'Oh, a grown-up. Well, that's OK then. Van-load do you, will it?' I realised he was pulling my leg.

'Just one, maybe more later.'

'That's what I like about you, Billy. Your huge orders keep my empire going.'

'Don't bother, then. I'll go and see Harvey!'

'Oi, don't start that old crap again. One bottle, here, tomorrow, same time, seven and six.'

'Bloody dear, ain't it?'

'Bloody scarce, ain't it?' he replied. 'And Billy, be careful. There's been some trouble lately, so watch yourself.' To emphasise his concern he tapped his newspaper on the table, giving off a dull thud from the tyre lever inside.

'What kind of trouble?'

'New people, Billy. Far too sharp for their own good!'

'OK. I'll watch myself. Thanks, Mickey. See you.'

Mum was delighted when I showed her the tray of eggs.

'You can only pick six, Mum. I have to sell the rest to pay for them – and *I* want the big one.'

'Egg and chips for tea, Billy. You peel the tatties.'

'How much for the other half-dozen?' I quickly worked out my profit margin. 'Two bob should do it.'

'That's not much less than David Greggs, Billy.'

'I know, Mum, but it is less and these are extras to the rations, see?'

'Oh, I see alright, you greedy little sod.'

'One and six then, but I'm robbing myself.'

She laughed. 'That'll be the day, Billy Brown,' and off she went.

'I'll have two more machetes, Tosh, and one of them trenching spades.' Since the arrival of the West Indian community and the sale of Nazi treasure I had become one of Tosh's best customers and confidants at his ex-army store. He bagged up the items and took my money, but something was wrong.

'What's up, Tosh? You look like you lost a half-crown and only found a sixpence.'

'Syrup, Billy. That's what's up.'

'Syrup? What are you talking about?' He waved me into his back storeroom, which was twice the size of the shop, with double doors to the yard. Before the war it had been a baker's, but the two brothers who worked for their dad had been killed at Tobruk, so the old man had closed the shop, never to reopen.

'Here, look, bloody syrup!' Tosh had prised open one of his job-lot ex-WD cases only to find it full of fifty one-gallon tins of Lyle's Golden Syrup and fifty one-gallon tins of Lyle's Black treacle, obviously destined for some army cookhouse somewhere.

'Why don't you put it out the front, Tosh?' I suggested.

'Can't. It's sugar, see, and what with rationing and all, I'd have to report it to the appropriate ministry – and I don't want those buggers sticking their noses in here so I guess I'll have to dump it.'

'Hold on. Let's not be hasty,' I said, putting my wheeler-dealer head on. 'How much do you want for a tin?'

'Ah, no, Billy. You're a good pal, but I wouldn't want to lumber you. I'll just have to get rid of it.'

'How about three bob a tin?' Tosh quickly calculated one hundred tins at three bob each was £15, only £5 less than he'd paid for the lot so he'd only make a small loss instead of a big one.

'Billy, if you can sell all this bloody syrup you'll be a friend for life!'

'Right, give us one of each as a sample, then. You know I'm good for the cash.' I loaded the two tins into the pram and covered them up with some old sacking.

'See you tomorrow, Tosh.'

'I hope so, Billy. I don't want this stuff sitting around for too long.'

'Hello, Horace. I've got your machetes.' I worked out that he had bought over twenty in the last year. Turning back the sacking, I revealed the tins of syrup.

'This any good to you or your friends, Horace?'

'How much you want for it?'

'Cor blimey, Horace, that was quick.'

'Me and Toby used to work at the Tate and Lyle processing factory in Trinidad, Billy. This stuff is liquid gold man, just liquid gold.'

'Five bob a tin, that's all.'

'I'll have dat, Billy. Just wait there a minute.' He went a few houses down and came back with another West Indian friend in a bright orange shirt.

'Daniel, dis is Billy Brown. A good man and you're gonna think he's fallen from heaven! Show him the baby, Billy.' I slipped back the cover on the two tins.

'Amen to that, Horace, Amen, Billy. You sure is an angel alright.' I had no idea what they were talking about.

'How much is it a tin, man?'

'Five bob. You can have syrup or treacle.'

'Treacle? Where we come from, Billy, dat's molasses. How much you got?'

'Fifty tins of each. How many do you want?'

'Fifty of the molasses and twenty of the golden syrup.'

'How much?' I asked, shocked. 'Wow, that's the biggest order I've ever had!'

'Well, Billy, you got to think big in de rum business.'

'You mean you're gonna make rum from it?'

'Sure t'ing, man, but not just any old rum, the finest sipping rum known to man. Now, when can you deliver?' I had to sit on the wall while I worked it out. I figured the pram would hold ten tins at a time, which made seven trips, but I might be able to do two a night. I explained this to my new-found friend, Daniel the rum-maker.

'You sure we can't come and collect it in one go, Billy?' he asked.

'No, no, definitely out of the question. My supplier wouldn't like it, if you get my meaning.'

'No, no, man. You just leave it to Billy. He'll see us alright. You just got to be patient and wait for the babies to be delivered.' Horace tapped the pram as he said it. They lifted out the two cans and Daniel paid me ten shillings.

'Thanks very much, but I'll have to have some money up front for the next lot.'

'Wait a minute, I'm not falling for dat old trick.'

'Shut up, Daniel. Billy's word is good. He's never cheated us before so why should he now?' Horace drew one of his machetes out of its scabbard. 'And if he does rob us . . .' he ran his thumb over its blade for sharpness and winked at Daniel. 'Yeah, man, he'll get the old sugar-cane chop!' They both laughed at Horace's joke, but I didn't see what was funny.

'Pay up and I might be back in half an hour with the first ten.'

Tosh was just closing up when I arrived back.

'Hello, you're back quick.'

'Told you I might sell some.'

'Oh yeah. How many? One, two, three, my little wheeler-dealer?' He still looked miserable.

'Seventy!' The long pole he was using to take down his display slipped from his hands, dropping army webbing all over the pavement.

'Seventy, Tosh. Fifty treacle, twenty golden syrup. Ten per load. Here's thirty-six bob for the two I've had, plus tonight's ten.' Tosh sat on a pile of grey blankets in the shop doorway and, pulling off his khaki woolly hat, scratched his bald spot.

'How the bloody hell did you do it? You've only been gone half an hour!'

'Can't say, but I want it all, one hundred tins. Payment on collection. Is it a deal?' I spat on my hand and offered it to him.

'Too bloody right boy-o. Deal!' He shook my hand and we went into the shop. Once the clings and dongs of his National till had finished we loaded the pram.

'Wait a minute, Billy.' Tosh returned with some old bits of wooden packing crates. Put this on top. Anyone

284

looking will think you've been to the market for your wood, OK?'

'Clever idea, Tosh. Maybe we should be partners!'

'Piss off, you cheeky sod. See you tomorrow.' And with that he went back into the shop, happy once more, and started singing some Welsh song about mountains.

It took me the rest of the week to deliver all seventy tins. On the last night Daniel was joined by another West Indian man.

'Dis is Rubin. He's my business partner. Rubin, dis is de boy I told you about.'

'Well, my, my, dat's a fine pram full of babies you got there, Billy. I think we can do a lot of business!' Horace came down his steps and was not pleased to see Rubin standing there.

'What you want, man? You leave dis boy alone. Daniel, you're a dammed fool!'

'Now hold on, Horace. I'm just being friendly.'

'Sure, sure you are, while it suits you.'

'Well, if it's like that, Horace, I'll say goodnight to you and your young man.' There's that 'young man' again, I thought. It never seems to do me any good.

'Listen, Billy,' said Horace. 'You gotta stay away from Rubin. He's not such a nice guy.'

'Really? He seemed friendly enough to me, Horace.'

'So does a tiger before he bites your arse! Just have nothing to do with him, OK, Billy? I'll speak to the reverend about this.'

'OK, Horace. I like him. He likes *The Light of the World*.'

'So he does, Billy, so he does.'

Within a week I'd cleared Tosh's stock of treacle and syrup. Rose in the Primrose Café couldn't believe her luck.

'That's my syrup ration for a whole year, Billy!' she exclaimed, taking delivery of five tins.

'You come in next week and I'll give you a free helping of sponge pudding with golden syrup. Don't suppose there's any treacle, is there, Billy?'

'Sorry, Rose, I'm all out, but I'll remember next time.'

'You're a good lad. Don't forget, now. If you can eat it or cook with it, I'll have it!'

'Sure, Rose. I might go into the sausage business!' She laughed at the reference to Big Mike's little earner.

'I'll mention it to Mike next time I see him!'

I didn't sell the last tin of golden syrup. I took it home for Mum.

'Billy. Wherever did you get it from? It must have cost a fortune!'

'It's from a pal, Mum. I can take it back if it's no good.' But I could see from the look of concentration on her face that she'd already written a mental list of all the things she could make with a whole gallon of syrup.

Mickey Finn was in his usual seat in the market café when I called in after school. Before I could ask if he had my whisky he handed me a brown carrier bag. Checking the contents, I looked back at him. 'I only ordered one.'

'There is only one whisky, the other one's vodka. Whoever you're getting the whisky for will certainly buy the vodka.'

'Is that good?'

'This is Black Label, strongest vodka made. Guaranteed to loosen any girl's knicker elastic, if you know what I mean.'

'I think so, Mickey. I'll take it. How much?'

'Same as the whisky, seven and six. You tell your man he won't find that in any off-licence!'

I paid Mickey and picked up the brown bag containing my bottles. Once stowed safely in my pram, I began collecting firewood, slowly working my way up Electric Avenue and into Station Road towards the fire station. Glad to have my winter coat on, I pulled the collar up around my ears as the sun faded and dusk set in.

'Well, well. If it isn't Horace's little pal.' I recognised him from Somerleyton Road. It was Rubin. I didn't know the other man.

'Hello, Mr Rubin. I'm just on my way home.' Trying to pass them, he put his hand on the pram and stopped me.

'What's your rush, man? What you got to trade today, Billy?'

'Nothing. I've got nothing, now let me go.'

'Nothing, eh? Well, I'll just have to see dis nothing

you're so scared about!' His friend started pulling off my stack of wooden boxes.

'Oi, you can't do that!'

'Can't, Billy? Who's gonna stop me?'

'I am!' I knew the voice instantly. George had heard the commotion from inside the arches.

'Piss off, Shorty, if you know what's good for you.'

'Let Billy go.'

'Oh, another friend of this boy. Is there any deadbeat he doesn't know?'

'I said let him go.' Rubin turned towards George, pulling something from his pocket. With a press of its button the flick-knife opened.

'Now I ain't gonna tell you again, Shorty. Piss off!'

Whether it was the knife threat or the 'shorty' insult, I didn't know, but George had had enough. Rubin didn't get to say any more. The ARMY fist exploded on his jaw, rendering him unconscious before he hit the floor. Rubin's friend rushed at George, who neatly sidestepped him and lifted him off the floor with the NAVY to the solar plexus. It was over in seconds.

'You OK, Billy?'

'Yes, George. How about you?' He held his two tattooed knuckles for me to see.

'Not a scratch, Billy, not a scratch.'

'Pity they both went down so quick. I was just warming up. Here.' He picked up the pearl-handled flick-knife. 'Souvenir for you. You get off home. Me and the boys will have a chat with these two clowns.'

*

Horace was stunned when I told him what had happened. After making me a cup of tea he went off for a few minutes, returning with the reverend.

'Tell him, Billy. Tell him what that bastard tried to do!'

'Steady now, Horace. Give the boy a chance. Here, Billy, finish your tea first.' Once the tea was gone I felt a bit less shaky. Telling the reverend of the encounter, he listened intently.

'And you're sure he intended to rob you, Billy?'

'Yes, sir. He was going to stab George with this.'

'Jesus Christ,' exclaimed Horace when he saw the flick-knife. 'That bastard. I'll kill him!'

'Horace, calm down and don't take the good Lord's name in vain like dat.'

'Sorry, Reverend, but dat Rubin and his pal are bad news for dis community.'

'I agree and I shall take care of this problem.'

'Were you hurt, Billy?'

'No, Reverend, but when I saw the knife I nearly shit myself!'

The reverend was trying hard not to laugh. 'What were they after? Do you know?'

'Well, I've only got Horace's whisky and a bottle of Black Label vodka in the pram.' Horace clamped his hand to his forehead and turned away, shaking his head and looking towards heaven.

'Have you, indeed. Well, you better go and fetch it.' The reverend admired the square bottle filled with dark amber whisky.

'Well, bless my soul. Bourbon. I haven't seen Bourbon since I left the West Indies.'

'Is that good?'

'Good? It's better than good! Horace, a glass if you please and make it a clean one!' Horace returned with two small glasses and a jug of water. Unscrewing the cap, he poured a small measure into the reverend's glass and offered him the water jug.

'When I'm thirsty I'll ask for water.' He tapped the glass against the bottle. Horace filled it nearly to the brim.

'Now, let's see.' Taking a big sip, he rolled it around in his mouth before swallowing it in one go.

'Ah, Billy, if only you were a man you could sample dis nectar from the gods and hear the waves on a sandy beach as the sun sets over the Caribbean.'

'Really, do you get all that from one sip?' He laughed again.

'Amen to that. Not having any, Horace?'

'Not just now, Reverend. I'm keeping it for a special occasion.'

'Do you want the vodka as well, Horace? My man says it will loosen any girl's knicker elastic!'

The reverend almost choked on his Bourbon. 'That boy kills me, Horace. Pay him his money before he buries you!'

Horace gave me three trays of fresh eggs.

'Two trays per bottle, Horace.'

'I'll have to owe you, Billy.'

'That's OK. I trust you. I'll just put it in my book!' I produced the old unused diary Dad gave me and, with a stubby pencil, I wrote: 'Horace owes me four dozen eggs'.

'I'll cross you off when you pay up.'

'You're getting to sound like the tallyman.'

'Well, I'll only forget otherwise. I've got more than one customer, you know. Oh, and three dozen for the big silk knickers. They're in the pram.' As I handed the bag to Horace the reverend intercepted it.

'Well, well. What have we got here then?' and, removing one of the garments, he held them apart with his thumbs.

'Hallelujah, Horace! Delilah's gonna be putty in your hands. I can feel a wedding coming on.'

'Jesus, will you listen to him. He'll have me married off before I can get 'em off!'

The reverend noticed me smiling. 'You shouldn't know about such things at your tender age, Billy.'

'I was just thinking back to when I told Miss Delilah not to get her knickers in a twist. I never thought I'd be supplying the knickers.'

The three of us couldn't stop laughing.

12

A Golden Crown and a Silver Compass

'When's she going to be coronated then, Mum?'

'Not coronated, Billy. Crowned at her coronation, see?'

'Oh, of course. That's what I meant to say.'

'It's going to be on Tuesday, June the second and we're all going to watch it on Florrie's new television set.'

'You looking forward to the party?' asked Dad. 'You'll be helping me on the bingo stall in the afternoon before the main party. Every child in the flats will be there. We've had to hire more chairs so you can all sit down together.' I tried to imagine what five hundred plates of jelly looked like.

'Will we have hats, Dad?'

'Of course we will. Your auntie Eaddie has collected boxes of them from your granny's over at Canonbury.' Dad was referring to my granny Brown, who did homework for Woolies making decorations and paper hats to be sold in their stores. Hundreds of outworkers, as they were called, did the same thing.

'We're all going to put up decorations. It'll be just like Christmas, Billy, but bigger!' I couldn't imagine anything better than Christmas and said so.

'This is a once-in-a-lifetime, Billy,' said Mum. 'A coronation. It's going to be marvellous. You'll see. Just what we all need.'

Not long after this conversation, Dad started bringing home packages from his work. Every night for two weeks, wrapped in brown craft paper and string, parcels arrived. My brother Bob and I wondered what was going on. Finally Dad opened all the packages and started to assemble the items. He had made each piece fit accurately together, forming an amazing display frame for a poster of the Queen, which he had got from a billboard company. He had also made Tudor roses in metal, together with telescopic poles holding Union Jacks. The most amazing part was yet to come. At the flick of a switch the whole display lit up. Someone phoned the newspaper and the next day Dad's display was in the news. It also won a competition for the Best Coronation Display, which earned him ten pounds in prize money.

'Queen Elizabeth, the Queen Mum's coming, Billy.'

'Where, Mum?'

'Here. She's going to meet your Dad.'

'Why is the Queen Mum meeting Dad, Mum?'

'Because he's won a national allotment competition and she's the patron so she's coming to see his garden!'

I couldn't wait to tell all my pals this news and rushed off to the playground.

'The Queen Mother! Billy, you're such a liar!'

'It's true, Jim! Dad's won the garden competition and she's coming next week at one o'clock.'

'It's true.'

'Oh, you'd say anything for him, Beryl.'

'No I wouldn't, not if he told a lie, but it's on the noticeboard outside the super's office!' We all trooped round to the noticeboard. Anthony adjusted his glasses and read it in silence.

'Well, what's it say, brainy?'

'The Queen Mother will be here at one o'clock next Saturday! To visit Mr Brown's allotment!'

'Bloody hell, Billy. You're gonna meet the Queen Mum. You'd better polish them shoes!'

'No, Jim, it's only my dad will meet her, on the allotment.'

'I don't think she'll come to tea. There's too many stairs for her!'

'Billy, you'll be famous!'

'Afraid not, Beryl. Dad might be, but not me.'

'He's already famous,' added Jim. 'Every bugger in Brixton knows who Billy Brown is!'

The day before the visit a detective and an officer came to vet the garden. The official carried a tape measure and Dad had to prune some of the climbing roses back to allow the Queen Mother access. She arrived exactly at one o'clock, to be welcomed by the Mayor of Brixton and our superintendent. Dad greeted her at the entrance to his allotment. We watched it all from our balcony. He looked so smart in his suit. Mum was crying again! After a brief walk around she shook his hand and waved to all the people watching. Dad cut a beautiful rose called 'Peace' and presented it to her. Accepting it, she passed it to her policeman and shook

Dad's hand again. It was all over in less than fifteen minutes, but my dad had met the Queen Mum and for him, the memory would last for ever.

The big day itself started off with a really good breakfast of eggs from Horace, sausages from Big Mike, bacon from Mickey Finn and mushrooms and tomatoes from the Monk brothers. This was all followed by toast and Mum's marmalade, courtesy of Mr Bentham's oranges from the docks.

After breakfast we all went down to Mrs Bentham's to watch the only television in our block. There were nearly twenty of us sat around the polished wood Decca set. As Richard Dimbleby narrated, we sat enthralled by the ancient ritual of crowning a monarch. All the mums oohed and ahed at the sight of four-year-old Prince Charles.

'I wonder if he's going to a street party tonight?' I asked.

'Be quiet, Billy, and don't spill that drink!'

I felt sorry for him if he wasn't and went back to thinking about what five hundred plates of jelly might look like. As the final fanfare sounded and the Queen emerged, I thought the speaker was going to shake the television to bits, it was so loud. When I asked Mum about it she explained that it was loud for the old lady from the second floor.

'She's almost deaf, you see.'

'If it goes any louder, Mum, we'll all be deaf!'

The coronation finally finished in the rain. The crowd loved the only other queen there, who'd come all the way from Tonga. She was the only one in an open carriage and refused an umbrella, despite the pouring rain, and the crowd cheered her for it. All the other dignitaries and guests in the parade sat in closed carriages.

Directly after the programme, there was a special news item. Edmund Hillary and Sherpa Tenzing Norgay had conquered Mount Everest. You'd have thought rationing Norgay had ended, what with everyone cheering and clapping. I thought it was better than the coronation. Then we all went off for lunch, together with the other twenty million viewers, a world record at the time.

By the afternoon the rain had stopped and, although overcast, our festivities began. A fair was held in the big playground and stalls of all kinds were set up. My dad ran the bingo wearing a large top hat with bingo cards stuck around the brim.

'Come along, ladies, try your luck!'

'I don't know what Eileen would say about that, Jack!' All the other ladies dissolved into fits of laughter, but I didn't get the joke. I found Beryl and we went off to all the other stalls. All our friends were at the Aunt Sally stall where, for tuppence, you could throw three heavy wooden balls and smash up old crockery.

'Come on, you two – have a go!' I took the balls from Jim's dad and paid the tuppence. I offered one to Beryl, but she declined.

'Go on, Billy. Smash the lot!' ordered Jim. 'There's boxes of it.' So, taking careful aim, I tried to smash an old white teapot right in the centre. The first ball just bounced off.

'What's it filled with? Concrete?'

'Throw harder, Billy,' advised Jim's dad. My next shot took the spout clean off.

'There. What do you think, Beryl?' She didn't seem to be interested.

'Yes, I suppose that was really good.'

'Suppose? Just watch this, then!' Taking careful aim once again, I hurled the ball with all my strength. The teapot exploded into a thousand pieces.

'Ha! How's that then, Beryl?' Jim and his dad were clapping. I looked around, but Beryl had wandered off.

'Probably gone to do girl's stuff,' I explained to Jim.

By the end of the fair I had won several prizes including a plaster model of a painted Alsatian's head on a plaque, which I was going to give to Big Mike to remind him of Jessie, who had recently died. At six o'clock the fair ended and was cleared away. I went off and found Mrs Prentis.

'I can't find Beryl anywhere!'

'She went up, Billy. She felt a bit sick. Too much chocolate, maybe.'

'She's coming tonight though, isn't she?' I asked.

'Of course. It's the party of the year. She wouldn't miss that!' I wandered back upstairs to put my prizes away safely.

'What's up, Billy? You look a bit down.'

'Beryl's sick, Mum. She left the fair early.'

'Oh, I'm sure she'll be fine for tonight. Probably too much chocolate or something!'

'That's what her mum said.'

'Well, there you are then. She'll be there. Whatever did you pick that horrible dog for? It's not going on my wall!'

By six thirty, the main room and the stage were filled with children waving Union Jacks and all wearing party hats. I soon found Beryl and we sat together.

'Are you alright now?' I asked. 'Your mum said you were sick!'

'I'm OK, Billy. It just got a bit too much, but I'm fine now.' She still seemed a bit quiet. The tables were filled by an army of servers. Mums and dads in party hats delivered sandwiches, cakes, chocolate fingers, bowls of jelly and packets of sweets. Mums came round with big jugs of orange or lemonade. The noise was deafening. I turned to Beryl.

'What a smashing party, Beryl. Are you feeling better?'

'I'm OK, Billy.' She still didn't seem to be right. She'd hardly touched her sandwiches.

'Don't worry, Beryl. I'll get a bag from my mum. You can take your cakes and sweets home!' When the food was almost gone the superintendent came on the stage with a microphone.

'Quiet now, please, ladies and gentlemen.' Once he had got order he proceeded. 'Ladies and gentlemen and children.' At the mention of the word children we all clapped and cheered.

'Now, now, quiet please.' We fell silent once more, except for a baby crying at the back. He continued. 'It gives me great pleasure to call upon Mrs Robson to unveil a magnificent portrait donated by Mr Jack Brown and his family on this auspicious occasion.'

'What's your dad done now, Billy?'

'I don't know, Beryl. He never said a word.' Mrs Robson pulled the string releasing the sheet. The whole room erupted into applause when they saw a superb copy of the painting by Pietro Annigoni of the new Queen Elizabeth. It covered the wall to the right of the stage above the exit sign. He had got it done by one of Hoover's top graphic artists without telling us. I was so proud of him I thought I'd burst!

The party ended with votes of thanks to all the helpers and organisers, who received a huge round of applause. Filing out into the now empty playground, mums helped their children put on coats and hats. Although it was June the rain was starting to come down again. Beryl joined me in her red coat and hat that I liked so much. We both stood on the concrete seat in the playground to get a better view.

'You still sick, Beryl?' I asked with concern. The first firework went off with a bang. She clung to my arm and put her face against my chest.

'It's only a firework, Beryl.' The sky exploded with crimson light. 'Wow, look at that.' I looked down at her. She looked up at me, crying.

'Whatever is it? Are you going to be sick again?'

'I'm going to South Africa, Billy.' I could hardly hear her above the explosions.

'What?'

'South Africa.' Bang, bang, the fireworks continued.

'That's a long way for a holiday, Beryl.' The tears streamed down her face.

'It's not a holiday, Billy. It's for good. Dad's got a job there.' The explosion in my brain was louder than all the fireworks and was only matched by the one in my heart.

'For good, Beryl, not coming back? When, when are you going?'

'In three weeks, Billy. I don't want to go, but Mum said I must.'

We didn't really hear the finale of the fireworks or see 'God Save the Queen' picked out in silver. We both got down and sat on the seat, Beryl sobbing in my arms.

'M-my dad works for a-a diamond company. He, he's been given a b-big job in South Africa. We're going to have a cook and a s-servant and a g-gardener. I don't want to go, Billy. I want to stay here with you.' I held her tight while she cried. I was going to lose my Beryl. My wonderful day was destroyed in an instant.

'You two still at it!'

'Go away, Jim. Not now.'

'She gonna be sick again?'

'No, Jim. She's going to South Africa – for good. Her dad's got a really good job out there.'

'Oh no, Billy. That's bloody awful. She's the prettiest girl in the flats.'

'She's the prettiest girl in the world, Jim.' I too now had tears in my eyes.

The fireworks finished, our group of pals gathered

around. 'What's the matter with Beryl?' 'Is Billy crying?'

Jim explained, adding, 'I think we should leave them alone, OK?' and they all wandered off.

'Goodnight, Beryl. Goodnight, Billy. See you tomorrow.' We were left alone in the empty playground with only the smell of saltpetre in the air to remind us of what we'd missed. Beryl was finally all cried out, her eyes puffy and wet with tears.

'I love you, Billy. I'll write every day. I won't miss one and you must write to me!'

'I'm not much good at writing, Beryl. I can't spell for toffee.'

'It doesn't matter. I'll still read them. Promise you will, Billy.'

'I promise, Beryl. I promise.' We walked back to her block. When we kissed goodnight it was wonderful and unbearable at the same time. I held her tight until her mum called down the stairs.

'Time to come in, Beryl. Goodnight Billy.'

The last three weeks were agony. Every time I saw her I realised just what I was going to lose. We spent a whole day together in Brockwell Park with a picnic both our mums had made. Straight after Coronation Day Mrs Prentis had Mum in for a cup of tea and a chat. She explained that Mr Prentis had worked for De Beers, the world's biggest diamond dealers, since leaving school and was highly regarded by the company. Due to his poor state of health he had been advised that a warmer climate would be beneficial to him.

When the post had arisen in South Africa it seemed like the ideal move, especially as it would double his salary. Mum had, of course, agreed that it would be foolish to lose such an opportunity.

'Don't worry about Billy,' she advised. 'He'll bounce back and it's such an opportunity for Beryl.'

'She's heartbroken, Eileen, absolutely distraught. I really think she actually loves your boy.'

'He can be an absolute terror if he chooses, but he's still a big softy at heart. We'll just have to let them get over each other in their own time.'

The sun shone the whole day whilst we sat against a giant oak tree outside the tearooms. We didn't say too much about her leaving, just staying together was enough. I hardly went to the market, except for Saturdays. It was summer anyway and the firewood demand had dropped off. The day before she was due to leave, Beryl came to say goodbye to Mum and Dad. Mum hugged her with tears in her eyes.

'You stay safe now and look after your mum and dad – and don't you dare forget us all.' Beryl was now crying.

'I won't, Mrs Brown. You and Mr Brown have been so kind.'

'Here you go, Beryl. This is for you.' Dad gave her something wrapped in white paper. 'Go on. Have a look.' She opened it carefully to reveal a small copper and brass treasure chest he'd made her. 'For your keepsakes, Beryl.'

She hugged him. 'It's lovely. Thank you, Mr Brown. I'll keep it for ever.'

'Steady on, Beryl. You'll have us all crying in a minute.'

'Haven't you got her anything, Billy?'

'Of course I have.' Out of my pocket I gave her a small blue jeweller's box. 'Here, Beryl. So you won't forget me.' Inside was a solid silver compass on a silver chain. 'It's so you can find your way back one day!' She rushed into my arms.

'It's lovely, Billy. I'll always wear it and think of you.' Mum was wiping her tears away with the corner of her apron. Dad was blowing his nose so loudly I hardly heard her the first time.

'Just like Florence Nightingale, eh, Billy?' We both smiled at the memory of the Crimea compass when I'd first kissed her.

We had our last kiss in the usual place, with her up one step higher than me. I couldn't see her off in the morning as I had school. I looked at her pretty face for the very last time.

'Any time you want to know where I am, Beryl, just look north. That's where I'll be.'

13

Toy Soldiers

Already a crowd of boys had gathered when I took my new stock of comics into the playground for the usual Sunday-afternoon sales. I was surprised that they were not waiting for me as usual, but were already engaged with someone else. Pushing my way through, I put my box down on the concrete seat.

'What's going on here then?' I demanded.

'It's that new lad, Peter,' Jim informed me. 'He's selling lead soldiers. I've just bought three for a shilling.'

I looked from the diminished rows of soldiers to the face of the new arrival. ''Ere, what's your game?' I wanted to know. 'This is my pitch – every Sunday afternoon – comics and mags.'

Peter was a year older than me, not as tall, but much bigger built.

'Free country, ain't it? Maybe they're tired of your old comics,' he said, indicating my late customers with a sweeping gesture.

'You've only been moved in a few weeks. I've been here since 1942!' By his 'so what' remark I realised he didn't yet know who he was dealing with.

'I'm Billy Brown,' I stated, as if this should settle any further discussion.

'I don't care if you're Winston bloody Churchill. I'm selling my soldiers, so sod off!'

'You can't let him order you around like that,' Jim told me. 'Give him a good hiding, Billy. Here, I'll hold your box for you.'

I'd already realised that the intruder would make short work of me, so I decided on the canny approach.

'No, no. He's new here and obviously hasn't been told what's what,' I explained. 'This part of the seat is my pitch, but, as you say, it's a free country, so if you wouldn't mind moving along, we'll stay friends, OK?' I offered my hand as a gesture of goodwill. Peter hesitated and simply glared at me.

'I'd say that is a very fair and sporting offer.' Turning towards the voice, I recognised Anthony's thick glasses instantly.

'Who are you talking to, four eyes?' It was Peter's big mistake.

'Oi, you can't say that to Anthony. He's our friend,' Jim said, and then the others started gathering around.

'We don't like bullies here, mate. Now, take your soldiers and piss off back to where you came from!'

'Yeah, Billy's right. It's been his pitch since 1942!'

The lads began to wander away from Peter.

'Look, I'm sorry. Nobody told me, see. How was I to know? I've only got a few left. Who wants 'em?'

'Stick your bloody soldiers,' Jim advised, safe in the knowledge that he already had the three he wanted in his pocket. A few more of the lads loyal to me added, 'Yeah, stick yer bloody soldiers, new boy.'

'How many you got left?' He was taken aback by my question.

'What?'

'How many? You want to sell 'em, don't you?' For a moment I thought he was going to hit me. Then, to everyone's surprise, he quickly counted his remaining army, still standing to attention on the concrete.

'There's nineteen of 'em left altogether.'

I mentally calculated six shillings at three for a shilling, with one left over.

'I'll give you four bob for the lot,' I offered. The crowd held its breath while he worked out the true price.

'It should be six shillings and sixpence,' he told me. 'You're a cheat!'

'Four shillings and sixpence. That's my last offer!' I said, adding, 'or you might like to try outside the flats.'

'You know I don't know my way around yet so there's no one else I *can* sell to. It's a deal.' This time he offered his hand and we shook on it, much to the cheering approval of my pals.

'Done 'im up like a kipper,' Jim told me, patting me on the back as I paid Peter his money.

'Right, now I've got comics. Two pence each or eight for a shilling and soldiers, three for a shilling,' Peter was sat on the wall counting his money, but looked up at me, smiling.

'Me and you should have a chat later, Billy.'

I nodded in agreement, then went back to taking

money. There was such a demand for the comics that I got Jim to help me count them into piles of eight. Half an hour later I was left with only three comics and four lead soldiers, which I gathered up and gave to Jim.

'Cor, thanks, Billy. I'll help you any time. Just say the word.' He wandered off with his booty.

'You just made two bob out of me.'

I turned to face Peter, glad that we were both smiling.

'Sure, but that's business and you, like me, sold out, so all we've got to take home is the cash!' I sat on the concrete seat beside him.

'Got any more of them soldiers?' I asked, still smiling. His reply took the smile off my face.

'Thousands of 'em. New batch every week!'

'You serious?' I asked inquisitively. He drew closer and lowered his voice.

'Well, I haven't got 'em yet, but I could have – or better still – *we* could have.' I was baffled, but seriously interested.

'Woolies,' he said. 'I nick 'em from Woolies. It's dead easy, but with two of us it'd be even easier.'

I let what he was suggesting sink in.

'I can't. My mum would kill me if she found out. She used to work for them before they made her redundant.'

'Well, there you are then, Billy. This is your chance to get yer own back for yer mum – and what's a few lead soldiers to Woolies?'

'No, I can't. I've never nicked stuff before. It's not my style. And it's asking for trouble!'

'Well, I'm going Monday afternoon. I'll be out by

the gate at four o'clock. If you're not scared or anything, I'll see you tomorrow, Billy!' He got up to leave but turned back. 'You're not scared, are you?'

'No, no, of course not,' I lied. 'Maybe I'll come.'

'See you, Billy.' Peter went off in the direction of his flat. I wandered along to where Jim and Anthony were sitting reading Jim's comics.

'I don't like him,' Jim announced. 'He's far too cocky for a new boy. Thinks he knows it all, but you showed him, Billy!'

'Very neatly done, if I may say so,' added Anthony. 'I thought he was going to hit you.'

'So did I!' I admitted. 'But he seems OK.' Anthony took his glasses off and squinted into my eyes.

'All that glitters is not gold,' he reminded me.

'Mum said that when I got her a watch that turned her wrist green!' They both dissolved into fits of laughter at my admission and I joined them.

'Well, it *was* only ten bob from Mickey Finn!'

The following Monday I was out by the front gates at four o'clock. I wasn't really sure about it or why I was there. Whether it was the thought of easy money or the fact that he said I was scared to do it I didn't know, but here I was.

'Hello, Billy. I knew you'd come. Good idea, the jacket. Nice deep pockets!'

On the way Peter explained the system.

'We enter at the opposite ends of Woolies and go to opposite sides of the toy counter. I'll go to the soldiers first and fill me pockets while you keep a look-out opposite me. Got it?'

'Yeah, I've got it, but what if someone comes? Like the sales girl or a grown-up?'

'Whistle, blow your nose, cough, anything to let me know. Once me pockets are full, we swap places and I look out for you. Easy-peasy, Billy! Soon as we've got yours, we leave as we came in, by opposite doors.'

I still wasn't sure, knowing it would be direct stealing. And from Woolies, which I still regarded as my extended family. I knew of other lads who stole sweets and stuff and they'd all bragged about how easy it was, but I'd never been tempted to join them. I was doing OK without the risks of shoplifting. Yet here I was.

'Not getting scared, are you?' Peter asked.

''Course not. Easy-peasy!' I told him, using his own phrase.

'Right, we're here, Billy. See you at the toys,' and with that he was gone. I waited for a while outside the double doors. Finally, deciding to go in, I pushed on the door but nothing happened. Looking up, I stared through the glass at one of the assistant managers pushing against me and froze in terror. His suit was immaculate and his brass Woolies badge shone like a sheriff's star. Opening the door inwards, he ushered me inside.

I'm caught, I thought. I was convinced he'd seen something in my eyes that had given me away and I tried not to look at him.

'So sorry, young man,' he said, apologising. 'Just off to collect my dry cleaning,' and with that he left the store. I couldn't believe it. The relief was enormous; so much had flashed through my brain – caught, police, Mum, Dad. I turned to go out of the store just as Peter caught my arm.

'Where the 'ell have you been?' he said, through gritted teeth. 'Come on. Let's get on with it.' He didn't let go of my arm until we got to the toy counter.

'Whistle, cough, got it?' I didn't answer, but went to the opposite side of the counter.

He was already examining the soldiers. I watched, fascinated, as he deftly held one in the palm of his hand before slipping it into his pocket. Glancing up and down, I could see the sales girl engaged with a lady selecting some coloured pencils and paper. By the time I glanced back at Peter he was staring at me, giving me the thumbs-up sign and making his way round the counter just as he'd said. I moved in the other direction so as not to pass him and was soon standing in front of the lead soldiers display. I immediately noticed a large gap in their otherwise compact ranks. I stood and stared at the two front rows of soldiers with their red tunics and white helmets, their rifles held out with fixed bayonets. *Don't touch*, they seemed to scream at me. I seemed frozen to the spot. This was nothing like the buzz I got from wheeler-dealing. All I could think about was getting caught and the shame it would bring. I was brought back to reality by Peter's loud coughing and looking up at him, he gave me the thumbs-up sign.

Doing as he had done, my pockets were quickly filled with the bayonet-wielding soldiers. It was then that I realised why Peter hadn't take any of them. The tiny bayonets caught in the cloth of my pockets and stuck into my legs. They were bigger than those stood to attention so you got fewer in your pockets. I looked up and froze once again. Peter had vanished.

'Hello again, young man.' I turned to face the assistant manager once more. My knees began to give way under me and my throat felt parched, images of the police flashing through my mind again.

'Dry cleaning,' he announced cheerily, holding up his freshly laundered suit. 'Hope you're not buying up all my soldiers. We only put them out this morning.' And with that, he was gone. Leaning back against the counter, I took several deep breaths. Once satisfied that my legs had stopped trembling, I headed for the exit. Suddenly noticing that I was walking crouched over like some demented goblin, I straightened up and slowed down to a more normal pace, hoping to avoid suspicion.

Stopping outside, I closed my eyes against the glare of the afternoon sunshine and sucked in the fresh air, the relief of not being caught washing through me.

'Gotcha!' I didn't even bother to open them at Peter's effort to scare me.

'Piss off! You don't scare me,' I retorted, with re-newed confidence.

'What did you say?' roared Constable Collins. He had been off-duty, shopping for his wife and had seen me in the store taking the soldiers.

'I . . . I . . .' His hand clamped on my shoulder.

'Piss off, eh, Billy Brown? Well, we'll just see what

your parents have to say, shall we?' and with that I was marched unceremoniously all the way home. Passing through the gateway, I almost ran into old Mrs Thompsit.

''Ere, 'ere, watch out, Billy. Almost knocked me over. Then where would we be?' I already knew where I was; in the deepest trouble I'd ever been in. The earlier flashes were back. The police were already here, next would be Mum, then Dad, then everybody in the flats would know Billy Brown was a thief! I was terrified.

Constable Collins had marched me so fast I could feel both my legs burning with cuts from the tiny bayonets and I was sweating with fear. Either all my pals were indoors doing homework or having tea, or they'd all witnessed the spectacle of Constable Collins dragging me along and made themselves scarce.

Mum had only just got in from work when he rang our doorbell. As soon as she saw him and me she knew I was in big trouble.

'What's he done now?' she asked. 'I hope it's not another broken window. His dad's only just repaired the last one.'

'I'm sorry, Mrs Brown, but it's a bit more serious than that!'

Mum stepped aside. 'You'd better come in, Colin – and you, young man!' She led us through to the lounge.

'Now, what's all this about?' she asked, looking extremely concerned.

'Well, Mrs Brown,' he began.

'Colin, we've know each other since he was born,' she told him.

'OK, look, Eileen. I'm really sorry, but I simply couldn't turn a blind eye this time. Empty your pockets, Billy,' he ordered. In silence I turned out my pockets, almost grateful to be free of the attacking bayonet-wielding soldiers.

When they were all finally out on the table he ordered, 'Inside out!' and I duly pulled all the pockets out to show that they were completely empty. With expert ease learnt over many years, he separated the items into three piles. Soldiers, money and hankie, string, conker and a brass plumbing fitting I'd found.

Mum sat staring straight at me while he continued.

'Caught him nicking them from Woolworths. Apprehended him outside.'

'He did what?' Mum's face was red with rage.

'I'm afraid that's not all, Eileen. When I grabbed hold of him, he told me to piss off and that I hadn't scared him.'

'I thought you were someone else,' I said.

'Who?' they both asked in unison.

'I don't know. Maybe a mate messing around.'

'Were you with someone else, Billy?' Constable Collins asked, coming up close.

'I-I was on me own,' I lied. Glancing at Mum, I knew she didn't believe me.

He sat and counted the money.

'Rob a bank as well, did you?' he asked.

'No, it's all mine.'

'Shut up, Billy!' I did as Mum told me.

313

'It's his, Colin, from his comic sales and all.' He flicked through the money, quickly adding it up.

'Lots of comics, Eileen.'

'And me scrap money,' I said. Constable Collins clasped his hand to his forehead while Mum shook her fist at me.

'Right, go to your room and shut the door,' she ordered. I couldn't get in there quick enough. I could just about hear Mum go to the kitchen and make a cup of tea. Then they chatted for what seemed like ages until the bedroom door suddenly opened and Mum ushered me back into the lounge.

'Sit down,' I sat. 'Now, the truth, Billy. Have you done this before?'

'No, Mum, not ever.'

'Is that the truth?'

'Yes, Mum.'

'Will you ever do it again?'

'No, Mum. I was so frightened.' The tears I'd held back began to stream down my face.

'I'm sorry, Mum. I'm so sorry.'

'Sorry you got caught more like,' she threw back at me. 'Well, young man, you can thank your lucky stars that it was Constable Collins that caught you and not another policeman.' I turned to Constable Collins, thanking him but not knowing what for.

'Right, Billy Brown, I'm officially cautioning you that should this offence reoccur, you will be arrested and taken before the Juvenile Court where you'll probably be sent to borstal.' The tears fell even harder. 'Do you understand?'

Y-yes sir,' I managed to stammer out.

'Oh – and next time you tell someone to piss off, make sure you open your eyes first!'

'Thanks, Colin. I'm very grateful to you.' Mum got up and went with him to the door, along with my soldiers now in a bag still trying to bayonet their way out.

'Now, young man,' she said, coming back into the room. 'You and me are going to have a little chat and you *will* tell me the truth. Who were you with?' I knew any resistance was futile.

'Peter, Mum. The new lad.'

'Did he put you up to this?'

'Yes, Mum. He said I was too scared to do it!'

'You stupid bugger! That's the oldest trick in the book and you fell for it. Have you done this before?'

'No, Mum – and I won't ever do it again. I don't want to be put away.' By now I was crying like a baby. 'Dad will kill me,' I wailed.

'No he won't, Billy, 'cos we're not going to tell him.' I stopped crying and sucked in air, unable to speak. 'As you know, your dad's not been too well lately, what with his migraines and all, and he certainly doesn't need this on his plate.'

'But, Mum,' I said, beginning to regain the power of speech. 'What about Constable Collins?'

'Colin agrees with me and considers the matter closed. Understand?'

'Yes, Mum,' I said, as if in a dream. 'Dad needn't know.' My relief was quickly dashed.

'Now for your punishment. Go and get your money.'

I'd been expecting that, but not her next words. 'And not your Mother Hubbard money box – your tobacco tin.' I turned towards her, horrified. 'Didn't think I knew, did you, Billy? Go on. Your dad'll be home soon.'

I was quickly back at the table with the two-ounce Old Virginia tobacco tin.

'How much, Mum?' I asked quietly. Without answering, she took the tin. Then, in the gentlest voice I'd heard since Constable Collins brought me home, she informed me of my fate.

'All of it, Billy! All thirty-seven pounds. And you can thank your lucky stars I don't empty Mother Hubbard as well!' I knew I couldn't argue so I didn't even try.

'Thanks, Mum. I'm so sorry.'

'So stupid, more like. Let this be a lesson to you: don't be led by fools! Honestly, Billy, since Beryl left for South Africa you've gone from one scrape to another, but this one is serious. You do know that, don't you?'

The tears turned from relief to heartfelt loss for Beryl.

'I miss her, Mum. I really do.'

'I know, Billy, but only time will heal that – and what if she found out you were a thief, eh?' I already knew the answer.

'I'm really sorry, Mum. I won't do it again, ever. I promise.'

'On your honour, Billy?' I made the cross-your-heart sign.

'I promise.'

'Well, then I shall say no more about it. This will be our secret – yours, mine and Colin's. And why are you fidgeting so much?'

Once I'd explained she helped me remove my trousers. Both thighs were covered in hundreds of tiny welts and scratches and were red raw. I was sure she was smiling, but she didn't say anything.

'Brambles, Billy. A little white lie to your dad. Now sit there while I get the Germolene.' She was back in no time with the pink antiseptic ointment and a cup of tea for me.

'Thanks, Mum.' I started to cry again with relief.

'One last question, Billy.' I looked at her face through tear-stained eyes. Now I knew she was smiling.

'Did you really tell Constable Collins to piss off?'

Having realised my stupidity and the error of my ways, I decided it was time to improve my cash-flow situation. I sorted out all the odds and ends of scrap metal in the pram shed. Supply had almost dried up from the bombsites as, one by one, they were fenced and levelled, ready for new flats to be built. Already, most of the Barrington Road sites were cleared, much of it by Big Mike's demolition team. Loading up the pram, I headed off to his yard.

'Billy boy. How the devil are you? Haven't seen you in ages.' We shook hands as if Stanley had just found Livingstone.

'Now, let's get this lot weighed.' He lifted out the few pieces of lead. 'Slim pickings, eh, Billy?'

'It's all the new building, Mr Mike. They're demolishing everything.' I passed him the small box of brass containing taps, fittings, a letter box, several door handles and a lump of brass with a corner melted. Tipping it out onto the huge flat pan of the Avery scales, he moved the balance along until he got the correct reading.

'Seven and six, brass,' he told me, and I chalked it on the weighing pan beside the four bob for lead. As he chucked the items back in the box, he picked up the odd lump. 'Wait a minute, Billy.' He showed me the melted corner. 'Jesus, will you look at that!'

I stared, but just saw a lump of old brass.

'So what? It's melted.' I still didn't understand his beaming smile.

'Billy, brass needs a really high temperature to melt, higher than copper.'

'So it must have got really hot,' I suggested.

'Not that hot, Billy, but hot enough to melt gold!'

'Gold? Did you say gold?' I replied, now wide-eyed. 'Let me see.' Taking the lump in my hands, I turned it over.

'But what is it?' I asked, returning it to him.

'I'd say that in its prime it was a very large solid-gold cigarette case, flattened in the bombing and melted by the subsequent fire.' From a shelf he produced a small wooden box containing a set of precision scales and three small bottles of chemicals. Opening one, he

318

placed a small amount on the case and waited a few seconds.

'Jackpot!' he exclaimed. 'You've hit the jackpot, Billy! It's twenty-two-carat gold.'

'Is that good?' I asked, excitedly.

'Not just good, the best!' he said, checking the case over carefully and brushing off every bit of dirt with his blue hankie. 'Now, let's see.' We both concentrated on the weighing process until he was finally satisfied.

'Jesus, Billy, it weighs just over six ounces.'

'Not a lot then,' I said, still thinking of the nearly forty pounds of lead I'd just delivered. With near reverence he came closer, speaking softly.

'Scrap twenty-two-carat, Billy Brown, is twenty-two pounds and two shillings an ounce!' In shock, I sat on the scale pan.

'How much?'

'Twenty-two pounds and two shillings, multiplied by six.' My brain was whirling; it wouldn't do the mental arithmetic, so I took his chalk and did it on the scale pan. I stared at the answer and then did it all again, unable to believe the total I'd come up with was correct. Same again; one hundred and thirty-two pounds and twelve shillings.

'It can't be, Mr Mike.'

'Oh yes it can, Billy,' he said, and proceeded to count out the cash from his huge roll of bank notes.

'But if it's so valuable, why isn't it on the price list?' I asked, pointing to the blackboard.

'Billy, use your brains! If I made it known that I dealt in gold, I'd have to deal with every petty thief in

Brixton, plus the bloody police, plus the bloody government! So I just keep it known to a trusted few. Now, put your money away safe and any more gold you get, you know where to come.'

We shook hands with the now obligatory spit and I walked back home, clutching the money in my pocket. Only a week ago, I'd been stupid enough to steal for five bob's worth of soldiers and had handed over all my cash to Mum. No wonder Ma Kingdom had always been keen to buy any odd bits of jewellery I'd acquired from some of the older girls.

That's it, I said to myself. Sod lugging pram-loads of scrap, especially as supply was dwindling by the day. Beryl's gone off to the land of diamonds; I'm going into gold.

I realised July 1954 was bad news for me when Dad looked up from his Sunday paper and announced, 'Well, that's it, Billy. You may as well shut up shop.' I stopped halfway through dipping my toast soldier into one of Horace's nice boiled eggs.

'What do you mean, Dad?' I asked, confused.

'It's official, Billy. Says it right here in the paper. All rationing is over. We can have anything we want and as much as we want.'

'You sure, Jack?' Mum enquired.

'It's in the paper, Eileen. Official rationing has finally finished so you can tear up the books!'

'Oh boy, Dad, you sure know how to put me off my breakfast!' My mind began racing through my stock of unsold items; stockings, condoms, two bottles of

Scotch whisky, rolls of knicker elastic, half a dozen mouth organs, nearly a full box of army jack-knives, comics and pin-up mags.

'You'll have to have a sale, Billy – you know, just like the stores do after Christmas, knock it all out cheap.'

I'd noticed of late how business had been slowing down. All my pals were growing up, just like me, and I was working in the market five nights a week and all day Saturday – and being paid well for it.

'The girls will still want nylons,' I said.

'Yes, but they're getting so cheap now, Billy, I doubt you're saving them much.' I let Mum's words sink in.

'But I'm too young to retire,' I announced. The two of them couldn't conceal their laughter.

'Billy Brown – you're only twelve. You can't retire until you're sixty-five!'

I looked at Mum and gave it some thought. 'Oh well, something will crop up!'

'Yes,' said Dad, examining the smoke from his cigarette. 'That's what worries me.'

EPILOGUE

Something did crop up. Rock 'n' roll with Bill Haley, Elvis Presley and Buddy Holly and girls, though of course there was always time for the occasional little earner. Like supplying the second-hand Rockola juke box and the furniture and fittings for a new coffee bar, or selling the twenty-three tons of coal discovered by Big Mike, which had been buried in an old school boiler room since the war. And I had a job in Brixton market. Even school had become a place of joy, at long last. I'd been enrolled at the Brixton School of Building and was being taught carpentry, bricklaying, stone masonry, plastering, tiling and painting and decorating. I couldn't wait to get there each morning. It was brilliant. Wheeling and dealing began to take second place.

By the time of my sixteenth birthday I had a regular girlfriend, Brandy, who was two years older than me, many friends and contacts and was ready for anything life would throw at me. But what I wasn't prepared for was my actual birthday.

I tried my key in the lock but it wouldn't open, so, just in case Mum was home early and had tripped the lock, I rang the doorbell. As soon as I did the door was thrown open and I was greeted by both Mum and Dad.

'Surprise, Billy! Happy birthday!' I kissed Mum and shook hands with Dad.

'Why aren't you at work?' I asked.

'We got the afternoon off to surprise you. After all, it is your sixteenth birthday. You're a man now.'

The lounge was all set for tea. Although it was only early May, Mum had made a ham salad with new potatoes and a hard-boiled egg, my favourites. There was a white iced birthday cake on a stand with the words 'BILLY 16 TODAY!' in blue icing, followed by trifle. And then, 'Right, presents, Billy,' and Dad went and got a large cardboard box.

'Happy birthday, son!' He sounded quite serious.

'If it's a puppy it's very quiet.' I joked.

'Just open it!'

At his insistence I opened the box and took out the brass and copper treasure chest which he had made me. The workmanship was amazing. He had made each filigree brass hinge from scratch. The whole thing was a metalworker's masterpiece.

'It's for your treasure, Billy.'

I was overwhelmed. 'Dad, it's wonderful.' Placing it on the sofa, I stood and hugged him. 'I couldn't have wished for anything better – I'll treasure it always.' I didn't intend it as a joke, but we all laughed.

'Open the lid, Billy. My present's inside.'

I did as Mum said. Inside, the chest was lined with polished wood and on the lid there was a brass plaque which read, 'To my Son William, may your chest always be full.' There were two presents inside and, taking out the smaller of the two, I unwrapped it. Inside was the chrome pocket watch I'd always wanted.

'Thanks, Mum, you're a real sweetheart!' I held the Ingersoll watch to my ear. 'Ticks like a battleship,' I observed.

'Now open the other one,' she ordered. I thought it was another birthday card until I opened the envelope. The Royal Blue Post Office savings book took me by surprise. It had my name on it, but it wasn't my one. Mine was dog-eared and worn from excessive use. This one was in pristine condition. I looked from Dad to Mum, confused.

'What is it?' was all I could say.

Mum's smile was radiant. 'It's every penny I ever took from you when you were bad or lost something. You know, satchels, caps, Billy. I promised myself I'd give it all back to you when you were sixteen – and here we are!'

'But Mum, I never knew . . .'

'Of course you didn't, you'd have spent it!' I was stunned. I turned page after page with nothing but entries, no withdrawals at all. When I read the final page I took a sharp intake of breath.

'Three hundred and twenty-six pounds and twelve shillings.'

'It's yours, Billy,' said Mum. 'All nine years of it. It always was; I just kept it safe all this time.'

I stood and hugged her, unable to stop the tears rolling down my cheeks.' Mum, you're mad,' I told her. 'And I love you.'

'I know you do, Billy, that's why I did it!'

As I took this in, I realised I'd had the most brilliant childhood any boy could ever have. Over a relatively short period, I'd wheeled and dealt in everything from firewood to nylons, scrap metal to condoms, even spiders and Nazi treasure. It had been an amazing education with all the people involved, each enhancing my young life in their own way. There was Beryl, my first true love, Jim, Derek and Anthony, my fellow musketeers, Big Mike, with his great boots, who had taught me always to shake on a deal and keep your word, and Jessie, who had shown me that the most ferocious can become a softy with kindness. Horace and the Reverend Stone had taught me that it's the person inside who matters, not the colour of your skin. Tosh, who showed me how to trade and entertained me with his long-winded stories and Mickey Finn who possibly taught me too much! Ma Kingdom, who was always pleased to see me, George, my saviour, Constable Colin Collins who turned out to be my fairy godmother, Sergeant Ted Norris of The Buffs and all the wonderful Woolies girls. But above all, there was my mum and dad. Throughout it all they had guided me, never stifling my adventurous spirit and filling my life with love and laughter, all a young boy could ever ask for. Now here I was, sixteen years old and nearly a man. In four months time I would leave school and start working for a living.

'Thanks, Mum,' I told her again.

'You don't have to keep thanking me, Billy. The money was yours all the time.'

'No, not for the money, Mum; for everything.'

THE END